QUACKY VOICES

STALE

Food, Sex, Wine, and Cigars—A Memoir

Written by
Lisa Stalvey

Strategic Book Publishing and Rights Co.

Strategic Book Publishing and Rights Co.
12620 FM 1960, Suite A4-507
Houston, TX 77065
www.sbpra.com

For information about special discounts for bulk purchases, please
contact Strategic Book Publishing and Rights Co. Special Sales, at
bookorder@sbpra.net.

ISBN: 978-1-63135-363-5

Design: Dedicated Book Services, (www.netdbs.com)

Table of Contents

Dedication

I dedicate this memoir to God above and beyond. He has changed me forever and now I know with Him I can do all things. I also want to dedicate this book to my mother, Marilyn as she saw my love for the kitchen when I couldn't. Her brutal honesty and open -minded attitude made me feel like I had a chance in this world to do anything I wanted. I want to also dedicate this book to my father, Dorrance. Even though he wanted me to be an artist, he reluctantly was supportive of my decision. He also taught me the value of honest hard work and to do what I loved throughout my life. He said if I am to be truly happy money alone does not do that on the soul level. I want to dedicate this book to my wonderful brother, Jeff as well. He was and still is the best brother any sister could want. I am so grateful to have him in my life. The best part about us is when we see each other we manage to make each other laugh until we cry!

I want to thank Kevin McKenzie, the chef from The Good Earth restaurant for pulling me off the floor as a waitress and throwing me into the kitchen over an omelet I made.

And a very huge thank you to my mentor, Wolfgang Puck, for giving me a chance in 1979 at Ma Maison and for being tough with me and believing in me. You gave me my first big position of my career, as head chef of Spago, Sunset in 1986. I will never forget that experience, ever.

And finally, thank you Mike, my ex-husband for putting up with my crap. I'm sorry I tortured you but you did know who I was when you married me!

Acknowledgment

I would like to first acknowledge the love of my life, business partner and best friend, Frank Coady, for supporting me throughout the process of writing this book. During this time, I found myself reliving quite a bit of this all over again, making me moody and depressed. I'm sure it was very difficult for Frank to handle, but he did. Thank you, Frank.

I want to acknowledge all of my friends, old and new, for reading this when it was totally unedited. I truly appreciate your constructive criticisms, support, emotional responses and a genuine interest in my book. It was great to go through this journey with all of you.

And finally, I also want to acknowledge my high school friend, Beth Dorfman-Bearer who has done this out of the kindness of her heart, for her amazing expertise in helping me format the black and white photos in my book and for my perfect cover design. Your expertise is much appreciated. She has a big dinner coming her way!

I want to acknowledge Brooke Warner, my coach and the *Founder of She Writes Press*. She literally changed my way of looking at the way I was writing. Although I am dyslexic and tend to be long winded, she never tried to change the way I wrote and expressed myself. She helped me improve my voice. For this Brooke, I am forever grateful. Thank you.

Introduction

I am owner/chef of Malibu Catering and The Malibu Chef. I have been cooking for over thirty-eight years now and am constantly working on my craft. As luck would have it, I trained under Wolfgang Puck at Ma Maison. After that, I went on to work at L'Orangerie and La Toque, and finally ended up as Wolfgang's head chef at Spago seven years into my career. After three years at Spago, I consulted for a number of restaurants and then finally took a break from cooking in restaurants and started to cook privately. I then had an opportunity to bring California cuisine to Reykjavik, Iceland. After four months there and five weeks in Europe, I came home to open Bambu, Malibu as the executive chef. While at Bambu I won two awards for one of the "Top 100 Chefs in America" in culinary leadership approaching the new Millennium. During my last month at Bambu, I met Paul Newman. He hired me to develop a steak sauce and French dressing for Newman's Own called *Newman's Own Steak Sauce* and *Newman's Own Parisian Salad Dressing*. I also co-wrote two cookbooks called *Newman's Own Cookbook* and *The Hole in the Wall Gang Cookbook: Kid-Friendly Recipes for Families to Make Together*. Since then, I have been catering and offering my services in private homes, delivering healthy meals for busy moms and families.

Food, Sex, Wine, and Cigars spans the first seven years of my now thirty-seven-year career and is my story as a professional chef who experienced unforeseen circumstances at the very beginning of my career when the unimaginable happened: three of my fingers on my right hand were severed in a Robot Coupe, a French version of Cuisinart, on a warm Friday the 13th, 1980. I was only twenty-four years old and very pretty, with huge dreams of becoming the most famous chef in the world. I was living the high life in and amongst

Hollywood's elite. I was getting ready to get married, too, which was to be the finishing touch to the "perfect" world I'd created, packed with destructive behavior and lies. It all came to a halt that day for me in the kitchen of the once-famed LA eatery L'Orangerie.

After the accident this became my world, swirling at light speed, caught in the dogma of my own spiritual and physical starvation. And yet I was being chased and suspended by God Himself. I almost died on several occasions, hearing the song of heaven. But even after that, I still chose to go down the wrong road and refused to grow and understand what had been revealed to me. I was caught in a superficial lifestyle, weaving in and out of trysts in my career and losing my grip and my battle with anorexia.

I have come to understand, after many years, that what happened to me was truly a gift. I now know the kitchen of L'Orangerie was God spinning the cocoon for my long journey, creating my rebirth in His way and perfect timing. God saw the bigger picture, as He is the Gardener of our lives, clipping away our weeds and our thorns. I guess in my case, I truly was "pruned," if you will.

My greatest hope is that *Food, Sex, Wine, and Cigars* will help others with what they are going through, no matter what it is. I now see that life is beautiful even when things are really bad. Our attitude is what is important as to the way we see things in life. There is *always* a reason for everything, especially when we don't understand why. We are supposed to live life in Faith. Finding Faith is what having a happy life is really all about. If you give yourself a moment to look at your situation dispassionately, I guarantee you that your reality of what you think is, isn't. Drama is never a good thing to nurture. I am fifty-eight years old now and I finally see the genuine beauty in the world and all by the grace of God.

Foreword
By Lisa Duffy-Atkin

Lisa Stalvey, my friend for over forty years continues to surprise and amaze me. I thought I knew all there was to know about the girl in school who was thought of as self -confident, spunky, cute and popular and who grew up to be the wild-child talented chef of famous restaurants on the Los Angeles culinary scene. To all outward appearances and even to those who thought they knew her best, her life was always on the upward arc of invincibility.

Unbeknownst to us, she was tortured by self-image loathing and as she writes in her book, it took her to great extremes of eating and purging, even as she conceived and created fantastic menus and dishes while at Spago. I had never heard of an eating disorder that involved chewing for hours and carefully spitting out everything that was chewed, so as not to ingest a single calorie.

Lisa takes you on an honest, no holds bar account of her life in her memoir. How her very personal issues shadowed her as she grew up in the dizzying atmosphere of Los Angeles in the 70's and 80's, where promiscuity, fast living and celebrity was the order of the day.

A horrifying accident with a food processor at the height of her career, in which she lost her three middle fingers halfway on her right hand, forced her to put the brakes on and re-evaluate the way she was living her life. As she lay in the hospital bed, she describes her out of body experience and the ethereal, golden love that enveloped her. This sense of serenity and illumination was a turning point on the long road to her new beginning. With determination she began her journey to heal herself and not only in a healthful capacity but also in a deeper spiritual journey that has transformed her life and continues to inspire her and through her writing and others. An enthralling, stimulating and moving memoir!

Chapter 1
The Accident

As Rochelle anxiously drove down the sidewalks of Hollywood to the hospital, I was suspended between disbelief and fear. My mind was racing in a number of directions as to why and how this accident could have possibly happened. I rewound the event over and over again, spinning at lightning speed, relentlessly, in my head. I had been making fresh pasta dough in that stupid machine for eight months, five days a week. What in the world did I do differently that day than any other day to cause such tragedy? When did my life take such a drastic turn for the worst? It didn't matter in hindsight. The damage was done and now I had to figure out how to cope with it.

It was 1980, Friday the 13th, an unusually blistering hot December day. Maybe I could blame what had happened on this renowned day of "bad luck." I wasn't a superstitious person, but after this accident I considered that maybe Friday the 13th truly was a day of bad luck. It also crossed my mind that I might die in the emergency room or even the operating room. I was skeletal—ninety-two pounds—and being 5'5" tall and small-boned I looked emaciated, or so Mike and my friends told me. All I saw was fat girl. I have no idea how or why I had dropped so much weight in only three short months. It was like the previous three months never happened. I don't remember that period of time at all. How could I have lost so much weight and not notice? I was a healthy 115 pounds before the weight loss, and happy as a clam that I was doing what I loved: cooking and playing beach volleyball. I was at my athletic peak, but what I saw in the mirror looked very different to me. I saw a 140-pound chubby girl. It amazes me now for all I've been through how our minds can play tricks on us. To have seen myself as fat is truly a testimony to how we perceive ourselves. I had grown to love the feeling of hunger pangs and the way my clothes felt on my body. I used to hate turtleneck sweaters and only because I thought they made my face look fat and round. I also thought my neck was short. I also never wore tight pants or belts because I felt as though I was suffocating.

Living in Los Angeles isn't easy on women. Constantly looking at pictures in fashion and tabloid magazines had its pressures for me, but I didn't know how much so until it was too late. I'm sure this happened to a lot of young women then and still today. I wanted to look like the models from those magazines. I had no idea they had the same disease I had. I'm assuming they did. Maybe that's why they didn't smile in photos; they were starving to death and miserable. And I had no clue those pictures were retouched to make them look perfect. Still, I wanted to look like them anyway.

Until the accident, I would have never thought of myself as anorexic, just skinny. My dad was thin and my mom curvy and sexy. It wasn't like I disliked food—in fact I loved food. During my teenage years I took over the shopping and preparation for dinner. My days seemed to revolve around what was for dinner and what I was going to serve. When I was twenty-three years old, I began to notice how little food I was eating. I cut out caffeine, white flour and refined sugar. I was obsessed about dying young or getting cancer when I turned twenty-four years old. That's the irony of it all. I had no intention of dying; I just wanted to be lean, not dead. It never occurred to me that it may have been emotional eating, but in hindsight it definitely was. I thought only fat people ate emotionally, right? The fact that I placed so many restrictions on what and how much I ate makes me very sad today. All that delicious food right at my fingertips in the best restaurant kitchens in Los Angeles and I didn't touch any of it. And there's no one to blame but me—but unfortunately I

"I'm number twenty-one at the top right corner."

blamed everything and everyone around me for my problem. I did this to myself. I had a love-hate relationship with food.

* * *

As a child I had tons of energy. I played outside all the time, climbed trees, rode my Stingray bike and made mud pies. I wasn't interested in make up, shopping or any girlie things until later. I had no interest in engaging in athletics in school but I was always doing something. It wasn't until the 7th grade that I became involved with the school athletic program. President Lyndon B. Johnson started the *Presidential Physical Fitness Awards* program in 1966. I was relatively popular, or so I thought. I had that one friend we all have in life that makes our lives seem more difficult. Her name was Sandy. She gave me my first kitten, Bootsie. He was grey with white paws and so sweet. We would play the

Ouija board for hours and were convinced we called in Boris Karloff one night on Halloween. But as we grew older, I felt like she was becoming more competitive with me and began doing not very nice things to me. She was on the committee for the "Best of Everything" contest who counted the votes fudging them so she would win. I had no friends that year as I decided all girls were mean and horrible and became somewhat of a recluse. Instead of confronting her I turned my disappointment and anger towards the athletic program. For the record, I won multiple Presidential Athletic Awards that semester.

After that experience I didn't join any athletic programs until I was a senior in high school. My grades were poor from a lack of interest in math and social studies. I was feeling like a failure, so to avoid my problems, I tried out for the varsity volleyball team. I watched the girls practice before and after school and thought I could definitely play the game. I never played volleyball in my life before I tried out for the team but felt like I'd played the game for years. I was surprised though that I made the team. I was a setter and made MVP that year. I was offered a volleyball scholarship to Pepperdine University, in Malibu. I didn't take it because they didn't have an art program and they required all students to attend Chapel three times a week. No way I was going to Chapel. This is the one and only reason I didn't take it really, not because they didn't have an art program. No one was going to make me go to church, but I have to say, this may be my one and only regret in life. I also never injured myself playing any sport, so I wouldn't describe myself as accident-prone. I hardly ever got even the tiniest scratch. Was this horrible accident making up for all that time?

The morning of the dreaded accident, I started off the day with the same two hundred–calorie breakfast: a concoction of nonfat yogurt, strawberries, bananas, blueberries, Muesli, and maple syrup. Sounds healthy, right? Not for me, because it was a deliberately measured amount of food which I always ate from my special six-ounce bowl. I measured everything

"I was about 88 pounds here at State Beach with the local lovely man Simon. This was in 1984."

I ate and later began documenting all of it. Looking back, I realize how exhausting that was. My obsessive behavior kept me from creating, resting, socializing, and most importantly, focusing on things other than myself. I compulsively wrote down explicit documentation of what I ate three times a day. I also resented the fact that everyone I knew told me I needed to put on weight, which was ridiculous from my point of view because what I saw was a fat girl. It was such a waste of time. I know that now. Here is the recipe for what I used to eat for breakfast then, and what I now call "The Anorexic Breakfast":

"Playing Volleyball with Daryl R. at the number one court at State Beach California. He was responsible for helping me to begin putting on healthy weight without me freaking out. It was one step forward and 20 steps backwards, but I managed to put on 5 pounds in a year."

The Anorexic Breakfast

1/2-cup fat-free vanilla frozen yogurt
6 blueberries
3 strawberries, quartered
4 thin slices banana
1/4 cup Muesli
Drizzle of maple syrup

Directions: In this order, place half the yogurt, then half the fruit, then half the granola and a tiny drizzle of maple syrup. Repeat once.

* * *

I stopped playing volleyball after I graduated high school but a few years later I wanted to play again. Someone told me about a famous beach called State Beach in Santa Monica,

California, which was the place to play volleyball so I decided to check it out. This is where I met my future husband, Mike. We played two hours of volleyball on that fateful morning, just like I did almost every day. If I didn't play with Mike I had the privilege of occasionally playing with the greats like Randy Stoklos, Singin Smith, Andy Fishburn, Darryl Ruocco, Wilt Chamberlain, Pat Riley- to name a few. Every single day without fail I would play three or four hours of volleyball and then swim three miles in the ocean. If that wasn't enough I would go to the gym and ride the stationary bike for an hour and lift weights—all on a two hundred–calorie breakfast. After the workout, I thought maybe I should order a sandwich because I was hungrier than usual, but I ordered my usual protein shake instead. It was 2:30 p.m. and that shake was supposed to hold me over until staff dinner at 5:30 after all that exercise? Not!

I'd been working at L'Orangerie, the only five-star restaurant in LA at the time, for eight months and loving every minute of it. It was also my second apprenticeship. Prior to this job, I spent the previous year at Ma Maison, where I mentored with Wolfgang Puck, the hottest chef in Los Angeles at the time. He combined French cuisine with the lighter California cuisine he basically pioneered. He taught me the basics and opened my mind. For that I am forever grateful. The kitchen at L'Orangerie was run by a fantastic, flamboyant chef named Jean Luc-Renault. He taught me a great deal about traditional French cooking and made it look so easy. It was a departure from what Wolfgang had taught me which was nice. I worked the line and was responsible for preparing many dishes. Even though it wasn't my job, there was a dish I was madly in love with. It was called, Le Oeufs et Caviar; eggs with caviar. It was L'Orangeries' most famous dish. It was served in its eggshell and filled with creamy scrambled eggs mixed with shallots, cream and chives, then topped off with Tsar Nicoulai California Estate Osetra caviar. I was responsible for main course dishes and side dishes, but what I looked most forward to preparing was the fresh pasta everyday.

The staff entered the kitchen from the back door, where our produce and meat were also delivered. The kitchen had a butcher station, which was unusual among professional kitchens. Meat normally came already butchered from the purveyors at the restaurants I'd worked in before, so for me it seemed rather extravagant. Space is always a precious commodity in a professional kitchen. As my career progressed, I only saw one other butcher station again and that was at Roger Verge's restaurant in Cannes, France. The "line," which is where food is cooked to order and then passed on to the waiter or expeditor through what is called a "window" also seemed relatively short for such an extravagant menu and a restaurant of this culinary magnitude as we turned out some of the finest French cuisine in Los Angeles at the time.

*   *   *

When I arrived to work that heartbreaking day, December 13th, 1980, I was forty-five minutes late and starving; so I went straight to the walk-in refrigerator for something small to eat. The shake hadn't done the job. Shocking. I grabbed a tiny crab apple to nibble on until staff dinner. Oddly, I had tons of energy. It seemed to me that the less I ate as time went on, the more I felt a wired and erratic energy. That coupled with the emptiness I felt, a feeling I had started to crave, was slowly beginning to wear me down.

It was the holiday season, and we were serving festive dishes like duck rillettes with baked crab apples drizzled with maple syrup and served with celery root puree. My specialty was a yam gratin, derived from the classic potato gratin, which was smothered in heavy French cream, fresh thyme, onions, garlic and aged Gruyere cheese. The walk-in was full of beautiful vegetables, fruits, and meats from Europe. I liked that the produce came in imported wood boxes, giving the walk-in a rustic European feel. It didn't feel like

Christmastime, though, because it was so unusually hot outside.

Since I was late, I was in a bit of a rush: I needed to get my pasta dough done and my special made by five o'clock so the waiters could sample it before we opened. As I began to create my special pasta, I nibbled on the tiny crab apple. This was the special pasta I was thinking of making that day:

Linguini with Porcini Mushrooms and Duck Breast

Serves 2
1 Muscovy duck breast, skin scored
3 porcini mushrooms, quartered (You can use any mushroom if you can't find this kind. A great substitute would be morels, chanterelles, or shiitake.)
1-3 Tbsp. olive oil
5 cloves garlic, sliced
1 white onion, small dice
3 Tbsp. sun-dried tomato pesto
1/2 cup fresh Italian parsley, chopped
4 Tbsp. grated Parmesan
1/2 lb. linguini, fresh or dried
Salt and pepper to taste

Directions: Sear the duck breast skin side down in no oil. Cook for 4 minutes on high heat and turn. Cook another 8 minutes. If you prefer well done, cook 10 minutes on each side. Remove from the pan. Boil water for the pasta. In the same pan you cooked your duck in (do not clean the pan), sauté the garlic, onion, and mushrooms, adding a little olive oil if needed. Cook until the mushrooms are soft, about 5 minutes. (If you are lucky enough to find fresh porcinis, they take about 2 minutes to cook.) Boil the pasta until al dente. Drain and toss in with the mushrooms and add the sun-dried tomato pesto, Italian parsley, salt, and pepper. Separate into 2 pretty bowls. Slice the duck breast as thin as you can on a diagonal. Split the amount in half and lay the sliced duck on top of the pasta. Sprinkle with Parmesan and enjoy with a fantastic Margaux or my favorite, a Pomeral. I'd recommend a La Gloria cigar after dinner.

* * *

As was routine, I put the flour, eggs, and water into the Robot Coupe. A Robot Coupe is the French version of a Cuisinart, except without the five different safety features. Most restaurant kitchens use this type of machine because of its functionality, power, and ease of use. I thought *all* machines were perfect, thinking they could never be faulty or dangerous. Just as I began to make the pasta dough, Virgini Ferry, the owner of the restaurant along with her husband, Gerard Ferry, came into the kitchen and called me over to have a word with her. I remember thinking how out of the ordinary that was. She never came to the restaurant early and hardly came into the kitchen unless it was during dinner service, usually to say that a customer was complaining about the food or asking why it was taking so long to come out.

Her tone was panicked and concerned. "You look weird," she said.

"I'm not tired," I responded.

"I didn't say you looked tired. I said you look weird."

"What do you mean?"

"You look odd and I want you to go home."

Not only was this a bizarre request, I couldn't understand why she came to tell me something so random. I'm quite sure she couldn't understand why she was telling me this either.

"Are you going to pay me to go home? Because I can't afford to go home."

"No."

"Okay. Then I'm staying. I'm fine, really I am."

At this point I should have asked her exactly why she was telling me this and why I looked weird, but I didn't.

"Okay, but please, be careful. You look peculiar. I can't really explain it."

"Okay, I will. Don't worry, okay? Everything is fine. Really, I'll be okay."

Famous last words.

* * *

I should have taken a moment to think about why she was telling me to leave and given some serious thought about how abnormal and out of context that conversation really was. She wasn't able to explain why and I didn't ask. That alone is weird, right? No! In retrospect, it was so random that I should have run, not walked, right out the back door and driven home. I chose to ignore her warning as it was impossible to understand where she was coming from. But in my defense, who would have thought in a million years that what happened in the next few minutes could have possibly happened? No one. The really dangerous thing about this disease is that not only is the body malnourished, so is the brain. I wonder – what if I didn't have an eating disorder, would I have heeded her advice and left?

After that little conversation, I resumed making the dough by pulsing the machine for about a minute to create a meal-like texture. Knowing the mixture would stick to the bottom of the plastic bowl, I turned the machine off and removed the lid to scrape the sticky mixture off the bottom. I always used my hand to incorporate the ingredients. Then the vibe, or whatever you want to call it that Virgini was feeling, unfortunately became my unforgiving reality. As I tossed the ingredients around the machines bowl it suddenly and without warning turned on for a split second, with my hand at the bottom of the bowl. There was pause—a short space in time where everything stopped, as though I had completely missed a second of my life. I heard and felt a thudding sound, the same kind of sound you'd hear if your car ran over a small animal. I immediately thought, *Oh my God, what just happened?* I couldn't hear anything or feel anything. Everything was moving in slow motion around me. I felt like I was in a tunnel, watching my co-workers running towards me in slow motion, asking me what happened. Something unquestionably bad had happened. I must have screamed or something.

My hand at that point was out of the machine and in my apron. Latifa, a beautiful and strong French woman, fellow line cook, and friend calmly said, "Let me see your hand."

"No. I have to look first. Just give me a minute."

"Are you sure you have a minute? Why don't you let me look first? It might be too upsetting for you to see."

"Maybe, but it's my hand and I want to look first."

I swear, to this day I have no idea how I found the courage or the clarity to look myself. As upsetting everything was, I was strangely articulate and coherent.

As I opened my apron to look at my hand I discovered I was missing some fingers. It was surreal. I was petrified to look too closely at them but I noticed that my little finger was dangling, barely hanging on by a thread. Now, that freaked me out. Just like that my body had changed forever. I had my whole life ahead of me and now this shit happens? What was going to happen to me now? I had huge dreams and expectations for myself and in one split second my life had changed drastically. I was now an amputee. What was I going to do about that? How was I going to live with this nightmare? I was perfect and then I wasn't. My ego and pride reared their ugly heads. I had no idea until that moment how vain and superficial I had become—or had I always been this way but had no reason to take notice? I was going to have a hard time dealing with this, I knew that much.

The reality that I might die before or during surgery because I was way too skinny crossed my mind, and it wasn't a good feeling. Maybe if I had eaten that fucking sandwich at the gym I would feel better about the surgery. I wanted a big, fat, juicy hamburger right then. This accident wasn't something I could put a butterfly on or bandage. This was the real deal. I faintly remember asking if someone could butterfly them at L'Orangerie. I remember seeing my blood, veins, muscles, and tendons. Yet I wasn't bleeding—something I found bizarre. The endorphins my body created from being in shock gave me a high I'd never known before. Even when I dropped acid I didn't feel like that. I felt like it was some kind of supernatural protection. I felt no pain whatsoever. I am a very visual person though and the image of my hand that afternoon is something I will never forget for the rest of my life.

I was feeling a bit faint, but passing out in front of my co-workers wasn't going to happen. I kept telling myself to snap out of it and hang on. Losing control and showing everyone how weak I really was, wasn't what I had in mind. What is really amazing to me as I look back is that I wasn't able to control what was happening yet I was still trying. If I could have I would have just bandaged my fingers up and kept on working. That's what I've always done. I burned my arm badly once at my first job at the Good Earth in Westwood. I was cleaning the griddle after serving almost 900 people breakfast and lunch and the grill brick slipped, causing it to slam into the upper right hand corner in a puddle of scalding hot oil giving me an immediate third-degree burn. I literally watched my skin come to a boil three times, popping every time until the third time. I'm telling you the truth when I say that severing my fingers wasn't nearly as painful as burning my arm. There was no endorphin rush for that burn. I still thought I could work but couldn't as the heat coming from that burn was so painful I had to keep it submerged in ice water for 4 hours before I could brave the drive home. Little miss tough girl. Don't show pain. Stay in control. It was all about control for me and I was never more out of control.

After I saw the condition of my fingers, I realized I couldn't go on working. It was Friday night! What were they going to do without me? I even said that maybe I could come back after they bandaged me! I was obviously in serious shock. I looked up and said in a terrified voice, "Okay, this is really bad. I have to go to the emergency room now."

Latifa was a wild and animated woman who was afraid of nothing and still isn't. I love her. We had been through some interesting times together while in the kitchen. She was more competitive than I was, if that's possible. She asked again if she could please see my hand.

"No," I said. "I have to get to the hospital now. It's really bad and I'm afraid if I let the pressure off my fingers they might start bleeding, and I don't want to die."

"You're not going to die," she said. "Are your fingers intact?"

"No! That's what I'm saying. Three are gone and probably in the dough and my pinky is dangling."

Looking back, I am astounded that I was capable of having a conversation.

"Oh my God! Which fingers are gone?" she nearly screamed. Realizing that someone had to retrieve my fingers, she yelled, "Someone get her fingers out of the bowl!"

Shiro, one of the pastry chefs who I worked with at Ma Maison before L'Orangerie, gallantly went over to the machine and calmly said, "Someone get a clean vessel of some kind and put a lot of ice in it with cold water." He bravely found my fingers amongst the pasta dough and put them in the ice water. I am quite sure I could not have done what he did that day. Meanwhile, Rochelle, another pastry chef, got her car to drive me to the hospital. The disbelief I felt was so intense that it was all I could do to not freak out. I truly believed I could get my fingers sewn up in no time and go back to work the next day. It was too much for me to engage in the seriousness of what had happened to me. My coworkers' voices continued in slow motion. Virgini and Gerard came running in to see what had happened to me, but I was already on the way to the car to be taken to the hospital. I remember turning to look at their faces, and they looked absolutely mortified.

* * *

Rochelle drove me to Cedars Sinai Hospital while I sat in Latifa's lap in the back seat, hanging on to her for dear life.

Rochelle was driving like a crazy person, traveling too fast dangerously down the sidewalk screaming out the window, "Get out of the way! This is an emergency!" I wanted to look at my hand again to make sure I wasn't bleeding profusely, but Latifa wouldn't let me. I could see spots of blood seeping through my apron though and it scared me to death. Holding my head close to her chest, she said in her thick French accent, "It'll be okay sweetie. You'll see. You're a strong woman and you'll get through this just fine. I promise."

Sobbing like a little girl in need of her mother, I said, "Shit! Why did this happen to me, man? I'm getting married in two months. Where's my mom? Did anyone call Mike?" I looked down and saw the vessel of ice water where my three fingers were floating, detached from my body. The sense of loss was overwhelming and inexplicable. My fingers had died. Would I ever see them on my hand again? I was convinced that Mike would leave me because I wasn't perfect anymore. Worse, if Mike left me because of this who else would want me? The gloom and doom I was feeling was so deep that I felt like I should go ahead and die. My life felt hopeless; how was I going to ever recover from something this traumatic? Everything I had worked so hard for over the last two and half years had come to a screeching halt. My career was over. Kaput. Death sounded great right about then . . . but I was also afraid of dying. I was totally screwed. If I died, at least I wouldn't have to go through what seemed to be most definitely unbearable and difficult. Why did this happen to me? What did I do wrong to deserve this? Why did I always have to use my hand to turn the dough in that damned machine? The chef always said I should use a spatula or a wooden spoon, but I didn't. I thought it was important to touch all the food I prepared. I thought it would make a difference in the way my food tasted. But making pasta dough in a powerful machine and sticking my hand in it was simply stupid, and now I would pay for my stupidity for the rest of my life.

* * *

Minutes away from the hospital, I had no idea what to expect. Even if they did reattach my fingers, how would they feel and look? Would they look similar to how Frankenstein was sewn up? Would they look like a zigzagged, chaotic mess? I imagined they would feel constant pressure, always swollen, making them painful. Would I have arthritis? I mean the damage would be significant so the possibility of arthritis was very real to me, constantly reminding me of what a stupid idiot I was. More than likely there would be more surgery required later on if they were able to reattach them, which I would hate. Maybe it would be better to just sew the ends up and call it a day. I knew my co-workers couldn't stay and that alone made me feel terrified. I didn't enjoy the idea that whatever was about to happen I had no control over. I was going to be at my most vulnerable and needy. I hated being transparent.

Chapter 2
The Emergency Room

We finally arrived at the hospital after what felt like an eternity to me. Did Mike and my parents know yet? I knew no one at the hospital. Could I trust any of them to know what to do? I didn't have a choice though, did I? I hated hospitals and still do. I took the health stuff seriously, but obviously I took it a bit too far; I became anorexic – just to avoid the hospital. How ironic.

Latifa gave me a big hug and said, "Stay strong, sweetie. You're in good hands now."

"Don't leave. I'm scared I might die."

"Oh sweetie, you'll be just fine and you know I have to go. I'm going to have to cover two stations tonight because of you!"

I actually laughed. She could do it without any problems. She was probably looking forward to it! Still, I felt horrible that she was going to be working her ass off because of me.

"I'll call you tomorrow, okay sweetie? I love you."

"I love you too." Latifa called everyone sweetie, and I liked how she said it: with genuine feeling.

There I stood, alone and scared to death. A team of nurses came rushing over to me, put me on a gurney, and rolled me into a partially private room. Did someone call ahead to let him or her know I was coming or was that my ego talking? Once I was situated in a semi-private area, I could hear other people behind the curtain dividers—some moaning, some crying and some talking with family members. They immediately plunged what was left of my hand into iodine and the fingers that had been severed went into a big bowl of ice with what looked like iodine too. I wondered if my pinky would fall off in the iodine. I wanted to look but couldn't bring myself to do it.

After what seemed like a lifetime lying there alone, I began to feel some pain. Scared to feel any pain I yelled for a nurse, asking her where the doctor was and if I could have something for my pain. Instead of answering me, they had a slew of questions for me instead—who to call, if I was allergic to anything, if I had AIDS, and whether I had any psychological problems. I said no to all of them except for the allergy question: I was allergic to codeine, penicillin, and to be safe I said anesthesia, too. And even though I wasn't okay psychologically, I said I didn't have any problems—though it was clear to anyone who looked at me that there was something going on. But it was my life and insisting on seeing a doctor immediately seemed reasonable. Time was of the essence, at least in my mind. I did, however, find it interesting that they weren't freaking out. That alone helped me stay as calm as I could, but I still had a few questions of my own.

"Why are you all so calm? My fingers were just severed off in a machine. Aren't you worried about me?"

One nurse said, "No. You are hardly bleeding and you seem alert."

"Where's the doctor?'"

The head nurse explained, "The hospital is flying in a highly qualified micro-surgeon from Chicago. He should be here in a few hours."

A few hours? Was she kidding? *I'll be dead by then*, I told myself. "What? That's forever! What if I die before then?"

"You are not going to die," the nurse said. "We couldn't operate on you now anyway because you just ate food thirty minutes ago. There could be a danger of you aspirating."

"You mean a tiny little crab apple is enough to cause that?"

"Yes," she told me, "even a tiny crab apple can do that. In the meantime, we are all here if something should happen."

I couldn't help but detect a bit of sarcasm.

"Please, can I have something for my pain?" I pleaded.

"I'm sorry, I'm not allowed."

I'm not allowed? Why not? She was so casual about the whole thing it was disturbing to me. Not even under these circumstances was I feeling any kind of love or compassion. I was feeling so alone and in need of both for what I was going through. It seemed she had no feeling for me and didn't care what had happened to me. I guess this happens to some people in the caring profession. When they do what they do for too long, they must automatically detach from all situations so they don't get eaten up alive by genuinely caring for a patient. I get it, sort of. I could never do what she did for a living. No way. I care too much about people and would become emotionally involved with my patients. She was probably a very caring person and I couldn't see it, I was so caught up in my problems. The truth is I had huge amounts of fear and was so hungry that no amount of love or caring would have helped, so I shifted my focus onto placing blame—and what better place than with her?

Sarcastically and in a condescending tone I said, "I'm hungry, and I'm sure if I don't eat I will die in there and it will be your fault. I want a hamburger."

I can't believe how rude I was. And the fact that I had an appetite while my fingers were soaking in iodine is astonishing for me to think about today. I realized right then how much of a deficit in calories I had and how much it was impacting my behavior. But in my defense, I actually felt I just might die in the operating room if I didn't get something to eat.

The nurse said in a clinical yet patient tone, "You know I can't give you anything to eat and you aren't going to die. I can give you an ice cube to suck on if you like."

"Seriously, look at me. I am clearly emaciated and need something to eat."

That was the first time and the last time I admitted I was beyond thin and it was the last time I said that out loud for the next fourteen years. I actually *knew* I was emaciated, but quickly dismissed that truth after I left the hospital.

"I'm sorry, Lisa," she said. "I can't do that. You'll be just fine. Good news, though. The doctor landed early and should be here in about twenty to thirty minutes. Sit tight."

Sit tight? Where was I going to go? Jogging? *What a stupid idiot*, I thought. There I was, lying in the emergency room with what was left of my fingers soaking in iodine for almost three brutally long hours with nothing to help me with the ever-increasing pain, and she wanted me to sit tight? I was also wondering why I wasn't bleeding after all this time. I started to panic. What if my lack of eating had caused my blood supply to lessen? Was that even possible? The natural endorphins that were protecting me from the pain were starting to wear off, and quickly. I was so scared—why wasn't she able to see that? I wondered how she might feel if the situation were reversed. But then again, I couldn't imagine how hard it must be in the ER. She'd probably seen many people die in there or who were in much worse shape than me. Where was my family? I hoped they would come before the surgery. I knew they were still working, and Mike was more than likely playing volleyball. Clearly, I wasn't behaving reasonably. That poor nurse didn't deserve the drama I needed to perpetuate my disease, even though I was unaware that I even had a disease at that time. All I knew was one thing and that was I needed to eat, and that wasn't going to happen for at *least* the next several hours.

* * *

While I waited for what seemed to be yet another eternity, I fantasized about the burger I really wanted. Any burger would have done right then, even a crappy Big Mac or the Jack in the Box bacon cheeseburger that I loved to "chew and spit" so often. But I wanted a nice, high-quality chunk of ground veal from Vicente Foods Market in Brentwood, California to make the juicy and succulent burger I was craving. Vicente Foods has been around for almost seventy years and carries the very best of everything- gourmet vegetables, excellent bottled oils and sauces, premium beef and incredibly fresh and expensive fish. I visualized myself biting into that burger, tasting it as I was building it in my head. I added my two favorite things to the mix: bacon and avocado. As I lay there *starving*, I could actually smell the fatty aroma of the veal and the bacon as it cooked. The smell of bacon always comforted me as a child and the aroma it released throughout the house as it sizzled made my mouth water every time. Even if I wasn't hungry, there was always room for bacon.

My imagination became larger than life. I saw myself pile on the mayonnaise, avocado, bacon, lettuce, tomato and a thick slice of Muenster cheese that melted slowly on top of it all. As I created that juicy burger in my head, I could taste it—and it tasted divine. At that moment, I found myself so incredibly sad that I had been denying myself these delicious foods that I loved so much and only because I thought I was fat. Why was I so afraid of eating? What the hell had happened to me and even more frightening, why didn't I think I was on such a dangerous path? I told God, which was the first time I'd included God in any part of my life except of course when I was swearing and using His name in vain which was a lot, I would make the burger I was creating as soon as I got out of the hospital. Here's the recipe:

Veal Burger with Bacon and Avocado

Serves 1
1/3 lb. ground veal
3 slices cooked bacon
1 sliced red onion
1 slice Muenster cheese
1/2 avocado, slightly mashed
1 piece of red leaf lettuce
3 Tbsp. mayonnaise
1 Tbsp. BBQ Sauce
Salt and pepper to taste
1 Hawaiian Bun

Directions: Season the veal with salt and pepper. Sear or grill the veal to whatever temperature you like. I prefer medium rare—yes, even with veal. When the burger is done, you may toast the bun if you like. The Hawaiian bun is awesome any which way. Then smother both sides of the bun with mayo and the barbecue sauce. Layer the avocado, bacon, onion, veal patty, cheese, and then the lettuce, and top with the bun. This would go great with a Hefeweizen beer and a nice light cigar like an Avo Uvesian.

* * *

Snapping out of my fantasy, I found myself still lying in that cold room starved and panicked, waiting for the micro-surgeon to show up and hopefully save my fingers—maybe even my life. I was more concerned about living instead of him re-attaching my fingers. The more time I had to think about everything I was developing bad thoughts about the surgery. My chances for survival seemed to be decreasing every minute I had to wait. The reality of what happened to me was beginning to sink in—trauma I wondered how I was going to heal from. Nothing could have possibly looked positive at that moment. How could I as a woman who *chose* to starve herself expect to live through a surgery that would more than likely take a long time? It's difficult to explain the plethora of feelings I was going through. I could go on and on, but I felt like a hypocrite. I had spent the last three months starving myself, which would translate into a slow death for some, and now I could die as a result of my ac-cident.

* * *

I went into another dream-like state, the same feeling I'd had on the way to the hospital. Strangely, and for the first time in my life, I felt an urgency to connect with God for real and promised to eat normally after I got out of the hos-pital. I was in full on panic mode and needed something or someone more powerful than me to step in and save me, but who was I fooling? I was in deep shit and promising God that I would eat normally after the surgery was a flat out lie. I needed Him to keep me alive. I'd heard He performed miracles and lots of them. Maybe He'd give me one even though I didn't believe. I hadn't once thought, cared or believed in God during my childhood. I believed in the universe though, which may have helped save my ass in life up until the accident, even though I'd spent twenty-three years as an atheist.

God, please let me live, I said silently. I felt stupid talking to something I couldn't see and didn't feel like I was convincing. I'd heard that prayer could be powerful, but since I'd never given Him the time of day my whole life, why should He answer my prayer now? I said quietly to myself, "I'll make a deal with you, God. If you let me live through the surgery, I *promise* that I will eat like a normal person again." What made me think I could make a *deal* with God, anyway? This was huge in any case. I was hoping He believed me and would save me. I had zero intention of doing what I had promised God I would do. I just wanted to live. But if He did answer my prayer and I didn't follow through, what would He think of me then? Would He ever answer any one of my prayers? I wasn't religious and worse, I had no relationship with Him whatsoever. I also had no clue how to pray. Has he saved me many times prior to this? I was hoping for a miracle. I had been taking my life for granted on a million levels for a long time. What were the life-changing ingredients I needed to live a more meaningful and fulfilling life? It occurred to me, ever so fleetingly mind you, that He might have caused this accident to snap me out of the shitty way I was going about my life. I asked God for help, and now I had no choice but to wait and see if He even heard me or cared.

* * *

I began to think about all the things I had done in the past that definitely didn't align with God's laws, like the first

From left: "Terry, me, Peggy Thurston and Nick Persian just before leaving for the Homecoming Party."

time I had sex. I was a tender fifteen and a half years old and was dating the most popular "bad boy" in school, Terry, when I had my first sexual experience. What was I thinking? Not only was I far too young to have sex, it was illegal. He looked like a Native American with a serious tan. Every girl in school wanted him and when you're a seventeen year old and a teenage male with raging hormones, why not accommodate them? I knew I was too young for sex but went ahead and did *it* anyway, cutting school and doing it on my parents' bed, no less. I had no idea how serious the consequences of my actions would be. What if I had become pregnant? What a total disaster that would've been. But my hormones were raging too, and that was all that mattered. It wasn't like Terry had a gun pointed to my head forcing me do it, but I didn't want to be known as a prude, and honestly I was curious.

By the time I realized it wasn't what I wanted it was too late, causing my 'first time' to be disappointing. It wasn't like Terry didn't know what he was doing, it was because I knew what *I* was doing was wrong. I felt shame afterward. I had no idea how special and intimate the act of sex really was until that moment, but knowing this didn't seem to stop me from wanting more in the future. In hindsight, sex isn't something you do haphazardly, but we do. To share one's soul with another shouldn't be taken lightly, but unfortunately it often is. Still, instead of using that experience as a lesson, I continued to sleep around for the next four to five years with people I barely knew. I needed the instant gratification sex gave me, which would mean to some that I had addiction issues. Back then, the only addictions I thought existed were alcohol and drug abuse and plenty of my friends had issues with those, I just didn't know it. Then I went celibate as I was grossed out with myself when I turned twenty-two years old. I didn't know I was a sex addict. I thought I was a normal, hormonal girl. But the fact remained that I was 'lost Lisa' and to make things worse, my promiscuity left me with a feeling of emptiness afterwards and every single time. It wasn't Terry's fault I ended up like this. He didn't know I was an insecure mess. It was my choice to move on in the fashion I did. But being the expert on placing blame, I did blame him for many years after. Oh how easy it is to blame others for our demise. Not having a relationship with God or being involved in any other kind of religion probably didn't help matters for me either. *I* was God. *I* knew everything. *I* paved the path I thought I should be on. *I* was the center of everyone's happiness. Yet all those paths were painful and lonely. My behavior was horrendous. I was the ultimate alpha female. Lisa the conqueror I was not. I ran around like a free spirit causing huge amounts of damage to others and myself. I was a disaster waiting to happen. Many years later, Terry contacted me and took me to dinner, apologizing vehemently for having treated me the way he did. He felt horrible and in many ways that helped me a lot to hear him say that. To add to the long list of things that happened to me because of my own stupidity, I contracted a venereal disease when I was sixteen years old. I was convinced I got it from a toilet seat because I couldn't fathom the thought of getting something like this from Terry or from sleeping with someone after we broke up. I didn't even know I had it until one night when I was working at the Brentwood Theater, a movie theater in Santa Monica. Suddenly at the beginning of my shift, I found myself lying on the candy counter in the fetal position in agonizing pain. The cramping was unbearable. My mom came and rushed me to the emergency room where I was probed by at least ten interns. To say I was in a very compromising position is an understatement. When I spoke with my GP about it afterwards I was with my mom, and if that wasn't humiliating enough, he said I contracted the disease about a month before and that if I had caught it at the beginning he could have treated it but it was too late. I was also facing an unknown amount of time of sterility (which was the good news), but it wasn't permanent because the scarring caused by the disease had damaged my fallopian tubes and there was no telling how long they would take to heal (which was the bad news). Still, I continued to have unprotected sex. I must have been a masochist. Why else would I continue to inflict so much pain on myself? Where did all of this shit come from? Oh, and I thought I was immortal too. Why did I think that way? Obviously I was starving for attention, but I certainly didn't plan on contracting a venereal disease. I was immune to everything. (Yes, I am being sarcastic.) Mortality was a very scary thing to me at the time. Even when my best friend died in a head-on collision when I was fifteen, I still couldn't accept the fact that we *all* die sooner or later. I was a frightened teenager; afraid I wouldn't get enough time in to do everything I wanted to do.

Then there was my second boyfriend, Terry. Two Terry's back to back—what were the odds of that happening? He was gorgeous, just like the first Terry, but while Terry the first looked like an Indian, Terry the second looked like a surfer. He was a gentle soul and introduced me to hunting and water skiing. His mother had a trailer in Lake Mojave, and he drove a bitchin' orange Blazer. He was the son of the handsome and gallant Robert Taylor, who was married to Ursula Thiess. We were together for about one and a half years when I began to go down the empty road of "jet-setting." We were nearing the end of our relationship anyway, so I broke up with him. I didn't want to hurt him. He was an amazing guy.

* * *

As I waited for the doctor, I felt like my issues with men had nothing to do with my father or mother—at least, I didn't think they did. Maybe they were too supportive of me and gave me too much freedom. They gave me tons of freedom. Maybe because they knew they couldn't control me. They seemed to care very little about my interests. They never attended the volleyball tournaments I was in or dance contests I competed in at various clubs around Los Angeles. Although mom would always help with the choreography with my dance partners in our living room, I still wished they had come to the actual competition. They did come to see me sing once at glee club in junior high school, and also when I danced *The Nutcracker Suite* when I was twelve and only because those were the fine arts they enjoyed—they never saw how important those hobbies were to me. I guess that hurt me more than I realized. For some reason history, geography, math and learning a foreign language didn't interest me at all. What did those subjects have to do with art, dancing, sports, music and my future? Nothing! Sports and physical activity somehow gave me confidence. Maybe that's why I liked sex so much—just for the sport of it. Knowing better and still not having the courage to make better choices, I continued to make bad choices, except when it came to cooking. Cooking seemed to be the only good choice I was making.

* * *

Slowly snapping out of my second "trance," I wondered while lying on the gurney how I was going to break free from the destructive patterns I had created for myself, which in such a short amount of time had caused me such great pain. The sad truth was that the pain and hurt I created felt good to me, yet it felt just as bad. I had created a bizarre type

"Here I was 16 years old and was cold after tandem surfing at first point in Malibu, California with some surfer dude."

of victimization for myself, and it fueled my eating disorder. I was spinning with memories and questions I desperately needed answers to and I wanted them immediately. That was who I was then—wanting answers now, not yesterday. I had no patience then, and didn't for a very long time. I had no idea what was going to happen to my fingers or to me, and that alone was terrifying to me. I had no choice but to let go of the outcome, but this was a stupid hope that didn't exist.

* * *

Finally, the doctor arrived. He had no idea what he was about to deal with. My hunger had turned into anger and gripping fear. When he introduced himself, I couldn't believe his last name started with "H-A-N-D." What were the odds of that? I've noticed throughout my life that doctors and other professionals with specialties seem to have a part of their name connected to their field—and his happened to associate itself with my accident? Weird.

"So Lisa, how are you doing?"

How am I doing? "I'm just fabulous. This is how I was planning on spending my Friday night."

I don't have any idea where that came from. My guess is that I was at my wits' end and my brain was seriously malnourished.

"Good to see you've got a sense of humor at a time like this. The nurse will be in to prep you for surgery in a minute."

I was in pain and had zero filters that day; I found myself completely paranoid and powerless to edit my thoughts and feelings. The paranoia I was feeling was so intense that I was incapable of trusting anyone to do his or her job, and it made it impossible for me to be polite or civilized. Then, out of the blue, I was suddenly horrified at the idea I might not be able to do the things I loved like cooking, painting, or using my right hand again for anything. Without self-control of any kind, I reached my left hand out and grabbed this poor guy's crotch, latching on to his testicles with reasonable pressure.

The look on his face was priceless. He couldn't decide if he should try to pull away from me in hopes of releasing the firm grip I had on his testicles, which would cause him substantial pain, or just stand there and wait and see what I was going to do next.

While squeezing his crotch I said with determination, "I'm in pain and I need something now; and if I can't paint, cook, or draw again, I will rip these things off of your body right now."

Shocked at my statement, he yelled for an IV of Demerol and Valium. Equally shocked at what I said, I realized I was hurting the man who had just flown many miles to operate on me and hopefully save my fingers, if not my life. I let him go and began to cry. It was as though someone else

"Terry Taylor and me at Lake Mojave, Nevada. I believe I was 17 years old here."

had taken control of me. I couldn't take the emotional roller coaster anymore and needed drugs.

Two nurses came running over to me and spent about an hour—and I am not exaggerating—trying to find a vein to administer the drugs. My veins were so small—due to my weight most likely that they couldn't find a vein large enough taking what seemed like forever to finally find one. Ultimately they found a spot—and on my left hand, no less. I was hoping the drugs would kick in immediately. I told the doctor how sorry I was and that I was obviously not myself. Being the understanding doctor he was, he assured me I was going to be just fine.

* * *

The drugs kicked in immediately—and thank goodness because I thought I was going to lose my mind. As I look back, I was functioning on raw and depleted energy, which had to have caused all of the chaos I was feeling that day and honestly every day before and after that moment. The drugs made me feel absolutely fantastic and free from pain. For the record I *hated* drugs and have my whole life, but this was a necessity. No choice here at all. I spent a year when I was fourteen years old smoking weed and listening to Led Zeppelin with severe munchies, but I only smoked that crap because I thought it was cool. I never did cocaine because the act of snorting something up your nose that got you high for twenty minutes and caused you to want more seemed pathetic to me. And the personality changes that happened further grossed me out. Man, I am so grateful I never went there. But in this moment nothing sounded better to me. I was higher than a kite and after waiting nearly four hours for the doctor to arrive, the surgery was about to happen.

Having had all that time to reflect I was convinced that if I died it would be just fine by me. I'd lived a pretty full life, so I thought. If it was my time to go, so be it. I acted like I didn't care but I really did and was terrified, even though the whole situation sucked. I couldn't fathom ever seeing my friends or family again, but what if I never saw them again, would they really care? I was such a pain in the ass and full of myself all the time. Where was everybody? Mom, Dad, and Mike had to know what had happened to me at this point. I was in deep pity mode—and in all honesty, I was probably enjoying every minute of it.

The doctor came in and said, "I'm almost ready to operate. It will be over before you know it."

I was so high I actually said, "I want to watch the surgery. I want to watch how you do it and if you are doing it right. I might have an idea you won't think of." As if I knew what to do more than the specialist did, and like I was in my right mind. "And I need to eat a burger or something because I might die during the operation."

Without skipping a beat or responding to absurdity of my request, he said, "You aren't going to die, and there are sufficient nutrients and calories administered during surgery."

"How many calories exactly, do you know?" I said in a panicked state.

Even then, I was concerned about the amount of calories that was about to be pumped into my body. Pretty sad, don't you think? I do.

"No, I don't know exactly, but it's enough so you won't die, I promise. I will see you in a few hours."

We all promise a lot of things during our lifetime, and boy do I know. I had just promised God and hour ago that I'd eat normally after the surgery. How was I supposed to trust him?

"How many hours—two, four, six? How many? Please tell me."

"You are very concerned about time, aren't you? Well, I have no idea how long this will take. It will be over before you know it and you will be alive, that much I do know."

How does he know I'm going to live? I thought. *He's not God.* All of a sudden I was the expert, and acting like God and I were best friends.

"You can't even give me an estimate?"

"No I can't, but if will help you relax . . . three, maybe four hours."

"Really? That's a long time, isn't it?"

"Okay, I have to get ready. I will see you soon."

I remember what happened next like it was yesterday. My hand was wrapped in a zillion bandages as I was rolled into the operating room. Three, maybe four hours—was he kidding? I was going to be saturated with drugs by then and that alone made me nervous. I was sure I was going to be addicted afterwards. As they hooked me up to the EKG machine, the nurses injected me with something that gave me a feeling like I was sinking into nothingness—like the floor was dropping out from underneath me. What a wretched way to feel. I can remember that feeling likened to the ultimate example of having no control whatsoever, which is not a favorite for the anorexic. Then I watched my arm and hand slowly fall over the side of the gurney, and when I looked over at my bandages I saw what looked to me like a waterfall of blood fall to the floor. I thought I passed out watching my blood pour out of my body, but instead my worst fear became a reality: I heard the EKG flat line. I was dying—or so I thought. The last few thoughts I had before I was totally out were these-*I am dying because I'm too fucking skinny. I really wish I had eaten that sandwich at the gym.*

Chapter 3
Hovering Over the Operating Room

Was it possible I was really dying? Now that it may be in front of me, it wasn't so bad after all. I really thought I was dying to be honest. I felt a sense of peace I'd never known before. I felt no pain, only bliss. And to my amazement, I wasn't feeling hungry anymore. I felt like I was being protected from all the pain of the world, yet at the same time I'd never felt so much—not physically but mentally. It was as though my heart was being filled up at heavens gas station, meaning God. How did I know? It was divine. I couldn't have thought of a negative thing if I tried. I felt definitely better than being in my body. I could hear everything that was going on, but I couldn't see anything. Was I on the way to being totally dead, or was I in a coma?

I heard the nurses run over to me. One of them told the others what to do. They began CPR, and when that didn't work, they brought out the paddles. Thank goodness I couldn't feel the pressure on my chest while they pounded on it trying to bring me back to life. I would imagine it to be very painful. It can't feel good when a person's chest bone is broken or they're body is zapped with electricity. I heard someone say they thought this might happen. I did too and I knew why. Sadly, I was too skinny. My blood pressure was probably so low causing it to drop rapidly, initiating me to go into cardiac arrest or whatever the hell was going on with me. While all of that was going on, I felt myself suddenly come right out of my body. I felt weightless, which was rather ironic to me. As I left my body, I rose towards the ceiling. Looking down I saw myself lying on the gurney, looking lifeless. What a trippy feeling it was to see myself lying there being worked on like that. As I rose further and further up in the room I could see everything in the operating room. I had no feelings of fear or panic. I felt peaceful, safe and warm in the arms that were wrapped around me, comforting me, and it felt great. But who or what was holding me? I had always wondered if there was an actual hell and whether it would be hot and horrendous like I'd read about and seen paintings of in books and in museums.

* * *

I knew I wasn't on the way there, or at least convinced myself I wasn't. Wait, could I be? Nah. Everything was telling me I wasn't and as an intelligent person I think I might have been feeling something way different. But was I really on the way to Heaven, or was I stoned out of my mind?

I suddenly felt a presence in the room that felt ethereal, powerful, kind, and definitely not of this world. I continued watching the nurses and doctors frantically trying to revive me from above, and I found myself amazed at how I couldn't feel what they were doing. Bizarre. I was impressed that everyone who was working on me relentlessly seemed determined to bring me back to life, even though it looked hopeless from my point of view. I had such a content look on my face, which was a big clue to me that I was definitely not in *that* body. If my soul was in *that* body, wouldn't I be awake by now?

I had never asked these kinds of questions before, but I knew I was experiencing something special. Was this God trying to tell me something? I felt He was there with me. That idea was intriguing to me, to say the least. Maybe it's something we all inherently know and are born with. Maybe we are reminded of this knowledge in the face of death, or maybe when we don't believe in God He wants to show us. Maybe this is why I had the accident—so that I could see that God exists. Maybe this is how God actually answered my earlier prayer to give me life if I'd eat again. Wouldn't that be something? Was I that special that I got to experience this only to come this close to meeting Him? He sure had gone to great lengths on my account. Or maybe it was my ego again, playing tricks on me. I wouldn't be surprised one bit.

Suddenly, a light appeared in the distance. It wasn't a big light but it was bright and it had certain mightiness to it. This definitely wasn't me waking up looking at a light in the surgery room; it was something else. It had to be the Gates of Heaven. I've seen paintings, videos and pictures of other people going through this same experience. The drawings and many paintings I've seen made it look large and grand, with angels blowing trumpets welcoming you in but this wasn't like that. It was personal. Not a big theatrical entrance into eternity. It was intimate and beautiful. There was softness in the middle of that light, which was encased in a very bright circle of light that was so inviting. My heart had warmth, unlike on earth. It felt cold and hard there. I tried to move towards the light, but it wasn't that easy. Maybe the closer I tried to move to it, I was that much closer to the entrance to Heaven and wasn't meant to go just yet. It was a surprisingly small and narrow entrance. I couldn't believe what I was experiencing.

* * *

I saw a movie called *Defending Your Life* years ago. It is one of the funniest movies of all time but had some very serious questions about Heaven. It presents the most fascinating idea about death and the process we may go through to see if we get to move forward or have to go back because of how we lived our lives. It captures how our fears keep us from achieving great things in life like joy, love, and comfort. This is something I can see clearly now. *Fear* was totally and without question controlling my life. I wasn't in the light. I was in the dark, thinking I could do everything and that I didn't need anyone. Fear is like a tumbleweed: it keeps gathering more and more fear, placing major roadblocks in front of us until we are frozen.

A big part of *Defending Your Life* is also based on bad decision-making. Albert Brooks and Meryl Streep are in a place called Judgment City, a sort of weigh station between Heaven and Earth. They are both on "trial" to see if they get to move forward or go back, being judged by two separate prosecutors and two judges in a courtroom-like setting. Parts of their lives are shown on big movie screens that are used to determine whether they're ready to move on or need to go back to Earth to continue on.

I wondered, as I watched my body being worked on, if I was on trial for making stupid decisions too. Sticking my hand in the machine wasn't the smartest thing to do, but I also knew as I hovered around up there that I didn't do it deliberately. It had never once occurred to me that a machine would turn on while turned off. I certainly had made very poor decisions prior to the accident, however—living haphazardly and thoughtlessly, thinking I was immortal. I chose to believe in reincarnation for those very reasons, but after hanging out near Heaven for a while, I realized there was no such thing as reincarnation—only eternal life. How did I know that? I didn't. I felt it. But I conveniently forgot about that later. I didn't understand eternal life, and I can't explain how I knew what that meant, but I knew that if I made better decisions I would feel the way I felt up there, hovering around in the operating room forever. I liked that idea because it seemed better than reincarnation and coming back to Earth for another round of life on earth. No thanks, especially if I was going to feel hungry all the time! If I was to return into my body and have a memory of my experience, I would definitely give what I learned serious thought.

Defending Your Life's idea of life and death made so much sense to me after going through this experience. I wonder if Albert Brooks died and saw this too or knew someone who did. So many people have experienced what I did that day, and I wondered if they saw the same thing and felt the same way I did. I wondered if some of these people actually got to talk to Jesus, or saw angels or talked to God while in between—and if they did and came back, did they tell anyone? Did they remember?

I knew one thing for sure: talking about this would be hard to explain to someone. I did wonder if I was in a coma, too. Would I wake up to find out it was one, five, or ten years later? Time was irrelevant, from my point of view. Did I want to go back? No, not really. Did I have a choice? Probably not. I had a feeling I would be going back, because as badly as I wanted to get closer to God, He wasn't letting me—and that made me feel sad in a peculiar sort of way. I wasn't afraid to move on any longer, not after experiencing that extraordinary moment, but I knew that if I did die it would certainly destroy my parents. They would never recover from something like this and I wouldn't be able to ease their minds by telling them what I saw and how I felt up there.

* * *

I have no idea how much time had passed, but the light seemed to be calling me closer, so I tried to move towards it again, but I still couldn't. I wondered if my true purpose in life was to cook—to feed the world. I wanted to think so as I enjoyed it so much. But I have to admit, I wanted a whole lot more. It sure felt great to be out of my body. There was no pain, no feelings of self-hatred or self-loathing, only supreme blessedness, something I had never felt on Earth. I also felt an abnormal kind of light within myself, and a self-confidence that was powerful and addictive. I was hoping I would come back to Earth feeling the same way.

I thought life would get easier as I got older, but it wasn't getting any easier and now that this happened it would more than likely be way more difficult. I didn't like that as I realized that maybe that was one of the many reasons I became anorexic. I didn't want to grow up. I wanted to stay a child so I could be taken care of—even though I was fiercely independent. What a mess I was. Frankly, I wanted to believe I was evolved enough to move forward, even if I wasn't.

If I was going to Heaven, I thought, what would I want for my last meal on Earth? I was equating this experience to Death Row somehow, but without the doom and gloom of waiting for my turn to die. I was convinced I'd get a last meal. I had no idea if there was such a thing as a last meal in Heaven. For some reason I didn't think so, but I didn't know for sure, so I decided to entertain the idea and decided what I wanted for my last meal. Though I was all screwed up about eating food, I wanted to think I could eat all I wanted and not gain weight, just like in *Defending Your Life*. Even though I wanted that burger I'd created in the emergency room, I thought of a better one: I saw myself gorging on a huge tin of Russian Beluga 000 caviar with shredded eggs, minced red onion, crème fraîche, and chives with a side of homemade potato chips. I wanted to wash it all down with a big shot of an ice cold Lemon Drop with shaves of ice in it, made with fresh Meyer lemons and Belvedere vodka. *How perfect*, I thought.

I'd had caviar several times before, and it was always just okay until I went to the Cannes Film Festival in 1994 for a movie I'd worked on as a food stylist called *Men*. That was definitely on my top-ten list of epic experiences I'd had in my life so far. The last evening we were there, Sean Young, the star of the film, was invited to a sheik's yacht. She invited my friend and me to come with her. That was very exciting stuff. We all wore white dresses. Mine was a full-length satin number, a gown Greta Garbo would have worn to a private party like that one. We all felt very elegant and important. It was by far the largest boat I have ever been on—it must have been 150 feet long, and it had two pools and a helipad. The view was magnificent as we watched the sunset. The clouds, which were riddled with beautiful hues of violets, reds and yellows that were reflecting on the Mediterranean Sea, moved me. It looked like a huge Renoir painting. My friend and I walked on the deck barefoot, feeling like royalty. I thought about how hard it must be to keep up with this kind of lifestyle, both financially and spiritually. How could one keep track of all that money and keep a firm grip on reality at that level? Who could they trust to manage all of their wealth? Who were their *real* friends? It all seemed so silly to me, like "look at me, I'm rich"—rather obnoxious, I thought—but I'm not one to judge. I do know that if I had that kind of money I wouldn't want to live like they did. I'm a minimalist and rather modest. It's sort of embarrassing to me to be so obvious about how much money you have. But we did have so much fun. I will always remember that week fondly.

On this yacht, there were at least five containers of Russian Beluga 000 caviar scattered about the yacht that I could see, and they came with blinis, crème fraîche and chives. There were 5 two-pound tins, each one bursting with succulent, wet eggs. Every egg was perfect and exactly the same size. That's when you know you've hit the jackpot when you see eggs like that. I went from tin to tin, hoping no one was watching. I must have ended up consuming at least two cups' worth of those fabulously firm, perfectly sized, and succulent pale grey eggs! If my calculations are right, I probably consumed at least $700 worth of caviar in about twenty minutes. Thank goodness I was no longer anorexic during this trip in 1994, or I would have missed out on the fantastic caviar on that enormous yacht and all of the other great meals we had while there. It was much more sophisticated than the last meal I'd had in mind. The following morning I was so bloated from the all the salt that my eyes were half-shut, but I would do it all over again if I had the opportunity. I felt like I died and went to Heaven that night, and now that I just might, caviar seemed like the right choice.

I will share the recipe with you here, though it's difficult to find Beluga 000 caviar. If you by chance find it, it will probably cost you a mini fortune. You can use Servuga, Osetra, or Vegan Caviar as a replacement. Try and find the palest eggs you can. You can also use salmon eggs or golden caviar.

Caviar on Shredded Potato, Crème Fraîche, and Chives

Serves 4 for appetizers
1 russet potato, shredded with the large grate; squeeze excess water out
2 Tbsp. crème fraîche or sour cream
2 Tbsp. chives
1 hard-boiled egg, shaved with a micro plane zester
2–4 oz. caviar
Olive oil
Black pepper

Directions: Mold the potatoes in a silver dollar–size patty. Heat the oil in a cast iron skillet on medium-high heat. Cook on each side to a crispy golden brown. Make twelve potato cakes and then drain them on paper towels. Cool for about an hour. You can make these in the morning for convenience later. Place a medium amount of crème fraîche on the potato cake, then a little shaved egg, then and a generous amount of caviar on top of that and sprinkle with chives.

Meyer Lemon Drop Shot

Serves 4
4 highball glasses, frozen
4 Meyer lemons
8 oz. Belvedere vodka or your favorite vodka
Soda water
Fine sugar

Directions: Freeze four highball glasses overnight. When ready to serve, dip the glass rim in the sugar, then fill with crushed ice. Squeeze the lemons and split into fourths. Split the vodka into fourths and top with soda water. Enjoy.

If you're hard-core like me, just sip a shot of ice-cold vodka while consuming your appetizer! I'm not sure a cigar is a good idea here, but if you must, find a high-quality cigarillo like Romeo y Julieta.

* * *

Snapping out of my caviar fantasy, I heard a voice whispering in the air that said, "Let go of everything, Lisa, so I can do my work on you."

Stunned and unafraid I said, "God? Is that You?"

"Yes," he said.

No way! Was The Almighty Father really speaking to me? I can't explain the depth to which His voice or energy filled my heart; with such love and warmth. It wasn't the kind of excited I would feel if I had just received a brand new car; it was much deeper than that, and that alone made me feel remarkably special. Would I still feel this way when I returned to my body? Even at that moment I still wanted to be in control, and I wondered if He knew it. Who was I kidding? I couldn't control anything up there or on earth, but up there I felt fine not being in control. It made sense and I loved it. For once in my life I could feel that God was in control of everything and not me. It was too much to understand in that moment. Was it possible to let everything go and let God, someone I couldn't see, take charge when I returned? Suddenly it became painfully obvious to me that I was headed in the wrong direction in life, or why else would any of this be happening to me? Was I being healed? I promised myself I would try my very best to let everything go, whatever that meant. To stop constantly talking about food always having to have the last word or always having to be right about everything, if and when I returned to my body. I would talk about art, listen more, not need serious amounts of attention, be the first one to know something and be comfortable in my body. Now those were promises I'd be shocked to keep, but I was feeling so good I thought maybe God was actually healing me so I could be healthy again. I was a walking contradiction when it came to food and my life—full of hypocrisies. I still had no idea that I was completely screwed up about eating food, as I'd only been obsessed with it for a few short months. However, because I loved food so much it wasn't registering. I couldn't cook enough of it or talk enough about it, yet I was afraid to eat any of it. I had no idea that this was another big sign that I had food issues.

* * *

After my short but intense interaction with God, I looked closely at that soft, brilliant, and forgiving white light just in case I was going back. I wanted to take it all in. As I gave into the idea of going to Heaven, I felt a warm breeze brush over me, similar to that of a breeze from the Caribbean ocean. I thought for sure I was on my way after that, but I was wrong. Suddenly, everything went black. The soft, beautiful and peaceful light that I was so drawn to and didn't want to leave was gone in a flash. All I could hear was the EKG beeping again. *I guess I didn't die,* I thought. *Shit.* Then I heard one of the nurses say, "That was a close call." After that, I felt myself fall into a fast and deep sleep. I didn't talk about my experience for years.

Chapter 4

The Surgery and a Few Other Revelations

Before surgery I told the surgeon I was allergic to anesthesia, which was a lie. I had anesthesia just three months prior to the accident. Sadly, it was for an abortion I wasn't planning on having. The feeling I had on anesthesia was so icky that when I came to, I felt nauseous; every time I moved I thought I'd throw up. And I hate throwing up. In retrospect, the abortion—not the accident—is when I really started changing my eating habits and started dropping weight rapidly, but for some reason I chose to ignore the fact that I had one and used the accident as the reason I was so thin. Of course this was not the case. I couldn't have lost that much weight overnight. But I couldn't imagine or admit how emotionally damaging having an abortion was. The accident only compounded it. I was still unaware that I had a problem, even though I begged for a hamburger before surgery, confessing that I was emaciated. I never allowed myself to grieve after the abortion. Karma can be a bitch. I had only been with Mike for about ten months when I became pregnant, and the guilt I carried afterward was pretty harsh. I brushed it into a very deep hole under a very shaggy carpet, lodging that nightmare away in the deepest part of my "I'd like to forget this event ever happened" file. I put the memory of that day away, nice and neat—or so I thought. Meanwhile, the abortion was eating me alive. I was in absolute and total denial. Desperate for answers, I entertained the idea that the guilt I was feeling might have something to do with the accident, but there was no way. I could never deliberately stick my hand through the small hole on top of the machine while it was running. The fact that the accident happened on Friday the 13th—I couldn't help but consider the idea that the day

44

had something to do with it. But since it was impossible, I put that idea out of my head.

* * *

The day I conceived, Mike and I had played a lot of volleyball. I felt unusually passionate that afternoon when we came home, and during our lovemaking, I could *feel* myself getting pregnant. Other women I've talked with about this phenomenon have experienced the same feeling. You just know.

Afterwards, I said to Mike, "I could swear I just got pregnant. Could you feel that? It felt very different than the other times we've had sex."

"Michael and me at my 10 year High School Reunion."

"I guess, I mean I felt something different from *you*. I felt like we were totally connected. Is that what you mean? "

"God, I hope that was all it was. Nothing personal, but my career is about to take off and there's no way I want kids now, or ever for that matter."

"Are you saying you think you just got pregnant?"

"Yes, that is exactly what I'm saying. But I can't imagine being pregnant. I'll get fat and probably have morning sickness. I wish there was a test I could take now to see if I was pregnant. Now I'll have to wait two, maybe three weeks."

"Maybe you're not pregnant. But I do remember you telling me that one day your scars would heal from the gonorrhea you had when you were fifteen."

"Oh my God, I totally forgot about that. The doctor said exactly that. He said it would come back, and out of nowhere. I was hoping all along that it was permanent. Thanks a lot for reminding me."

I was in such denial about the possibility of being pregnant I couldn't possibly process this idea.

"I'm sorry, but I had a feeling you forgot. We'll deal with it later—that is, if we have to. Okay?"

I knew I wasn't ready for a baby and never would be. I had been at L'Orangerie seven months and loving every minute of it. I was like a sponge, sopping up all I could about the culinary arts and what it took to be an executive chef. I was becoming more aware that being a great chef is basically a really amazing cook that knows how to handle food cost, order food, keep an inventory, food rotation and temperature. I desperately wanted to become an executive chef some day. I would dream about food at night, sometimes creating specials that I would prepare the next day.

* * *

Poor Mike, he looked so hurt hearing me talk like I did—and who could blame him? We had just possibly conceived a child, and for me that wasn't a warm and fuzzy thought—it was a nightmare. How unromantic, not to mention rude and insensitive. God, was I really that selfish? Pretending I wasn't pregnant became more and more difficult to do as the weeks went by. I was in such a state of denial I didn't buy a test when I should have. A month had gone by, and I began to notice my appetite was becoming more ravenous, I was constipated and gaining weird weight and my boobs hurt. I was emotional, and my attitude sucked. All I wanted to do was cook—to be the world's best and most famous chef for the rest of my life— not to be pregnant. I craved deep-fried ice cream, chicken tostadas, and fresh peach margaritas at my favorite Mexican Restaurant, Carlos n' Pepe's in Santa Monica. I found myself thirsting for that food almost three times a week during that month, which was abnormal for me. I ate a whole Chinese air-dried duck at L'Orangerie *after* eating a huge stack of pancakes with eggs, bacon, and sausage just three hours before. The next day, I decided to buy a pregnancy test.

I was experiencing such profound rejection of a child growing in me I pretended to think I was recovering from my anorexia. I thought I was overreacting about thinking I was actually pregnant and was terrified to get a pregnancy test. But my little inner voice kept nudging me, telling me I had better get one immediately. So I did—actually, I bought two. When I got home I grabbed a glass of wine and thought about how I was going to react if it was positive. After I took the test, I was too terrified to see the result, so I waited an hour to look. When I finally did look, it was positive. It couldn't be true. No way was this happening to me. Even after seeing proof right in front of my eyes, I still refused to believe it. Mortified and full of terror, I drank a glass of water and took the second test. It was positive too, and in a few short minutes, my world went from perfect to shit-again.

I sat at the dining room table of our cute little white picket fenced house in Pacific Palisades with my head in my hands, feeling both shame and, ironically, joy as well. I was pregnant after being sterile for all those years; what woman wouldn't be happy to know she could still have children? Me! I felt shame because I knew what I was going to do about it and I felt horrible about that. In retrospect, it felt great being pregnant. There was a life inside of me and I remember feeling as whole as I had ever felt as a woman. But being a woman was an uncomfortable place for me. I was working in a man's world. I think I would have had a great pregnancy. No signs of morning sickness at all, just a humongous appetite. But my world had just gone from amazing to disillusionment, and my first and only thought was to wonder how Mike would handle my decision. What a horrible place I was in. I truly can't explain the lack of class I was feeling. For me back then, people who had abortions were bad people—but I also thought how great it was that we had the option, and not from some back-alley butcher. I was in the same position as the women who had gone before me, and now I knew how they felt: both relieved and ashamed.

What a messed up place I was spiritually. Not once did I think about going full term to give my baby up for adoption, perhaps to a couple who weren't fortunate enough to have children of their own. And as we all know by now, keeping the child was nowhere near the vicinity of an option in my unstable state and because of my fear of puking. It never crossed my mind. It was as though no fiber of love and compassion existed in me. I felt nothing. I also thought how embarrassed I was going to be when I had to tell my gynecologist I wanted an abortion. Did my gynecologist even believe in abortion? And how much was it going to cost? Shit!

* * *

I sat alone at the dining room table, crying, drinking wine and waiting for Mike to come home. I actually wondered if I kept on drinking it might cause a miscarriage. That's how out of my mind I was. And I was dreading the conversation I was about to have with Mike. I knew he wasn't going to feel the same way, but there was no way he would be able to talk me out of it.

When Mike walked through the door he took one look at me and could see I had been crying. "You're pregnant."

"Yes."

With a smile and tears of joy rolling down his face, he said, "That's so great. It's incredible. I'm so happy."

"I'm glad for you, but for me it's not so great. I am in shock and horrified, really. I'm sorry Mike, but that's how I feel."

"So, you want an abortion, is that what I'm hearing?"

"Yes, I do. I'm not ready to have a baby, and honestly, I don't know if I ever will be. What if I get morning sickness? I'll gain weight for sure, and you know how I feel about that too. And I won't give up my career. And who can guarantee the health of this child after me having an STD, anyway?" I was rationalizing every way I knew how to talk myself out of having a baby.

"How far along do you think you are?"

"I don't know, maybe four to six weeks? If you want kids, maybe we should rethink moving forward with our relationship. We've only been together nine months, we'll get over it."

If I had been Mike, I would have taken the offer and left me. That was a huge red flag for him as I saw it.

"No! Don't be silly. Okay, if this is what you really want I'll pay for it—but to let you know, I think we could handle it, at least I know I could. I'll look for a higher paying job, maybe in management, if that helps."

Of course I started to cry at that point. The guilt went from bad to worse, beyond infinite and deep, way too painful to really think about. I was, however, grateful that he respected my decision and didn't try to place a guilt trip on me.

When I told my parents, I was surprised at my dad's reaction. His eyes welled up over the idea that he would be a grandfather. His reaction struck a deep chord in my heart. I wasn't expecting that kind of reaction from him at all. I thought all he cared about was his music. He was very supportive of my decision, but he also said he would do all he could to be supportive as a father and grandfather if I changed my mind. That information didn't help as it made me feel worse but his words helped me see him in a totally different way. My mother, on the other hand, was tough as nails about my decision. She said she'd be supportive as well, but also said that I should *never* sacrifice my dreams like she had—which of course made me want to have the child just to spite her. It was a mixed message from her and a shitty thing to say. She was basically sounding like it was my dad's fault she hadn't accomplished her dreams, like he'd put a gun to her head and proceeded to ruin her life. Her comment really pissed me off. She made it all about her.

I had no idea my mother had grown into such a resentful place with my dad. He had apparently told her she had to give up modeling and playing the piano if they were going to get married. I have to admit that if a man I loved said that to me, there's no way I'd marry him. That information also kind of made me disappointed in my dad—but it was the fifties. That's what couples did back then. They got married and had kids anyway and I'm glad they did. I had to tell Gerard, the owner of L'Orangerie, about my pregnancy. I needed a week off to deal with what I had to do, and because I valued my job and respected him, I felt the only way to save my job was to tell the truth which was extraordinary in itself. When I told Gerard, he wasn't at all surprised. He said it explained my behavior and the mood swings over the previous few weeks. Relieved and feeling hopeful, I made the appointment with my doctor, despite my moral contradictions—and as I suspected he might, he refused to do it. He did refer me to another doctor, but not without trying to talk me out of it first.

My doctor's refusal didn't make me feel any better about myself at all. When it was over—it only took a few minutes—I woke up nauseous and starving. Hence, the side affects of anesthesia. I couldn't imagine eating anything, but I knew I had to eat. After several hours, I finally felt good enough to move and go home, but still I couldn't eat anything. This was the first time I noticed how much I enjoyed the feeling of being empty inside. Little did I know at the

time that my emptiness wasn't hunger—it was the emptiness I felt for ending the life of a human being, my unborn
child. As I look back from my present, healthy state of mind,
this was probably when and why I began my long journey
into denying myself food. Not to say that losing my fingers
didn't help perpetuate my disease. It more than likely sealed
the deal. My joy was nonexistent, too. Looking back on this
time in my life I feel like every emotion, including my sense
of compassion, died inside me when I got the abortion,
though I didn't notice it. That's how numb I was. Who was I,
a monster? Where did I go? Who had I become? Why was it
so terrifying to think of having a beautiful child?

After the abortion, I remember that I could eat only three
or four bites of food at a time. Food started tasting different
to me too. It had a strange sourness to it, and it was almost
a chore to chew it. Completely unaware I was screwed up,
I kept spiraling further down into total denial of who I was
as a person and as a woman. I was an erratic and insecure
zombie. I didn't dare let myself feel any of it. I chose to go
on with my life like nothing had happened. I also didn't need
or want to forgive myself for what I had done to my child
or myself. That would mean taking responsibility for what I
had done, and I didn't want to. Instead, I went ahead with my
life for a long time thinking that day didn't exist. This was
one of the many reasons that started my long journey into
the anorexic world of self-loathing and self-hatred. The endless hours, days, and years of pain became unbearable later.
Constantly feeling hungry is a very painful thing.

* * *

The morning after, Mike and I played volleyball all day
like nothing had happened—or at least I did. My invisible
guilt rapidly began to eat away at me. I continued denying
myself the nourishment I so desperately needed, after the
abortion and for years after. From September 1980 to December 13, 1980 I went from 120 pounds to 92 pounds.

Mike tried to talk to me about the abortion again, but I never wanted to talk about it, and because of that our sex life began to disintegrate. I was afraid I was going to get pregnant again, and I certainly didn't want that. I didn't want to use birth control either, especially the pill. The pill was a chemical—a weird sort of prevention I couldn't understand at the time. I still don't get it, to be honest. I hardly ever put anything in my mouth that wasn't from the earth into my body. A pill that could prevent pregnancy had to be bad. I also hated condoms. Why bother if I couldn't feel anything? The diaphragm and the IUD were not an option either because any kind of foreign object that was semi-permanent always bothered me—at least the idea of it did. I liked the natural feeling of unprotected sex and I continued to enjoy it that way. Even after what I had gone through, I was still irresponsible about protecting myself. I more than likely set myself up for another disaster. I sometimes think about how my life would have turned out if I'd had that baby. I would have loved living a part of my life through my child's eyes. Of course I know I will never know what that's like and will always be responsible for my decision. After the accident, I hoped one day soon I would find out why it happened, and after thinking about it, I'm sure the machine was entirely at fault. It had to be. I also didn't feel one way or the other about living after almost dying and knowing how great I felt up there; I really didn't care whether I was alive or not. I wasn't doing such a good job of living, that's for sure.

* * *

As I slipped into a deep sleep after almost dying, I still wanted to wake up during surgery. The curiosity was killing me. I wanted to see how it was done. I don't know how far along I was in surgery, but as incredible as this is going to sound, I did eventually wake up. As I opened my eyes, they felt heavy, and I was groggy, but I was able to see a big television screen in front of me with an image of my hand on it. I looked up and saw the doctor looking at my hand through a long pair of telescopic glasses and into another huge telescope.

I looked back at the monitor and saw him attempting to sew my fingers back on. "Wow, this is so cool!" I said.

Dumbfounded, everyone in the operating room looked over at the doctor. After a short pause, he said, "Jesus, give her more drugs! This girl has the strongest will I have ever seen!" The anesthesiologist gave me more drugs immediately, and as I faded away again, I thought how amazed he would have been to learn how close I'd come to meeting Jesus Himself, just a few short hours before. I really did want to live and it seemed that someone up there wanted me too as well. Even though the surgery was in progress, there was still a chance I could die, at least in my mind. After it was all over, I woke up to Mike holding a cup of something. I was hoping it was my hot toddy. Thank goodness I wasn't feeling nauseous, and seeing Mike was actually a relief to me. I was surprised at how I remembered every bit of what had happened in the operating room, but I didn't tell Mike because I knew he would never believe me. I was beyond voracious and craving breakfast something fierce. I wanted bangers and hash. I have no idea why, but it sounded so good. I think it was one o'clock in the morning, and I thought if I didn't eat something, I might die from starvation. Now that would have been something after all I'd been through. Here's the recipe:

Bangers and Potato Hash

Serves 4–6

4–6 English bangers or breakfast sausages, sliced into 1/4-inch pieces

3 russet potatoes, diced into small, bite-size pieces

1 red onion, diced

3 garlic cloves, thinly sliced

3 king oyster mushrooms or regular oyster mushrooms, diced

1/2 stick sweet butter
1/4-cup olive oil
Salt and pepper to taste

Directions: In a sauté pan, heat the butter and oil together. Add the onions and garlic and cook for 2 minutes. Add the potatoes and sauté for 8 minutes. Add the mushrooms and sausage and sauté another 4 minutes. Test the potatoes. If they aren't fully cooked, throw the entire mixture into a baking dish at 400 degrees and bake for 6 minutes. Serve in a porridge bowl with ketchup on the side. If you like, have a hearty beer or Bloody Mary with this dish. It also makes for a great lunch.

* * *

"Lisa, I'm so glad to see you. I brought you a hot toddy, but without the booze for obvious reasons."

I loved my hot toddy before bed, but with the booze, of course. I thought that was a very sweet gesture.

"What time is it? How long was the surgery? Were they able to reattach my fingers?"

I was remarkably coherent.

"It was about 6 hours. It's 1:30 a.m."

I could see Mike was dreading what he was about to tell me. He could never conceal his emotions.

"And no Lisa, they couldn't reattach them. They tried but couldn't. I'm so sorry."

I could see the sadness he felt for me all over his face. I could see that he would have traded places with me in a minute instead of watching me go through something as hardcore as this.

"Oh. Why? Why couldn't they?" I asked, with tears welling up in my eyes.

"Your veins are atrophied."

"That really sucks." I began to whimper with what little strength I had left after a very long surgery and the loads of drugs churning through my veins.

"You'll be able to hold a knife again though, and that's good news, isn't it?"

That should have been good news, but it wasn't. I wanted to go back in time and take the advice of Virgini and go home. I wanted my fingers back the way they used to be.

"Mike, I would give anything to go back in time."

"I know you would. I offered my big toe for you."

I actually chuckled; Mike's big toe was huge!

"You smiled! I was serious. If it would have helped you, I was willing to donate it."

How sweet I thought that was. Mike was hardly ever selfish. He would have given away everything—and not just for me, for anyone.

"Your mother and father are waiting for you in your room and are worried sick about you."

"You wanted to donate your big toe? You would have never been in balance again. But that was very sweet of you."

"This is why I love you so much. After what you've been through, you can actually say that I wouldn't have balance again? You are a classic."

Pausing, and with great sorrow, I asked Mike a very painful question: "Do you still love me even though I am not perfect anymore?"

Trying to hold back his tears, he said, "What a ridiculous question. Of course I still love you. And who said you were perfect before this accident, anyway?"

Mike had always had a great sense of humor, especially in the midst of tragedy. I asked him my second dreaded question.

"Do you know how much of my fingers are left? I mean, they were so short when I looked at them right when the accident happened."

"Let's talk about all that later. Your parents are very anxious to see you, especially your mom."

"No, I want to know now. I can take it."

Reluctantly, he answered, "Your three middle fingers are half gone. Your ring finger is very short."

"Please tell me he saved my pinky."

"Yes, he was able to sew it up nicely."

"Why couldn't he sew together the other ones?"

Of course he'd just told me why, but I was so sad I couldn't accept it. He told me over and over again how sorry he was and how much he loved me and I was more beautiful to him now than ever before. We were to be married in three months. My gut told me it wasn't going to happen though and that it would be better to wait. Just thinking about walking down the aisle in a wedding dress as an amputee made me sad. God only knew what I was going to go through after this experience, but this was not the time to talk to him about it. When we got to my room my parents were standing outside waiting for us looking horribly distressed. I almost felt worse for them than me. As Mike rolled me into my nice private room, I was exhausted and still very high and didn't know what to say.

Mom and Dad came over to me, kissed me on my forehead, and gently hugged me. I think they may have aged 10 years because of this.

"Sweetheart, we were so worried. I'm so sorry we weren't here before the surgery," Mom said with a crackle in her voice.

Dad said, "Honey, I'm so glad you're still with us. We've been worried sick about you."

I smiled and said, "I'm okay dad and mom. I'll be cooking in no time at all."

Chapter 5
The Hospital

Needless to say, I was feeling groggy, disoriented, and stoned the following morning. My parents were sitting next my hospital bed looking frazzled and exhausted. My mom looked especially sad, but she had her usual "tough love" armor on, even during this catastrophe. Dad looked rather pissed off. I wasn't sure if his anger was focused on me or on how this could have possibly happened to his daughter.

I said, "Is it Christmas? Or is it Super Bowl Sunday?"

"No sweetheart. It's Saturday, December 14."

Slurring my words, I said, "Oh, well how come there's football on then?"

"I don't know, sweetie. Are you feeling okay?"

"I'm higher than a kite, Mom. I've never been this high except when I dropped acid. Remember? Have you ever been on these kinds of drugs before?" I think after that comment my mom left me for a moment to find out how high my doses were, because I was never that screwed up again. I do remember really liking the feeling Demerol gave me though.

Early that afternoon, the phone started ringing. Some very close friends called me not knowing how to talk about my loss. The owners of L'Orangerie called saying they and the staff sent their love and hope for a speedy recovery and were also sending dinner that evening, and for the whole family too. To my elation and surprise, Wolfgang called. I hadn't spoken with him in about nine months, and I can't tell you how happy that made me and how nice he was. He was always nice to me, even though I still cried almost every night on the way home after a shift at Ma Maison. Looking back, I know he was only trying to toughen me up and also wanted to make me a better cook. Virgini and Gerard said my favorite dish was coming later on in the evening. This was also a popular dish at L'Orangerie- a clean mix of stewed chicken, carrots, celery, and onions. It had a clean, fragrant scent that made me feel warm and fuzzy inside. It was served with potato galette on the side, which is a dish of yummy, creamy, and crispy French-style potatoes. They were also sending over apple tarts made with homemade puff pastry by master pastry chef, Claude Koberle, who I worked with at Ma Maison. And, to wash it all down with, was a surprise wine they said I'd love. I was hoping it was my favorite wine—a 1959 Petrus Pomeral, which is to me, one of the best French Cabernet Franc's of our time. I'd had the pleasure of experiencing this inconceivably magnificent wine several times at the restaurant. Pomeral was, and still is, quite possibly the best wine around, and is certainly the most amazing I'd ever tasted. It cost over $800 a bottle retail back then. People spent money like that on wine back then without blinking. Today, that same wine—if it's been kept at the proper temperature for fifty-four years and hasn't been moved around too much—could easily cost anywhere between $3,000 and $5,000, maybe more. Here is the recipe to my best recollection:

Chicken Casserole with Potato Gallette

Serves 4
1 small whole chicken, cut up
6 carrots, peeled and sliced 1 inch thick
2 yellow onions, large dice
5 celery stalks, cut 1 inch thick
8–10 cups water
Salt and pepper to taste

Directions: In a Dutch oven, place the chicken and the broth. Bake for 30 minutes at 350 degrees. Add the veggies and bake for another 20 minutes at 375 degrees. Season with salt and pepper to taste.

Potato Galette

Serves 4
Pre-heat oven to 400 degrees
2 russet potatoes, thinly sliced with a mandolin or a Japanese slicer
Olive oil
Salt and pepper

Directions: In a skillet, heat the oil. In a circle starting on the outside, place each potato slice about 1/4 inch apart until you reach the middle, then season with salt and pepper. Repeat. Cook on medium heat until golden brown; turn over with a spatula. Cook 2 more minutes and place in the oven with the chicken. Serve the casserole in a bowl with the broth and the potatoes on the side. Enjoy a French Chablis or Sauvignon Blanc with this and a nice Padron cigar. Of course, if you happen to have a Pomerol on hand, please feel free to drink it with this satisfying stew.

* * *

This wonderful recipe had all the qualities of a typical American-style chicken soup—nurturing and medicinal, nature's penicillin. While we waited for the food to come, my mind was racing with thoughts like how long would it be before I could play volleyball again? This was especially disturbing to me as that was my primary form of exercise besides bicycling. How would everyone at the beach react to me? Would they even care—and why would I care if they did or didn't? I barely socialized with them outside of the beach, but I did spend a considerable amount of time with them. I would soon find out who my *real* friends were and that was unnerving for me, to say the least. How were my co-workers going to deal with me coming back to work? Would they avoid me? Would they be afraid to ask to see my fingers, or would they act like it never happened? Would I even *want* go back to work? I imagined that no one would look at me in the eye because they would be too busy following my hand around, and I would hate that. How would it feel to hold a knife again with my three middle fingers halfway missing? Would I be able to set the volleyball for Mike as well as I used to?

* * *

It also dawned on me that what if I had told Sam Elliot that I was ready to get married, would I be in the hospital right now? Maybe. In 1977, I met Sam. I was almost nineteen years old. It's a very interesting story, as meeting him the way I did seemed it was meant to happen. I went to the movies with my high school friend one afternoon before work. We were dying to see *Lifeguard*. I saw it only because of Sam. He was so hot and that deep rugged voice was enough to melt a rock. As we were watching the movie I told my friend to mark my words: I was going to meet him and be his girlfriend, possibly even his wife. She looked at me like I was on crack. I just knew I was going to meet him even though I had no idea how or why. After the movie I went home and changed into my satin wraparound dress, and for some reason I took the bus to work and needed to stop at the drug store for some Midol—I was having wicked cramps. When I walked into the pharmacy, I walked to the aisle where the Midol was and there he stood, looking for something. I can distinctly remember almost collapsing I was so shocked. He picked out a deodorant, walked right past me, glancing at me for a moment. I couldn't believe it. I grabbed my Midol and quickly walked to the checkout counter because the bus was going to be at the stop and I didn't want be late, but I was hoping he would at least say hi to me and if he didn't then it wasn't meant to happen. Then, it happened. He said "Hello" in that deep voice of his, looking right at me. I turned so red I could have sworn my face was on fire—and worse, I knew he could see that I was extremely nervous. I said, "Hi." Then he said, "Where are you off to in that pretty satin dress?" I found it difficult to speak. I wasn't expecting him to ask me a question. "Uh, well I'm on the way to work and my bus is here." I felt like such a dork. A bus?

Frazzled, I said the even cornier thing – 'Have a nice day and bye!' I couldn't have walked fast enough to the bus. As I got on the bus and looked out the window, I saw Sam waving good-bye to me. I waved back and then he blew me a kiss. I nearly died. I frantically pulled the wire on the bus, hoping the next stop wasn't too far, but it was. I sat down and started to cry. I thought he probably does this with every woman who flirts with him. I mean seriously, what were the odds of meeting him after seeing him in a movie that afternoon? Then, running into him only a few hours later? Really? It had to be kismet. I wished I'd been more confident and missed the bus.

I was on the way to Dillon's Disco in Westwood, California where I was an espresso bar server. It was a three story high building that had a restaurant and bar in the ground floor. The other three floors offered different types of venues: disco, rock and roll, and swing. That night I was going to hostess. I was the disco queen back then. I loved dancing and danced every night I wasn't working and sometimes after work. I loved dancing to Donna Summers songs mostly. I was on American Bandstand, danced with the choreographer of Soul Train, won contests all over town, and got into ballroom dancing.

I was in too much pain to work. I was sporting a nice big zit on the side of my nose, too. I asked if I could go home and thankfully the manager, Bill, said yes. Thank goodness it was a Monday night. Monday's were typically slow. While waiting for my mom to come and get me, I sat down at the bar. Bill offered me a Grand Marnier. Yeah, I was under age, whatever. While I was sipping on my drink, Bill came over to me and said, "There's someone who wants to meet you."

"Really?" I said.

"Yes, he's right across from you at the other side of this bar."

I looked up and nearly spit my drink out. It was Sam! He smiled at me and lifted his beer to toast me. All I could think about was that fucking zit! What were the odds of him being there? Then Bill said, "He wants to talk to you, would that be okay?"

Okay? Hell yes it's okay!

"Yes, of course!"

Bill walked me over to him.

Sam said, "We've met already, right? But now I need to know your name."

It was as if no one was in the room. This time I managed to not blush and tried to act confident, although I was dying inside with nervousness and insecurity. "My name is Lisa and we met at the drug store earlier, right? How bizarre is it that you're here!"

Of course he knew where we met. Man, did I feel like an idiot.

"Bill and me are friends and have been for a while now."

I had no idea he knew Sam.

Well, one thing led to another so I snuck away for a minute and called my mom to tell her not to come get me. We must have spent four or more hours talking at the bar on the third floor. There was no band that night, so it was quiet and dark, which I hoped hid my zit. It was like we'd known each other for years. There began our dating for almost two and half years. I loved listening to him talk. He was supportive of my dream of wanting to be a model and loved that I had a passion for cooking. I was and am still way too short for that but he made me feel like I could do anything. He bought me a leather portfolio case to put my pictures in for interviews that never happened. Even though I was in love with him, I always knew deep down we wouldn't last. I was emotionally way to young back then and was terrified he'd get bored with me and leave me or get a starring role with some fabulous actress (which happened) and leave me, and because of this I did everything I knew how to screw it up.

Sam got the lead in a movie with Katherine Ross called *The Legacy*. Well, that didn't go down too well for me at all. I did my best to not be jealous, but I was green with envy. I hate the feeling of envy and jealousy. It's so self-destructive and makes the person who is, look like an insecure person. I tried not to show it when he told me, as I wanted to be cool and grown up. And Katherine Ross was so beautiful, and still is. I remember seeing her in *Butch Cassidy and the Sundance Kid* and being blown away at her beauty, both inside and out.

When Sam returned some three months later I could *feel* that something had changed. I actually knew it when I talked to him on the phone while he was filming but I was in denial. Soon after he returned he took me to my favorite restaurant, Stellini's on Pico Boulevard. I loved that restaurant, especially the house salad. During dinner, Sam asked me if I was ready to get married. Sadly, I heard, "Will you marry me?" I was convinced it was a trick question, testing me to see where I was in the relationship, I was sure of it. But, being the tough I don't need anyone gal, I said no. Deep down I really wanted him and hoped he would fight for me just a little. I wanted to show him I was independent and needed to start my career first. I thought he really wasn't ready either, but it turned out he was. I think he asked me if I was sure. I said yes. He then announced he was going to ask Katherine to marry him. Just like that it was over. I felt like my heart was literally splitting in half. I had to maintain, though.

Maybe that's when I truly began to shut down, but Sam easily could have been one of the billions of excuses I used to blame my anorexia on. It wasn't his fault, he was mature and I was a child. I was madly in love with that man but at too young of an age to really know what love was. It took me a long time to get over him. I would drive around Westwood looking for him for the first several years after we broke up, and one night I saw him walking in the rain with his cowboy hat and raincoat on. I stopped the car and rolled down the window. He stopped walking and looked over at me. I said,

"Please, I want to talk to you one more time." He agreed. I drove him to his car and told him I'd made the biggest mistake ever thinking he was testing me. But that was all in the past and I truly wished him lifelong happiness with a wonderful woman. He told me he would always love me and to never forget it. He kissed my cheek and left. That was the last time I saw him for many years. I punished myself for being too strong a person. What was I trying to prove?

Over the years from time to time, we'd run into each other in Malibu, which has been very healing for me. He's always been kind to me and interested in what's going on with my life. I will always feel a special connection with him. But still, I couldn't help but wonder what might have happened if we had married. Maybe if I'd said yes I wouldn't have had the accident. Who knows? I will never know. I do know this though: nothing could have stopped me from cooking, not even Sam. But I also knew he wouldn't have ever stopped me. He wanted me to happy, that's all. And nothing could have stopped me from meeting Sam either. It was meant to be. But still, I can't help but wonder why we did meet. Depressed and not knowing the answers to any of these questions provoked me to ask a nurse for some more Demerol. Of course she said no. I was imagining that the pain post-surgery might be worse than the actual accident. After all, he had stitched and re-stitched my fingers over a six-hour period. The pain to come had to be worse, right?

* * *

My family sat with me in my room in uncomfortable silence while we waited for the food to come. I could almost *hear* what my parents and brother were thinking it was so quiet. I knew they wanted to ask me questions about the accident, but they seemed to not know where to start. A child, being the innocent beautiful beings they are, would never give a second thought to asking what happened. Kids have no boundaries, just huge innocence. They ask questions that most adults wish they had the courage to ask. I know this because kids have flat-out asked me where my fingers went many times throughout the years. It's simple curiosity. The parents almost always say, "Susie! That's not polite!" and I'd say, "It's okay, really." I'd explain how it happened and said it just like this: "Keep your hands out of all kinds of machines. They are very dangerous." Most of these kids were as young as five years old, and it's the way they ask me too that I especially liked—with a raw innocence and a genuine curiosity. In hindsight, I think those kids helped me heal in some small way.

Maybe if I hadn't been so stubborn and headstrong my whole life, my family wouldn't have had a problem approaching me. As I mentioned earlier, it was all about fear for me, and it never occurred to me they might not want to ask for fear it might upset me. All I wanted was the truth from them—how they felt. I was the *queen* of telling people what I thought the truth was, but God forbid my friends told me my truth! Maybe that's why my family felt hesitant to ask me anything. My mother always told me to face fear head-on, but the facts were that I was a liar, a cheater, a masochist, a narcissist, a fleeting alcoholic and a control freak. Not to mention anorexic and promiscuous. And I wondered why I was so misguided and messed up? Addictions of all types have been around since the beginning of time. Anorexia, drug addiction, alcoholism, smoking, sexual addiction, and overeating, to name a few, have been problems for millions of people over the centuries. It's all about "medicating" our pain so we can't *feel*. But if we crush our difficult experiences in life through medicating our pain, we can't grow spiritually. I was crushing mine by sleeping around and not eating. Pain is a huge drag, and I was in more of it than I realized long before the accident. Losing my fingers and having an abortion inside of three short months wasn't the plan I had for my life, that's for sure. I already had walls around me. I sure could have done without those experiences. Was the accident some form of punishment to me for having an abortion? And if it was, was it God trying to save me from much worse later on, or was it simply an accident? What was I supposed to do? The really bizarre part is that I remembered every part of my experience with God in the operating room but chose to ignore it. I looked at every other option for a strong spiritual belief system other than God. What else was supposed happen to me before I woke up and truly understood what I needed spiritually?

* * *

The food wasn't supposed to be at the hospital for another two hours, but I hoped it would come sooner than later so we could at least have something to talk about other than my wretched accident. Geez, all of it was so lame. The silence was awful. I must confess that I'm not sure I would know what to say at a time like this, even to any of my family members. I couldn't bear the silence any longer, so I spoke.

"So, did anyone call from the restaurant to ask about the accident or me yet?"

Relieved, my mother said, "Yes!"

"When did they call and what did they say?"

"Virgini called this morning and expressed how sorry she was and said to get well soon and whenever you're ready, please let them know when you want to come back to work."

"That's all she said? She didn't talk about what happened?"

"No."

I could tell she was lying, but I was too exhausted and out of it to get into it with her. What was the use, anyhow? I mean, there must have been something said like, "How's Lisa?" or "We found some evidence as to why this happened" or something else pertaining to that day. What did it matter anyway? It happened, and here I was. I knew it wasn't L'Orangerie at fault for some reason. Still, I thought maybe there might have been some kind of discussion about *me*.

My dad asked, "How could this have happened? I just don't understand it."

"I don't either, Dad. Honestly, I am surprised it didn't happen sooner."

"What do you mean? You knew it was dangerous, didn't you?"

"I've been using the machine the same way for the last nine months, Dad. The machine went off by itself, I just know it, and for the life of me I can't figure out how and it's torturing me."

"What does 'the same way' mean?"

I was just being honest.

My mom looked at him with her ever-so-famous evil eye and said, "Dorrance! Please! This is not the time. She just had surgery yesterday! She's been through hell, can't you see that?"

I started to cry at his words because I was just as confused as my dad was.

"I'm sorry, Lisa. I'm not thinking clearly. I am very upset about this and worried sick about you. Fucking machines!" This kind of response was typical of my dad when he couldn't fix something or didn't know how to express his feelings.

* * *

Finally, the food came. They actually had a messenger service deliver it, and my wish came true—I got a bottle of that 1959 Pomeral! The relief of having something else to talk about was a huge weight off. I powered the food down like I hadn't eaten in years and with no thought of how many calories I was ingesting and it felt great. This was transparently pleasing to my family and Mike. Looking back on that meal, I enjoyed it immensely. I remember how good it felt to eat like a normal person and not think about my weight. I felt genuine pleasure eating that magnificent meal. But naturally, that was a one-time deal. I was dehydrated from the long hours of surgery and the drugs and worried that I would not be able to have a bowel movement, which was interesting because I barely went anyway. There was no food to poop out! No way could I allow myself the luxury of enjoying food *that* much ever again.

During dinner, we had the most superficial conversation ever. We talked about nothing but the weather and other mundane things, and in retrospect, it was a blessing. Too many heavy conversations have ensued in my family during my life and in a very short amount of time on Earth, so talking about nothing deep was fine by me. I didn't drink too much of the wine because Dad was concerned that mixing the wine with all the drugs I was on might cause a reaction or worse. I thought it was so cool that we were eating five-star cuisine in a hospital.

* * *

My parents were intense, open-minded, and creative people. They never treated my brother or me like children, which is a good and a bad thing. We were always spoken to as though we were adults, and they expected us to understand them. I liked that they didn't treat us like kids, but I do wonder occasionally what I would be like today if we had been raised like most kids. You know - Barbie dolls and other girlie things. Only educational and artsy things were under our Christmas tree. I really didn't care. I wasn't the typical "princess" most little girls were in my class. My mom wanted me to dress more like a girl as I grew up and she did on special occasions, but I was more comfortable as I got older wearing hip-hugger jeans, corduroy's and Pendleton shirts. I dug climbing trees and making mud pies. I was a tomboy, in a word.

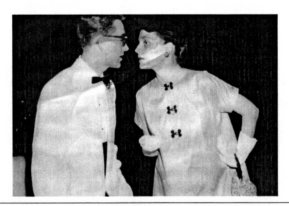

"My Mother Marilyn and my Father Dorrance leaving a jazz gig where my Father played Saxophone. She was checking to see if she could smell alcohol on his breath! That was me she was pregnant with. I think my Mother was absolutely gorgeous."

My parents looked at everything abstractly and loved digging into our psyches, hoping to pull out some kind of enlightening thought in hopes we would discover something new about ourselves. They never told us who or what we were supposed to be. They wanted us to figure things out by ourselves—who we were as people and what we wanted out of life. More than likely this is where I got my interest in people's innermost psyches and private thoughts. It's a hobby of mine. There wasn't a simple explanation for anything, according to my parents.

As I grew older, I noticed that people felt comfortable discussing very personal things with me. For a long time, total strangers would bare their darkest and deepest thoughts and feelings to me. Many times throughout my life I could be sitting at a bar or wherever, alone or with a group of people, and someone would strike up a conversation with me and before I knew it they would tell me their deepest and most ugly secrets and ask me what they should do about them. Like I knew?

Mom and Dad were groovy East Coast hippies. Dad was a composer and taught music at Immaculate Heart College for money, where I ended up going to school to study art. Later, he became the director of Monday Evening Concerts at the

My mom always cut our hair the same way. This was on my 5th birthday I believe.

Los Angeles County Art Museum and held that position for thirty-three years, until his death at seventy-four years old. As a result of that, he won the prestigious Juilliard Award three times for creative programming. He also started Friday Night Jazz Concerts at the museum, which were hugely successful and are still going on today. Dad started out playing in jazz clubs in Cincinnati, Ohio, where my mom was a concert pianist at the Conservatory of Music in Cincinnati. They met one night on the way to a jazz club, invited by mutual friends. There was no room for my mom in the backseat of the car, so she sat in my dad's lap, and before they knew it they were making out, falling instantly in love.

My mom resembled Marilyn Monroe and my dad resembled James Dean, mostly because of the dated bouffant hairstyle he wore. When mom played piano, I would close my eyes and I could swear Bach himself was in the room playing the piano. Mom ended up working at the Rand Corporation for a while. After that, she became the executive secretary for Igor Stravinsky. As I got older I thought that it was so cool she worked for such a genius. Later she worked at The Sever Institute, until her death at sixty-four years old. I wonder sometimes if my mother was satisfied with her outcome in life. She seemed to grow resentful over time that she gave up her dreams of becoming a famous concert pianist for my father's dreams. I could be wrong, but I often wonder. I believe she would have been a seriously famous pianist. They also didn't have any spiritual beliefs between them at all, which more than likely didn't help them through difficult times. My dad, however, was a huge Carlos Castaneda fan, and Mom wanted to try acid after I told her about my experience but her therapist wouldn't let her.

* * *

The only rule we had, which was strictly enforced, was having dinner together every night during the week. Usually an argument would ensue, mostly because of me. I didn't

Dad on the beach in his early twenties in South Carolina where he was born and raised.

like anyone disagreeing with me or questioning me about anything because I thought I was always right. I would almost always leave the table pissed off about something and not finish my dinner. I would eventually run to my bedroom, slamming the door and collapsing into a full-blown tantrum. Maybe that was how I got out of eating everything on my plate. I never understood the concept of cleaning my plate or forcing myself to eat long after I was full anyway. I was a sort of torturous to me. One time when I was around twelve years old, mom served Birds Eye green string beans with dinner, as she seemed to serve almost every single night— I had grown to hate those tasteless, limp vegetables—and finally I just couldn't eat them anymore. But that night, if I didn't finish them there would have been no television for two weeks or dessert, and at the time that was equal to dying. So I sat at the table alone after everyone had left, trying to eat the beans without gagging. I sat there for more than two hours.

Periodically I'd say, "Mom, I can't eat any more. I'm full."

"Okay then, no television, and definitely there will be no dessert."

So after another hour or so, I decided to take a chance and lie. I knew there was no way I could eat them or I'd puke, and I hated puking, even then. I also hoped she wouldn't come back to check on me because if she did, I'd be seriously caught with my pants down.

"Mom, I'm finished!"

"Okay honey!"

With macerated green beans stuffed in my cheeks, I said, "Aren't you going to check?"

"No sweetie, I trust you!"

I was flabbergasted! It was incredible. The lie worked. I got up and went straight to the bathroom and spit it all out in the toilet. Even the act of spitting food into the toilet made me gag—that's how much I hated the idea of puking. I think maybe that was when a very potent and dangerous seed was planted into my brain regarding my issues with eating. I also think this may have been when I learned to lie. We were allowed a minimal amount of television when I was a kid, unless it was my father's favorite shows, like *Star Trek* or *The Twilight Zone*. We always spooned on my parents' bed while watching our shows before bedtime. Not only was she my mom, she was my best friend too. On Mother's Day I miss her and more so as the years go by. I think that's because I have so much I want to tell her now. But she had one very annoying habit—she loved flicking her big, thick, perfectly groomed toenails together while watching television. It was weird to me that she even had long toenails in the first place, but to hear that clicking noise always irritated me but I would do anything to hear that noise from her now. I must have seen every *Star Trek* episode at least ten times, and I loved them all as Dad did, but never while eating. Watching television while eating was never an option in our home, and what a great lesson to have learned as a child. Even though I was a rebellious young girl, those rules helped me a great deal later on in my adult life because I really can't stand watching television while eating. In fact, I really don't enjoy television anyway. Maybe that's because I was always cooking during dinnertime, and when I wasn't working I wanted to converse and enjoy the company I was with, the way my mom and dad taught me. I also understood the value of food. We weren't rich and had enough if not more than many in the world but food was a blessing in our home. Every penny counted. My mother said we should always be grateful for our family, for the food put in front of us, and the clothes that were on our backs. She couldn't stress enough how important it was to pay attention to what we were eating. I never understood that until *way* later. We were also told if we didn't like what was on our plate then we'd go to bed hungry. There weren't choices in our home when it came to food and thank goodness dad was a health nut. We were also expected to bring our plate to the kitchen when we were finished eating. As insignificant as it may seem to most kids today, this was a very important part of our family dynamic, and it indirectly taught us teamwork and self-respect. As a kid I fought discipline like hell; I think most kids do in order to find their voice. Nonetheless, I needed the discipline desperately, even if I threw a tantrum over it.

* * *

When we finished eating dinner at the hospital, visiting time was over. My mother asked the nurses if she could stay with me an extra hour. Thankfully, they said yes. My dad and brother went home, leaving Mom and me alone. That night we lay together watching television spooning, just like we did when I was a kid. I have no idea what we watched, but it didn't matter. We didn't speak one word to each other. We just held each other while tears of sadness and deep depression rolled down my cheeks. After Mom left, a nurse came into my room hinting around for another pill cup full of wine in exchange for a shot of Demerol. Really? She could have lost her job and her license over that. But the fact was, I wanted more Demerol and they wanted more wine. So throughout the night, they got their wine and I got my shots. Lying alone in that huge, uncomfortable hospital bed, I began to grasp how alone we all really are and how difficult being a parent must be. The stuff my parents had endured over my brother's bad decisions and my countless moments of poor judgment must have sucked for them. How many nights, I wondered, did they stay up waiting for one of us to come home? Many, I'm quite sure. I can't imagine. Even after a child leaves the nest, the parenting doesn't end, ever. I'm sure my parents never thought anything like this would ever happen to their daughter, and neither did I.

We are born naked and alone, struggling to get out into a very difficult world through our mother's womb. I think that is an extraordinary thing, even though I rejected mine. Women go through so much pain to experience the joy of giving birth to a life. I wondered if newborn babies feel anything as they came out into the world through a very tight canal, screaming their heads off. Do they feel one way or the other about it, or are they even aware of what's going on? Are they afraid of leaving that safe, dark, liquid place they lived in for nine months only to enter a cold, well-lit delivery room covered in placenta and blood? Do they ask themselves what the fuck just happened? Recently, I watched a video on how a child develops, and at forty-five days—the exact time I had my abortion—my child had already started developing a heart. I had no idea it was that fast, and that makes me very sad. So much develops in such a short amount of time, and as I watched that video I felt a sad reminder that what I did has never left me.

* * *

As I continue to grow spiritually, I find myself weeping over how many people abuse their pets, children and spouses and have no regard for our planet. And how we allow people to hunt animals for enjoyment provokes me to pray for their souls. It's so not cool anymore. And when we die, are we just as alone on our journey to Heaven? After what I saw and experienced in the operating room, I should have been convinced we aren't alone. Now I know it was a gift from God to show me how wonderful it is going to be traveling to Heaven and have eternal life. I think God wanted me to understand this early in life so I could relax and do what I was supposed to do in what is such a short and fleeting time on Earth. I didn't get this until much later. I had no idea what a gift I was given then. Most of us have family and friends around us as we die but we are still totally alone, on our journey to Heaven. I know this because when both of my parents died they had such peaceful looks on their faces, which was remarkable to me. Even though they were both riddled with cancer and suffered greatly as a result of smoking all their lives—non-filtered cigarettes, and two packs a day, no less, which I found ironic as my dad was a major health freak—both of them had ethereal looks on their faces. There was no pain, or at least I don't think so. They were on heavy meds too, so hopefully they didn't feel any pain. I saw my mom just twenty-four hours before she passed and my dad only eight hours before he passed and it looked as though they were both already on the way to Heaven. And as extraordinary as this may sound, the last words out of both their mouths to me were exactly the same: "What am I going to do without your beautiful face?" I knew they were going be together again in Heaven when my dad said those words to me ten years after my mom passed. A week after my mother passed my alarm went off. The song on the radio was from R.E.M called 'Everybody Hurts." That was amazing to me as I was hurting deeply. Then after my father died, they both visited me, shining in white light, and told me that they were happy again and in no pain. They said they were looking forward to seeing me later on. They were holding each other. I will never forget that. Again, God was showing me that they were okay and I'm still not getting it. Later, in 2009, I found something my mother had written down on a piece of paper. I found it through a psychic I worked with at Passages, a famous rehab in Malibu, during a hypnosis session. I was the executive chef at Passages at the time. The piece of paper that was crammed into one of her journals—exactly where the psychic said it would be—said, "Vitza Kawaba Cha," meaning, "I am the beginning and I am the end." It was in some kind of African language. She loved Africa and always wanted to go on photo safari. I think she knew she wasn't going to be here too much longer and was searching for a reason as to what her purpose was in this life. I believe she was right—we are the beginning and the end. I understand now that this really is our only shot in this life, confirming what I felt and saw in the operating room. Going through an abortion and then a major accident were major losses in my life, and within such a short period of time too. I knew it would be a long while before I would recover from these two events, and that the fallout would probably be immeasurable. A permanent loss is a permanent loss and it's something that can't be ignored, but I did my best to do just that. I would have to look at my fingers as a constant reminder of how stupid I was to stick my hand in that fucking machine forever. I wondered if other people would ever completely understand what I was going through. Would they ever get how horrendous this whole thing was, or would they think I was overreacting? Ultimately, it really wasn't important to me how they felt about my pain, and why should it be? But it dawned on me while feeling sorry myself in the hospital that I cared more about what people thought of me than I realized. Before the beginning of what was to be my lifetime profession, I was running around town going from party to party with men much older than me, and worse yet, superficial men. I somehow thought that lifestyle was important. Staying up late with a bunch of guys who just wanted to have sex with as many women as possible, sometimes two to five in one evening, seemed intriguing to me. It was in fact a dark, meaningless lifestyle. I was introducing many clueless and helpless girls to guys who cared about only thing: getting laid. I was actually indirectly responsible for the consequences these girls may have suffered later on due to the selfish acts of these childish men and myself. How could I have partaken in that kind of thing? I mean let's say it like it is- I was a 'pimp' in some way, except I didn't get paid. Did I need to be liked so much so that I would put women in harm's way? Why was I so drawn to those people? Was my anorexia also punishment for this kind of behavior, adding to a longer list of bad decisions than I thought? I used my age at the time as an excuse for my behavior, but that was bullshit.

* * *

It was the second day after my surgery. My eyes were puffy from crying and I was in need of a bath, so when mom came to see me, she offered to bathe me. She could see that I had been crying but didn't say anything about it. She also hadn't seen me naked in almost seventeen years and that was a little uncomfortable for me. While she bathed me, I could feel she was disturbed by something. Then she asked me the worst possible question she could ask, which shouldn't have been shocking to me.

"Lisa, I can see your ribcage and your spine very clearly. Have you been eating? What the hell is going on here? You look like you just left a concentration camp, for Christ's sake."

Mortified, I said, "Mom! I just lost three fingers and this is what you want to talk about right now?"

"People usually lose weight in the hospital, but this is ridiculous if not scary, to say the least. It's been a long time since I've seen you naked, but your ribs are sticking out almost an inch, Lisa!"

Stunned that she was more concerned over my weight than my accident, I had nothing to say except "Stop it mom! I'm not that thin!" Let's get real here. I knew I was in deep shit Idaho with my eating disorder, and I was totally embarrassed that she called me out on it in such a vulnerable moment. In hindsight, it didn't occur to me that she'd notice how thin I was because I thought I was fat. I thought she would be proud of how I kept in shape, but instead she saw how sick I really was. Unfortunately, I did not. As she bathed me in silence, I could sense her confusion and concern for me and how helpless she felt over my disease.

While drying me off, my mom said, "Please, talk to me, Lisa. We have always been open and honest with each other since you were a little girl. You told me about your first sexual experience and shared your acid trip with me, which are scary things for a mother to hear. That's very personal stuff most kids never tell their parents. So please, tell me, how long have you not been eating?"

Honestly, she was being very rational in her questioning me, but I still resented it.

"Mom, please, that's enough! I've been off dairy and sweets and exercising a lot. I'm fine. I have enough on my plate right now and this conversation is totally out of left field!"

I knew this discussion was nowhere near over—it was just beginning—and I wasn't looking forward to future ones with her, either. After having that little exchange about my ribs, I felt like I was now under a microscope. Mom would pay more attention to me now more than ever while I ate, causing excess distress for me. The pressure would become unbearable for me, and it would only make my condition worse. She had no idea that her words were actually contributing to my disease; no well-meaning person would understand. Negative comments about my weight only made me more determined to prove everyone wrong, causing my disease to get worse and sending me further in denial.

We ate lunch in silence because I knew she was angry with me. She wasn't getting the information she needed from me. But dealing with this accident was all I could handle. I was an adult, and I didn't have to explain anything to her. After lunch I said, "Mom, I want to be alone tonight. It's my last night in the hospital and I need to be alone, you know, to think about things."

"Okay, but it's not because of what I said about your weight, is it?"

"No! I just need to think about things alone. I have a lot to think about. Please understand."

Yes, I was very pissed off, just for the record.

"Of course I do, but please make sure you eat your dinner, okay?"

"Mom?"

"Okay, okay, but if you need me . . ."

"I will, and I know."

Even though I was upset at her comment, I didn't really want to be alone but I wanted her out of my face. Looking back, I couldn't look at myself through her words. She was totally right, and I didn't want to hear it. I was also amazed

I had the guts to ask her to leave because I was terrified. Maybe I was much stronger than I gave myself credit for. I knew there was going to be so much to deal with, and only God knew for how long. I ate only a few bites of food when dinner came because it was horrible. I guess hospital food has to be bland, boring, and tasteless since there are so many kinds of illnesses floating around in there. I was still feeling profoundly sorry for myself and equally as flummoxed as to why this happened. I almost couldn't bear the thought of dealing with this for the rest of my life.

* * *

During the night, a nurse came in for the last bit of wine I had left, and in return, I received my last shot of Demerol—maybe. I can't really be sure if it or any of the other shots were a placebo or real. As I lay in bed dozing off to sleep, I was as unhappy as anyone could be. Would I really be able to work at the restaurant again and face the machine and my colleagues? Worse, was I still going to want to cook? I'd had such big plans for myself before this happened. I had become addicted to cooking and wanted to be a famous chef, maybe even have my own cooking show someday. But who would want to watch it? No one wants to look at an amputee on television, especially a chef who lost her fingers in a kitchen accident. They would probably be disgusted at the idea of how I lost my fingers and couldn't watch the show because of that very reason. I wanted to write cookbooks and become the next Julia Child, which was still a possibility and thank goodness. Before the accident, I had always wanted to have an extraordinary story to tell someday. Maybe this is why the accident happened.

What about my love life? I was engaged but I knew deep down where I was headed—straight for unfaithfulness. Because I was already insecure, I was certain I would be even more insecure after having the accident and would more than likely want to test the waters with other men to see if they thought I was still an attractive woman. I was far too afraid to leave Mike but wanted to be free at the same time. It was all so unfair to Mike. He didn't deserve such a selfish person like me. He offered his big toe for goodness sake! Would anyone else genuinely love me besides Mike? Probably, but I wasn't able to see it. He must love me because if he didn't he would have left me. The fact that we had gone through two very life-altering changes together in three months gave me some hope, not for him but for me. I loved Mike mostly for how uncon-ditional he was. He was funny, sensitive, and a perfect gentle-man. He always opened the door to the house and the car and always pulled out chairs for women when they sat down at a table. Once he even put his coat down over a puddle so my new shoes wouldn't get dirty. He was and still is a chivalrous man. I loved that about him. But marriage was a big deal, and I still wasn't anywhere near ready for it. All my parents seem to do was argue constantly, especially if too much alcohol was involved. If that's what marriage was, I wanted no part of it. Mike and I never fought interestingly. He was easygoing, maybe to a fault. Did he compromise with me more than he wanted to just to make me happy?

* * *

I finally drifted off to sleep, but was awakened in the mid-dle of the night by a nightmare. Whatever the dream was about, it triggered a profound epiphany in me. At the age of five, I did a lot of drawing. In first grade, I created a crayon drawing that my dad thought would catapult me into being a full-blown artist later on in life. He thought I was going to be the next Marc Chagall. He gave me my first art book, called *Marc Chagall*, and wrote, "Lisa, the artist. Love, Dad." I went to art school where my dad taught music, Immacu-late Heart College in Hollywood, California, which is now the home of The American Film Institute. He bought me a high-tech drafting table with a hydraulic lift, and when I de-cided I wanted to learn airbrush painting—thinking I could do multimedia work that would be the first of its kind—he bought me an airbrush. I owned a Minolta and Leica camera because I decided in school I wanted to be a fashion photographer. I no longer have the cameras, the airbrush, or the high-tech drafting table, and for the life me I have no idea what happened to those cameras. The things that manage to get lost in moving amaze me.

My parents, especially my dad, were hoping that I would be a famous artist someday and when I announced I wanted to pursue a career in cooking, I think dad was disappointed. I could be wrong, but I remember sensing disappointment from him when I told him that cooking was what I wanted to do the rest of my life. I felt like he thought I could have done better in my life—but what could be better than cooking? My mom on the other hand, was thrilled for me. She saw my interest in cooking when I a kid, and since I took over the shopping and cooking in my teens of my own accord, she wasn't surprised that I gravitated towards cooking. Cooking is a form of art and the fact that I was creating art on plates and getting paid for it at the same time was excellent. I wasn't going to be the starving, suffering artist (that is what artists did, at least according to my dad). He wasn't rich enough to support my painting and photography, and I wasn't marrying for money. I know, that's a mouthful. But all of this seemed logical to me. I enjoyed cooking because it was physical, something I absolutely needed to be at a job if it was a forty- hour workweek. Cooking professionally is a total workout, and you get eight hours of it a day, if not more. I had the best of both worlds. I got to exercise, cook, and make money! For me, I had hit the jackpot, and there was no way I would ever be sitting at a desk all day. No sir, that's wasn't for me.

The profoundness of my epiphany relates to when I was eighteen years old. I began to obsess over the fact my middle right finger wasn't "perfect." I noticed it had bent to the right a little and had developed a callous on the first knuckle. I hated that middle finger so much that I wished it would go away. I tried forcing it straight, I tried filing off the callus, but none of it worked. It occurred to me while lying there in my hospital bed: Did wishing my finger away actually manifest itself into the accident? Could it be that my extreme hate for that finger had something to do with the accident? Deep down, I knew that was impossible, because as I mentioned earlier, there was no way my hand could have fit through the small hole at the top of the lid of that machine. But I couldn't help but wonder if there was a possibility of it happening because of some kind of bizarre karma. I'd do anything to take back all that hate. More interesting to me was my parents always said beauty was on the inside so why did that finger bother me so much?

*   *   *

Later on, I began to read all kinds of self-help books and one in particular: *You Can Heal Your Life* by Louise Hay. She believes that physical issues are a direct cause of how we feel about bodies and ourselves. Surprisingly, what my fingers represented in Ms. Hay book was very accurate. According to Ms. Hay, the index finger represents ego and fear. I think my ego was huge, and because of that I was in full fear mode about failing at everything. But at the same time, cooking gave me power and confidence, which hardly makes sense. I felt a deep feeling of satisfaction while cooking, especially in a professional kitchen with all those men around me. I knew I was able to keep up and even do better than them, and of course performing well without their physical help was a big challenge for me but I did it – even after the accident. I knew I could conquer just about anything in the kitchen, and since men were a special challenge, it made me want to succeed.

The middle finger represents anger and sexuality. Maybe the anger I was carrying was because my finger wasn't perfect before I lost it. And now that it's permanently gone, I get to look at an equally ugly finger for the rest of my life. It also represents my creative side. I should have looked at my old finger as an artistic masterpiece, but instead I was angry it didn't look like a model's hand. Now that it was halfway missing, there was no chance I would ever have a model's hand. And the sex I needed and sought out for a good amount of time must have been validation for me that I was still an attractive woman but this doesn't explain my behavior prior to the accident. If I had to come to some kind of conclusion about my promiscuity, I might have used sex to get attention early in life and to deal with my anger for having lacked the courage to just say no. It could have been that simple.

The ring finger represents unions and grief. I think my first union was so deeply hurtful to me that I became distrusting and disconnected in relationships. And finally, the little finger represents family and pretending. I always wanted my family to be like the *Leave It To Beaver* or the *Gidget* brand of family, but of course it wasn't. Ours was anything but close to a brand. All families have their dynamics and problems, and we certainly had our fair share. But looking back, we didn't have it all that bad, even though I thought we did. I didn't like the surface of life around me untidy, yet there was plenty of it.

* * *

I drifted off to sleep again thinking how uptight a person I was, incredibly defensive and super-controlling. What a burden. Now that I'm in my mid-fifties I sort of think I may know why. Maybe it was because there was so much fighting in my family as a teen; I was afraid the family would fall apart, so I felt the need to take over everything like I was going to be able to fix things. Now that my fingers were missing I certainly felt uglier than ever before. I wondered how I was going to address all of these issues as time passed. I was going home the next day and I had to figure how I was going to go about getting myself together and how to heal from this.

Chapter 6
The First Day of the Rest of My Life

When I woke up the following morning, my eyes were puffy *again* from crying all night. I looked at my cumbersome cast and wondered how long I was going to wear it. It wasn't the usual-looking cast. Normally, casts on the arm stop at the wrist or wrap around a thumb. This one covered my whole hand and people would certainly be curious as to what happened to me. I was anxious, mostly because I was leaving the comfort of my drugs and the isolation of my hospital room, which was a scary thing for me. I was reluctant to re-enter the world; even though my world had changed, everything else in the world was still moving round. I was also wondering what *could* happen in my new world. What would I do if my stitches were to open? Or what if I went into convulsions coming off the cocktail of drugs I'd been on for three days straight, especially since I have never done hardcore drugs like these before? What if I couldn't handle living with three half-missing fingers? Was I capable of suicide? Would I become a drug addict or an alcoholic to add to my already hellacious anorexia to deal with the pain? I knew I would have to tell my story to countless people over and over again, like a broken record, constantly reminding me of what happened—most likely for the rest of my life. The next few days, months, and years were unknown to me, so much so I almost couldn't handle thinking about it. When Mike came to take me home, he could see I was anxious. He helped me get what little things I had together while I sat on the bed not wanting to leave and holding back a total breakdown. I had a lump in my throat the size of a baseball, but I dared not lose it. I had to be strong in front of Mike. God forbid I become vulnerable showing him—or anyone, for that matter—that I needed him or anyone more than ever.

Just as we were leaving, the nurses who had helped me through those very difficult days walked in. I stood up from the bed, holding my cast in my left arm like I was holding a baby. As we were leaving, I apologized to the nurses for my shitty behavior and hoped the doctor was going to come by and say his good-byes, but only for one reason: so I could ask him for Demerol. One of the nurses said I didn't have shitty behavior and to not apologize. She said she would have been much worse than me. Then, thank goodness, the doctor came to say good-bye.

"Lisa, how do you feel today?"

"Okay, I guess. A little scared to go home, and so soon too."

"There's nothing more we can do, and the sooner you get back to your normal routine, the better. And if you experience any unusual kind of pain whatsoever, please call me immediately."

"What do you mean by that?"

I needed something else to worry about, as if things weren't scary enough.

"I mean if you feel any kind of shooting pains going up your arm or excruciating pain or odd sensations in your hand, I would like to know."

"Okay, but what are the chances of something like that happening?"

"Very little, I just want you be aware of it, that's all. I'm sure it's fine. Don't worry."

Don't worry? I was still in a fog from all the drugs I'd been on and still dealing with the trauma of it all, and he was asking me not to worry?

"What's the percentage? Do you mean I might get an infection after all of this? And are you going to give me something for my pain?"

"Lisa, you have nothing to worry about, okay? I'm giving you Darvon. It kills the pain without knocking you out."

I wanted to be knocked out. I wanted the Demerol and wanted to still ask for it but I didn't want to sound like I was addicted to it already even though I was.

"Okay, thank you. I want to apologize for behaving as badly as I did in the emergency room. I wasn't myself. I was just so scared."

"Thank you but no need to apologize. Please take it easy and rest. Before you know it, you'll be back at work."

I had to ask for the Demerol.

"I would rather have Demerol instead. It worked so well with me and to try something else may not work."

"No Lisa, I'm sorry. Darvon is a very effective drug for this situation."

"Are you sure it's strong enough? I'm nervous that I'll be in a lot of pain and the Demerol worked great."

"Yes, it's fine."

He knew what I was getting at, and that was embarrassing enough.

"Okay. Well, thanks again for everything."

"You're welcome. I want to see you a week from tomorrow to change your bandages and see how your stitches are healing up."

Really? So soon? How could it be that I would see my "new" fingers for the first time since the accident in a short week? Was I going to be ready for that? I really hadn't seen them all that well when it happened because my hand was nestled in my apron, so I had no idea how much of my fingers were gone, and I wanted to postpone it as long as possible. I could have waited a month for this.

"So soon?"

"Yes, you'll be surprised at how fast the human body heals. If you have any concerns, just call me. Take it easy and *rest*, okay Lisa?"

"Yeah, I will."

As Mike and I walked to the car I stressed about how I was going to deal the pain or life in general without my Demerol. What a miracle drug that was. It took away *all* my pain. Thank goodness my addiction of choice wasn't using drugs. That's all I have to say. It's *far* worse than anorexia— *not*! At least I had control over my eating—*not*! Drugs take us over, anorexia doesn't—*not*!

*   *   *

When Mike and I got to the car I began to sweat—a nasty, cold sweat that wouldn't stop—and my skin felt prickly. Was I withdrawing from the drugs already? I didn't really know what detoxing felt like, but I guessed that was exactly what was happening to me. I was squirming around in the car and itching like I wanted to jump out of my skin.

Mike noticed and said, "Sweetie, are you okay? You're sweating."

"No, I am *not* okay! I want more Demerol."

I felt like I was like a lion trying to escape from a cage. I was scratching my nails against the glass and breaking out into multiple cold sweats that seemed to never end—one wave after the other, like big waves crashing on the shore during a violent winter storm.

"Honey, you aren't getting anymore Demerol. He gave you a Darvon prescription and we should get it filled."

I screamed, "No! I want Demerol, damn it! You must know someone at the beach that can get you Demerol. Please Mike, I feel like I'm dying right now. I am in so much pain."

"Honey, you haven't tried the Darvon yet, so you don't know how it will work until you take one. And the pain you're in is emotional. I've been where you are right now and believe me, it sucks."

"It can't be as strong as the Demerol was. Can it? Have you had it before?"

Mike said in his very sweet way, "No, I haven't, and you aren't dying. You're having withdrawals. It will be over soon because it's only been three days that you've been on it. Imagine coming off of hard drugs after using for years. Trust me on this. I'm going stop at the next pharmacy I see and get it filled."

Mike had a point and I guess he was right, but the fact was, I wanted Demerol. I'd never felt better than I did while on that drug, and for a person who hated drugs that was a very dangerous idea. It took the pain away and made me feel like I was floating in air. Mike filled the prescription and got some aspirin and I continued to squirm around like an uncomfortable snake.

* * *

The minute we walked through the door of our home, I couldn't deal with being there. The last time I was home I was happy about my career and excited to see where my journey would take me. It should have felt great to be home but it didn't. My gut said to stay with Mom and Dad for a while and heal. It also became clear to me that I wasn't going to be able to do the things I used to do as well, if at all, and I couldn't deal with that either. How was I going to make my breakfast or make the beds or do laundry? I felt like such a failure. I felt weak because I was going to have to rely on my mom and Mike for everyday things that I took for granted. I never allowed myself to think what I'd do without the luxuries of running water, toilets, showers etc. I mean the list is endless as to the amount of things we take for granted daily. I decided to call Mom that minute and asked her if I could come home and stay with her and Dad for a little while to heal. Of course she said yes and that she was actually looking forward to having me around for a while, just like old times. Mom always made me laugh, sometimes to the point of crying, and I needed that medicine more than ever.

"Mike. That was Mom. I think it's a good idea to stay with my parents for a while. I might need help with stuff and you have to work. Are you okay with that?"

"Of course, whatever you need, baby, but you know I can and will take care of you if you want me to. You know that."

"Yes, I know. I just feel like I need to be home with my parents right now. I think it's best for the both of us."

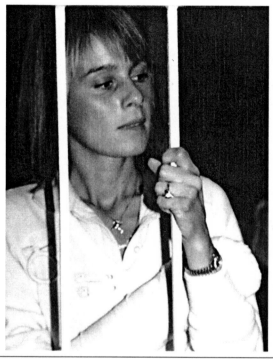

Here I am in my cast just a few weeks after the accident. I am not happy, and what was I thinking wearing those baby pins? Obviously I wasn't well.

The real reason I wanted to go back home was I wanted to decide for myself when *I* wanted to leave the nest, and not on my mom's terms. Mike and I had been dating about eight months at this point and my mom told me to move out and right in front of Mike and since Mike and I seemed to be in love, we should move in together. I was absolutely devastated. Actually embarrassed. How could she do this to me in front of Mike? I had no idea she was even thinking about kicking me out. I only imagined how embarrassed Mike probably was. But Mike, being the gentleman that he was, said, "Sure. I'm fine with it as long as Lisa is."

I wasn't anywhere near ready to move in with Mike, or any man for that matter. I couldn't afford to live on my own, and frankly, I didn't want to move out yet. But I also didn't want to move in with one of my friends, so what recourse did I have? Even though it was time for me to be on my own, I was terrified. I was twenty-three years old and was way overdue to move out, but this wasn't the way I'd imagined it would go down.

Mom said, "See? I told you he wouldn't mind." I was so stunned over what they both had said to me that I couldn't say anything. I felt like I was up against a wall and would look like a bad person if I said no.

I said, "Mom, don't you think you could have discussed this with me in private? You are embarrassing me."

Mike said, "Lisa. It's cool, really. Actually, I was going to bring this up with you anyway. What do you think?"

I said the only thing I felt I could say under that kind of pressure: "Sure. We can give it a try, and if it doesn't work out, we'll deal with it then, if and when the time comes."

Mom said, "See, that wasn't so hard, now was it. Take a month. No rush."

No rush? Was she kidding? A month to find a place to live seemed like two minutes to me. I felt like I'd just made a business deal with my mom and it sucked! I used to fantasize about the day I moved out. I'd dream that I'd be swept off my feet by my Prince Charming, who would ride us off into the sunset on a huge white horse. I used to wear my mom's frog ring in high school, rubbing it hard, hoping my true love would appear out of nowhere. That might have been the only "girly" thing I did as a young girl—dream of my Prince Charming. I was an unrealistic romantic, but the reality was that in my young years I wanted to wait until I was married to live with a man. By the time I was thirteen, I remember wanting to save myself for my husband. I'm a Virgo after all—The Virgin. Boy, that dream fell far from my emerald tree. I don't know what sent me so astray.

Feeling slighted, I made it my mission to find a place as fast as I could, just to show her and as luck would have it, we found the cutest little house in Pacific Palisades the following week. The move was very difficult, though. There had been torrential downpours for over two weeks, closing parts of Sunset Boulevard and causing us to make innumerable trips using long routes and side streets to get to our new home. I, of course, took that as a sign that we shouldn't be moving in together. Why else was it so challenging? Nothing should be that hard. But anything worth a shit is hard, isn't it?

It was too late to change my mind and honestly I was looking for a way out, just like I was from everything in my life—except for cooking. This might be a good thing after all. When our cute little house started to come together, it actually felt great that I finally had my own space and could do whatever I wanted as far as where things like art and furniture would go and how I set up my kitchen. Mike enjoyed watching me in this process and let me have my way. I was "playing house" on a whole new level for the first time in my life. Thank goodness Mom made it mandatory for me to learn how to take care of myself. I knew how to budget money for food, clean the house, and wash clothes. Decorating was fun and easy for me as well because of my training in art school. The only art that ever hung on the walls at home was stuff that mom and dad found, or something Jeff or I created or was given to them as gifts. They loved art, especially abstract art. Also quite a few pieces I did in college hung on those walls, too. Now in my new home it was all mine, except for the huge Salvador Dali painting Mike bought before we were married. I also found myself unexpectedly worrying about Mike's personal habits. I'd never shared a bathroom, kitchen, or home with anyone but my family. Was he the kind of guy who would leave the toilet seat up? Would he squeeze the tube of toothpaste at the top? Would he leave his clothes all over the place when he undressed, leaving it up to me to pick up after him? Would he leave the lights on everywhere he went? He was violent sleeper, tossing and turning in bed like we were in a wrestling match, which was difficult for me as I am a very light sleeper. Luckily, we both had California King beds, and thankfully they fit into our bedroom perfectly. It was wall-to-wall bed and I loved it.

It never occurred to me to ask Mike about these things before moving in together, and now it seemed useless mentioning it since we were already moved in. Why was I so afraid of change? Was I that set in my ways already? Or was I seriously doubting our relationship and didn't have the courage to have a go of it on my own? We had only been dating for four months after all. There were so many wonderful attributes to Mike, but I was wondering if anything was good enough for me. Mike wanted to stay with me the first night I was at my parents' house to make sure I was okay, but I didn't want him to. I was also incapable of paying attention to him at the time, and I wanted the least amount of energy put out for that kind of thing. Mom asked me if there was anything she could get for me to eat before I came. I said no, because my famous breakfast couldn't be prepared by anyone but me. During the night, I woke up realizing how in the world was I going to make my breakfast, since my right hand wasn't usable for while? I figured that I'd need to learn how with my left hand and spent a good two hours trying to visualize how I'd accomplish that. I decided I could do it.

* * *

The following morning I walked straight to the kitchen, hoping Mom was gone already for work. I was determined to make my famous "anorexic breakfast" myself, but Mom insisted on making it for me. She was worried I would be frustrated and feel worse about myself than I already did. Feeling obligated because I was staying in her house, I let her. Naturally, it wasn't right. I told my poor mom that it wasn't layered properly and the fruit was cut all wrong. Of course she thought I was being ridiculous, and of course I was. Why should it matter how the fruit was cut or layered? It all tastes the same in the end. But the fact was, she couldn't possibly understand how important it was to me that it was done right, and why should she? Even though she knew I was a mess with my eating, she couldn't have known how much so. I was the one with the problem, not her. I reluctantly ate the breakfast anyway because I could see I had upset her with my relentless and neurotic behavior. I was, after all, in *her and my dad*'s house now.

Since moving out, I could feel my space was gone. It was no longer my home where I spent most of my formative years as a teenager and young adult, and this made me sad. It seemed to me that they had adjusted to my leaving as well, and that made me melancholy. I apologized to my mom and ate the breakfast, praying there weren't more calories than there should be.

After my parents left for work, I decided to share the epiphany I'd had in the hospital with Mike. When I finished telling him, he said with tears in his eyes, "That is absolutely ridiculous, Lisa. Your thoughts about how you felt about your fingers when you were eighteen years old did not manifest itself in the accident. The accident happened at the fault of the machine. You'll find out what happened when the lawyer does. In the meantime, try not to think about it."

"Yeah, maybe you're right. I've been going crazy trying to figure out what the fuck happened."

"I bet, and I don't blame you one bit sweetie. The doctor gave you the number of a therapist to call and I think you should consider seeing him."

"No! I don't need to see anyone, Mike." Moving into self-pity mode, I said, "I'm broken in so many ways. How can you possibly love someone like me?" In hindsight, I was probably looking for compliments.

"I love you because you are open, honest, and strong. The accident happened just four days ago and you are acting as if it's been a year since it happened! I'd be in bed right now, hiding under the covers, milking it so hard just so I could wallow in self-pity, and doing as many drugs as possible just so I felt nothing. You're an animal! I've never seen anything like it. You are also a great volleyball player, incredibly talented at cooking, and very funny. You aren't broken to me—not even close. To me you are perfect in every way. I'll never forget when we first met. Remember when I came to dinner at Ma Maison when we first started dating and you made that pigeon dish for me? It was incredible! It was cooked perfectly and was served in a nest of port-soaked sliced pears. I can still taste it."

"Yes, I do remember."

"You have come such a long way since we met, and even after all we've been through we are still getting married."

My heart sank. I knew I had to tell Mike soon that I wanted to postpone the wedding. The wedding wasn't going to happen, at least not then.

Here's the pigeon recipe:

Sautéed Pigeon Nestled in Port Wine Pears

Serves 4
2 pigeons, or squab, cut into sections
Salt and pepper
1 Tbsp. olive oil
2 red pears, sliced a 1/4-inch thick and split in two
1/2-cup port wine
1/2 cup red wine
1 1/2 sticks of sweet butter

Directions: In a bowl, place the sliced pears and cover with the port and red wine; marinate an hour. In a sauté pan, heat the olive oil on medium to high heat and season the squab with salt and pepper to taste. Place in the pan and cook for 4 minutes. Turn over the squab and cook another 4 minutes. Turn off the heat and cover with a lid. Meanwhile, melt a quarter of the butter and sauté the sliced pears for 1 minute. Remove and set on a plate. Reduce the port and red wine another 2 minutes. On very low heat, whisk in the butter. On 4 plates, make a small nest of pears, top with 1/4 of the squab, using all parts equally. Drizzle liberally with the sauce and enjoy!

I recommend a high quality Syrah from Paso Robles, Alexander Valley, or Napa Valley with this delectable bird—and if you like cigars, a La Gloria cigar would be the perfect choice.

* * *

I said, "I want to go for a little walk. I have something I want to talk to you about."

"You're joking. You can't exercise yet. He said the blood would rush down into your hand if you had any physical activity. You're supposed to keep it elevated as much as possible. The doctor said to rest."

"I just got out of the hospital four days ago and I refuse to let this fucking accident rule my life! I can't stand it that I'm not exercising and I'm getting fat. I've gone from five hours a day of exercise to nothing. Nada."

"For once in your life can you do what someone asks you to do? You need to rest."

Unfortunately, that was impossible.

"I said just a walk, not a workout. I'm going stir-crazy."

"Okay, but a slow walk, and try to keep your hand elevated—and you are not getting fat. You could stand to put on a few."

Wrong thing to say.

"No I couldn't! Why does everybody think I'm skinny?"

Mike looked at me like I was nuts—and I was. But he was a smart man, and he knew better than to argue with me.

"Okay, you're right. Let's go."

He was learning that it was useless—I wasn't going to listen to anyone concerning my weight.

"I should probably take an Advil before we go."

"I'll get it for you, but you have Darvon too. Do you want that instead?"

"No, I don't want it unless I feel like my hand is going to explode. I've decided that I am going to feel everything I am going through."

"See what I mean? You are a remarkably strong woman. Like I said, if I was the one going through this, I would be on every drug imaginable, all the time. I would not want to feel anything. When God made you, He certainly broke the mold!"

"I've never heard you mention God before."

"It's a saying, that's all."

"I know. But we've never talked about this stuff before, have we? Do you believe in God, Mike?"

Mike answered quickly and without thought, "I don't know, maybe. I've never thought about it."

"Either you do or you don't. There's no in between."

Here I was, the expert, not!

"I guess so. I don't know. Maybe. Do you believe in God?"

I thought I was the authority on *everything*, literally. I found myself slow to respond and came up with this answer: "No, I believe in a higher power."

"Isn't that the same thing?"

A little caught off guard by Mike's response, I did everything I could to answer without flailing.

"No, it isn't. I've never been to church except for one time. It was Midnight Mass one Christmas Eve when I was fifteen years old. I took Communion and didn't even know what that was and still don't. I haven't read the Bible either. I only know the first sentence and a few other stories."

"So what? You can still believe in God and not know the Bible or go to church."

I thought his answer was absolutely amazing, but I wasn't about to admit it. Why? That was another thing about myself I didn't like. I never gave too many compliments back then. I was always jealous of something, or so it seemed.

"Okay, I'll tell you why I don't believe in God."

"Okay, but why do you feel the need to talk about this right now?"

That was a great question too, and I really didn't know why it was so important. I guess it was because of my near-death experience. I was starting to feel that there was a reason it happened, or maybe I felt like bragging.

"You mentioned God and how He broke the mold when He created me. I think we need to talk about our thoughts on this because something happened before surgery that I haven't told you about yet."

"What happened?"

"I'll tell you after."

"Okay, go on then."

"Mom and Dad decided it was a good idea to put us in Sunday school when I was seven years old and Jeff was five and a half years old. It was a Presbyterian Sunday School. We'd been in this school for only a few weeks until one morning while we were studying the story of Mary and Joseph and their immaculate conception, Jeff decided to ask her how that was possible. The teacher was rather taken aback by his comment and after several uncomfortable minutes she explained that it meant that God gave Mary the Holy gift of a child. My brother proceeded to explain that mom told us babies are born through an act of love, in a marriage between a man and woman. She responded with this: 'Profanity is not allowed in Sunday school. You must be punished.' After having said that, the teacher walked over to my precious little brother and hit the top of his knuckles with her ruler, scolding him for talking dirty. Talking dirty? Profanity? Really? Naturally, he began to bleed and cry. I couldn't believe what I had just seen so I ran outside and called mom from the payphone. I told her what had happened and my horrified mother immediately came and got us. When she got there she had quite a few unpleasant words with the teacher. After that day, she decided to let us choose our religion when we were ready, if at all."

Mike said, "Wow, that's awful. So what's your point?"

"I really don't know what my point is, but maybe if Mom hadn't given up on us and religion and tried another school I might have learned to believe in God, causing me to make better decisions in my life. The accident has to have been some kind of wake-up call for me, don't you think? I mean, God showed himself to me in the operating room, and even after that I still don't believe in God as I tell you all of this. Why? What else has to happen to me for me to get on a better path?"

"What? He did?"

I explained the whole thing to Mike.

"How could you not believe in God after that? I'm confused."

He was full of good questions that day. How couldn't I? What else did I need to go through to believe in God? For Jesus to come down and give me my fingers back? I've heard that happening to people before, so why not me?

"I don't know. That's a good question. I'll have to give that one some thought."

"That's pretty heavy stuff, Lisa."

I knew deep down in every part of my heart, that if I were to come to God, I would have to take responsibility for my sins—and I'd committed plenty up until that point—which might have healed my anorexia ironically. Then I would have been free from feeling guilt or shame, but I wasn't ready. I was digging the drama, big time.

"Well, since the accident happened only five days ago, give it some time. Maybe you'll change your mind."

"Whatever. That's when I thought how good could God be if He put a teacher that evil in charge of a Sunday school? At least I believe in a higher power now. I was atheist for almost fourteen years before coming to a higher power. The whole church thing, the little bit I knew or heard about it, seemed psycho and hypocritical to me. And from that day forward and up until several years ago, I chose to be an atheist and believed in reincarnation. Now I believe in a higher power. That's some improvement, isn't it?"

"I guess, but I still don't see the difference. And not every person who teaches Sunday school is like her, and not everyone gets to meet God and come back. Maybe you should give God another chance. I think He's trying to tell you something."

I was in no way expecting Mike to respond to this like he did. I was rather impressed.

"Well, what about you?"

"I believe there is a God, yes. But I can't understand how there would be a doubt in your mind after what you've gone through. I do know that if I had a bitchin' experience like you did I would give it a go, that's for sure!"

Looking back, it's incredible that Mike was actually pushing me to believe in God. Mike and I had never discussed anything this heavy up until then or after. When Mike suggested that when God made me He broke the mold, I never dreamed he would respond the way he did about it all. I think I fell in love all over again with him that day—or at least I thought so.

* * *

I struggled with my desire to connect or believe in something more powerful than me for almost thirty years after the accident. I looked to anything but God—trees, apples, Tarot cards, discos, sex, cigars, wine or alcohol—none of which did shit for me. I just thought it made me a "deep" person. The so-called "New Age" way of thinking never found me at peace, but I liked it in some ways. It still gives you the easier way out, and I liked the self-empowerment it encourages you have. That in fact *we* are God. According to this idea, we get to control our destiny, which was attractive to me because I needed to be in control. I had found the perfect "religion" within that concept.

"Was this the reason you wanted to go for a walk?"

"No. The actual reason I wanted to go for a walk is to discuss something else entirely different."

"I enjoyed that conversation, I really did."

"Yes, so did I. Let's go for that walk now."

As we walked outside, I couldn't remember the last time I'd appreciated the sun, the trees, or the flowers around me like I did that day. They were brighter than I ever remembered them to be. The air smelled sweet, like honeysuckle, and was unusually crisp and clean. I had never been so happy to be alive, even though I was depressed. It was weirdly quiet, almost deafeningly so. I could hear the birds chirping, and their songs were clearer than ever before. I felt uncommonly close to Mike, too, and that felt great and also scary. I needed depth with a man apparently, but not all the time. Mike was obviously willing to give it to me, but I was scared to death of that kind of closeness. But it felt so good—I have to admit..

Mike said, "So what's up?"

"You know I love you, right?"

"Yes, and you know I love you too."

Mike had this look on his face like, "What's she going to say now?" I was a bit apprehensive since we'd had the conversation we'd just had, but I had to let it out.

"Okay. I want to wait to get married." I suddenly felt lighter than ever. Man, what a relief to finally say it.

Mike stopped walking, and for a minute I thought he might be angry—which was lame of me to think, because Mike was *never* angry with me, at least so far. "What? You're upset now, right? I'm—"

Interrupting, he said, "No, not at all! Have I ever been upset with you? I was upset about your accident, but not this. Go on."

What did I tell you? He was never upset with me.

"Thank God! I am going through so much already and can't imagine what I am about to go through over the next few months, maybe even years. It's all so overwhelming for me."

Smiling and with a thankful look on his face he said, "I totally agree and understand. You can't know how relieved I am."

His words were like music to my ears. I said with love, "I am so grateful. I was worried you would leave me and I wasn't sure I could handle that."

"No way! I wanted to bring this up with you too, but I was afraid you would think I didn't love you anymore and wouldn't want to be with you any longer because of the accident. I want you to be totally into it."

"Oh, thank God."

"Right now, I don't see how that's possible and honestly, I'm not ready right now either. A lot could change and it would be horrible to get a divorce."

"Right?"

"I really think it's a great idea. What's the rush anyway, right?"

"Right."

Feeling a ton of pressure lifted off of the both of us, we stopped walking for a moment. Mike turned to hug me, and as we hugged I looked up at the sky and there were big and glorious, puffy clouds moving quickly. I looked for some kind of sign that this was the right decision we made.

The following morning, I announced I was going to make my own breakfast from now on.

"How, honey? You're right-handed," my mom replied.

"I am going to become ambidextrous. I need my independence, mom. I can't stand the thought of being reliant on you or anyone. I am going to wash myself from now on, too."

"Well, you have always done things your way; why should this be any different? I've never been able to tell you what to do or how to do it since you could talk. If you change your mind or need help with anything, I'm here for you."

That morning and every morning after that I cut, sliced, diced, and spooned everything with my left hand, layering it the way I liked in my special bowl.

* * *

I couldn't believe the week had flown by so quickly. It was time to change the bandages. I was extremely nervous about it because I hadn't seen my fingers since the accident. I had no idea what to expect. Mike tried to explain over and over to me how much of my fingers were left, but I still couldn't imagine how they looked. When we arrived, the doctor got right down to business.

"Are you ready?

What was I supposed to say, no? "I guess."

"I want you to look up at the huge light box against the wall."

When he turned the lights on, I saw a vast display of photos he had taken before and after the surgery, and what I saw was very difficult to look at. It was as though I had been through a war. The first set of pictures showed my hand before the surgery, on a cloth covered in iodine and spots of blood. The iodine made the whole image look worse than it was. The ends of my fingers looked jagged and frayed. From the looks of them, the blades seemed to be dull. Otherwise, it would have been a much cleaner cut, I would think. Also, my ring finger was even with the other fingers *before* the surgery. In fact, all of my other fingers were the same length as my little finger where they were severed. Above each finger was the other half of my fingers. That was almost nauseating to look at. I looked closer at my little finger and noticed that the piece that was hanging on by a thread was lying next to the rest of my finger. I saw the tiny piece of skin holding them together and that was almost harder to look at than the missing ones.

Then I looked at the second set of photos. I assumed these were taken sometime during the beginning of the surgery because I noticed my ring finger was much shorter. I wondered why. The last set of photos showed my fingers sewn up. They looked very swollen and red—almost double the size of my other fingers on my left hand. My middle finger's knuckle at the end of my nub was wider than the other fingers. It looked like a small mushroom cap at the end of my nub. I was not happy with how it looked it at all.

"Wow."

"I know, Lisa. It's hard to look at, but it will help with your healing."

"I wasn't sure what to expect, and you're right, it's really hard to look at, yet I can't stop looking at them."

I found my mind switching from a fear-based mindset to an analytical one. I decided at that moment I would assess the situation analytically rather than emotionally.

As the nurse unraveled my bandages, I looked at my fingers and couldn't believe how much of each one was missing. They looked much shorter than they had in the pictures on the light box.

"Why do they look so much shorter in person than on the light box? And my ring finger is super short. Why is that?"

"If we didn't cut them back you might have become very sick. The fingers were infected."

"Really? Is that because the blades were dirty?"

"It doesn't matter how well the blades were washed, and the real reason I couldn't reattach them is because your blood wouldn't flow through your veins. I tried re-attaching them three different times, waiting an hour in between to see if they would take. Unfortunately, they kept falling off."

Suddenly, I remembered Mike telling me this in the recovery room.

"Your veins are atrophied because of your weight. That's why the surgery took so long. I had no other recourse but to make sure you wouldn't get sepsis, and that meant cutting them back in order for you to not get very sick."

"So you're saying that if I was heavier, you might have been able to save them?"

"Well, that would have been helpful, but there were other factors too. The gangrene wasn't helping, and it was spreading very quickly up your fingers. There are never any guarantees as to the outcome in a situation like yours."

The truth was that had I been a healthy weight, I would probably have my fingers back, and that made me angry, and all because of my fucking disease. My fingers were gone forever because of whatever I thought was important about being skinny had changed my life permanently. What a jackass. Fucking fashion magazines.

"If I hadn't eaten that crab apple before the accident, would I have gone immediately into surgery, and if so, would there have been a better chance of reattaching them?"

"Probably not, Lisa. The time between the accident and the surgery wouldn't have made a difference."

I studied the photos a little more closely as the nurse finished re-bandaging me and I noticed that the air was stinging my nubs, and so were the bandages that were touching the ends of my nubs. It was very painful.

I asked the doctor if my nubs would always be this sensitive. Saying the word, 'nubs' was so hard to say, I can't begin to tell you.

"Not forever, but don't hit, scrape, or brush the ends of them against *anything* for a while, it's going to feel like your fingers are running through broken glass."

"What if I do hit them accidently? Will I bleed, or will the stitches open up again?"

The doctor looked at me with concern. "No, that's not going to happen. I gave you the name and number of a good therapist. You should use it."

Mike said, "Honey, I think that's a great idea."

"Whatever. I've said before, I don't need anyone, do you understand? I'll get through this myself and hopefully with the help of you and my parents. Other than that, I don't need any help. I'll be fine."

The doctor said, "I hope you reconsider. I want you here in exactly four weeks for permanent removal of your bandages. Immediately after that you'll be seeing an occupational therapist to help you to deal with the machine. We want to see you back to work as soon as possible."

"Is that long enough? I mean, are my wounds going to be healed?"

"Yes. You'll be just fine. Any other questions or concerns, feel free to contact me."

Incredible as it sounds, I actually thought I could actually deal with this shit. I didn't want to see a therapist. I truly believed I could get through the whole ordeal by myself and with the help of Mike and my parents.

When Mike and I returned to my parents' house, I was very depressed and in tremendous pain. I decided to take a Darvon because I thought my hand was literally going to explode. I took it on an empty stomach and suffered a stomachache worse than the pain in my fingers. When my parents got home, I was lying on the couch in the fetal position, bawling my eyes out. This was the first time I had actually allowed myself to fall apart since the accident. Mom came rushing over to me.

"Honey, what happened?" she said with deep concern for me.

"Why did this happen to me, Mom? What did I do to deserve something like this? Everything was going so well and now this has ruined everything. I'm a freak now. None of my friends are going to want be around me because they won't know how to handle me or how to act. It's a clusterfuck of shit."

I didn't think of what kind of pain my mom and my dad might be in, I was so caught up in my own.

"Oh Lisa, we are so sorry for what you are going through. So much so that we feel we need to be strong for you and we know you are going to be just fine."

It didn't matter how strong they were going to be for me, it was *my* fucking journey. It's so interesting to me how people, even parents, see things from their point of view—though now that I look back, how could they have seen it any other way?

"You are a very strong woman and we know you won't let this bog you down. Just give yourself some time and a break. We know how impatient you can be, but this happened only a week ago."

"I'm allowed to be impatient. You fucking try this shit. It sucks, big time."

I felt bad saying that, but they needed to know how lame they sounded. Not a damn thing they said mattered.

"That's true. We love you, and the friends who really love you won't care this happened to you. Think of your accident as the truth. From now on, you'll know the truth about people and how they really feel about you. Look at it as your new 'truth meter.'"

What a cool way to think about what had happened. She had a special knack of helping me see things differently all my life. I compare our relationship to a movie I saw many years later called _The Horse Whisperer_, directed by Robert Redford. It is a 1998 American drama film directed by and starring Robert Redford, based on the 1995 novel by Nicholas Evans. Robert Redford plays the title role, a talented trainer with a remarkable gift for understanding horses who is hired to help an injured teenager and her horse back to health following a tragic accident. Scarlett Johansson, who played the part of Grace MacLean, lost the lower half of her leg while her horse protected her from being hit by a truck that was carrying a large load of logs on an icy road. Grace's mother, Annie MacLean, who was played by Kristin A. Scott Thomas, was a lot like my mother, never giving me one break, not one second more than necessary and for my benefit, thank God.

After I calmed down, I had a glass of wine and never took another Darvon again. In fact, I threw them all down the toilet. I was going to tough it out like I said I would in the first place. I'm not sure how healthy that was, but it was the only way I knew to get through the whole ordeal and I hated how those pills made me feel. I had the sense, even then, to know that pain is a necessary part of growth. During dinner, while eating my usual whopping three ounces of fish and eight ounces of steamed vegetables, I announced that I was going to sue the company that had imported the machine from France.

Dad said, "We can't afford a lawyer, Lisa."

"The lawyer I found is a friend of a friend's father, and he agreed to represent me on consignment."

My mom said, "Honey, are you sure you don't want any potatoes?"

I was talking about suing, and she was concerned about eating potatoes?

"Mom! Please! I thought we had a talk about this already."

I knew the time would come, sooner than later, that I would be ready to go home just because of her constant monitoring of my eating habits.

Dad said, "Okay, you two. That's enough. Honey, are you sure you want to sue?" My dad was really big on karma. I wasn't lying about any of it so there was no karma attached.

"Yes, and just so you know I'm not suing for the money. I want to make sure this doesn't happen to others, and if a nice financial settlement comes out of it, great. A young team of lawyers also called me today. Another friend of mine told them about me, but they wanted me to lie and say that I couldn't cook anymore because of the trauma; they said I could easily get two to two and a half million dollars if I lied. No way am I lying, so I told them no."

"That's my girl."

No way was I going to lie in front of God and a jury for two million dollars to stop doing what I loved most. That brings bad mojo to one's world. My dad was proud of my decision, especially of why I wanted to sue. I am in love with cooking and couldn't imagine doing anything else with my life. If I had lost my thumb then maybe I might have gone for the two million with the greedy legal team. It might have been impossible to handle a knife without my thumb. Two million was a lot of money in 1980, and I occasionally won-der how my life would have turned out if had I gone for it. But then again, how could I have considered it since cooking is in my soul—God's gift to me? The truth is, all the money in the world couldn't bring back my fingers.

New Year's Eve was rapidly approaching. Two and a half weeks had passed since the accident, and I wanted to go to

L'Ermitage restaurant in Hollywood to celebrate. It was the first time in a long time that the whole family was gathered together during the holidays and unfortunately not for the greatest reason. L'Ermitage was an exceptional French restaurant that I had tried get a job at for years. When I finally asked for one, the chef said he didn't hire women. If I were a feminist I would have called Gloria Allred to handle the situation. Thank goodness I wasn't.

It was a bittersweet New Year's Eve. My dad seemed especially melancholy and particularly reflective toward me that night—reminiscing about my childhood and how adorable I was. This was not something he normally displayed on an emotional level, yet I was never more "Daddy's little girl" as I was that night—it was a very sweet feeling.

That dinner was epic, but there was one dish I had that still sticks out in my mind today. It was called Foie Gras En Croute, and it was served as an appetizer on a bed of sautéed spinach, nestled in puff pastry and finished with a rich port wine butter sauce. It was startlingly exceptional. Dad brought a 1972 Château Lafite from home. He loved Lafites and collected them up until the earthquake in 1971. I'll never forget that earthquake. It was in the early morning hours just before school. A sudden, violent shaking woke us all up and the first thing I did was run to the bathroom to flush the toilet. I had heard in school that if you flushed a toilet during an earthquake the water would swirl down counterclockwise, and it did! My dad's first instinct was to run to his precious Lafites, which were sitting on the top shelf in the dining room. He grabbed a chair and stood on it, guarding his wines for dear life. My brother slept through the whole thing, and my mom prayed there would be no wine lost. I'll share the recipe with you, though finding Foie Gras is difficult these days.

Foie Gras with Sautéed Spinach, Puff Pastry
and a Port Wine Glaze

Serves 4
4 slices Foie Gras, cut a 1/2-inch thick (this can be found
   at very high specialty stores; if you live in LA, Surfas
   in Culver City has Foie Gras)
1 bag fresh baby spinach, wilted in 1 Tbsp. olive oil
Salt and pepper to taste
1 package frozen puff pastry, partially defrosted
Egg wash

Port Wine Sauce

2 cups port wine
1-cup balsamic vinegar
1-cup sugar
Salt and pepper to taste

Directions: Pre-heat the oven to 425 degrees. Place a sheet
of puff pastry on the counter while partially frozen. Roll out
with a rolling pin to a thinner piece. Use a 2-inch round cut-
ter, punch out 4 circles, and place on a baking sheet. If you
don't have one you can cut into 2-inch squares. In a small
bowl, mix together 1 egg yolk with 2–3 tablespoons water
and beat with a fork. Using a pastry brush, brush the egg
wash on top of each round of puff pastry. Place in the oven
and bake 7-10 minutes. In a sauté pan, wilt the spinach with
olive oil and salt and pepper to taste. Make the sauce by re-
ducing the port and balsamic together until reduced by half.
Add the 1 cup sugar and lower the heat to medium; cook until
the sauce starts to thicken. Add salt and pepper to taste. I'd
go a little heavy on the pepper. After you have all that done,
now it's time to sear the Foie Gras. Pre-set your four plates
and place the spinach in a mound on the middle of them.
Heat a non-stick pan with no oil—there's enough fat in the
liver, trust me. When the pan is hot, add your 4 pieces of

Foie Gras very quickly. The fat will come out immediately. Cook for 5 seconds, flipping them over quickly, then cook another second and remove, draining on paper towels. If you cook it too long, it will melt like butter. When you complete this successfully, place the Foie gras on top of the spinach. Drizzle some of the sauce on the Foie Gras and around on the plate. I would use a squeeze bottle with a small tip to have more control. Then place the puff pastry square off the side of the mountain of spinach and the Foie Gras. You can use the puff as toast, or take bites of Foie Gras with the spinach and then bite the puff. This is great with dry champagne or a ruby port wine.

* * *

Dad drank way too much that night. Drunk, he said over and over again how sad he was about my hand and how he hoped I could cook and paint again. Dad was the kind of man who would hide his emotions in his composition of music, avoiding the day-in and day-out stuff of life. Mom always handled all of that. But this was something he couldn't disguise in his writing in the corner of the living room. On the way home, he burst into song, singing "Auld Lang Syne." We all joined in, and when we got home my dad fell out of the car and threw up all over the lawn. He was indeed drunk, and only because he was more upset about me than he could ever express.

The next day, Dad had a horrible hangover and so did Mike. I'd never seen Dad or Mike like that before. Mom had put a stainless steel bowl next to Mike in the living room just in case he puked. I've never been drunk like that, not before or since.

* * *

New Year's Day. What better time to go home? I told Mom and Dad I was ready to go home, and honestly, they seemed relieved. I could see they wanted their home back again and I was ready to start living in mine. On the way home I suggested we move closer to town, maybe to Brentwood, or close to it. The drive to Hollywood was too long, and I wanted to be closer to Mom and Dad.

"Don't you think you're moving way too fast? It's been only two weeks since the accident; now you want to move to Brentwood?"

"I do everything fast."

"Yes, I know, but you are dealing with a major trauma and can't be thinking clearly."

"I'll do some looking around to see what's out there and if I find something before going back to work, which could be in a month or so, we can move closer to town."

"We have a house for only $1,200 a month in The Palisades, Lisa, with a huge backyard and beautiful front yard. It's close to the beach and in a very nice community."

"Yes I know, but I really want to be closer to work and my parents."

"Okay, do what you need to do. I really don't want to move, but if it's that important to you, I'll consider it."

The next day, before we went to our favorite restaurant that night, the phone rang. It was the workman's compensation lawyer. He wanted to set up an appointment the following week to determine how much I was going to receive financially for the accident. The week before my appointment, I went to the beach every day. Frankly, I was enjoying not working. I've been working since I was sixteen years old and it was nice to have a break for once, but I wish it were under different circumstances. I watched my friends play volleyball, trying to figure out how I was going to set the ball again. I would have to wait another several months before I could try. I couldn't imagine the volleyball hitting my nubs knowing the kind of pain they were going to be in. I knew it would be a long while. I had also heard about the "phantom" finger phenomenon thing. I apparently was going to look forward to feeling the ends of my fingers still attached to my body that would move appropriately with my other body parts. So this meant that I would naturally set the ball before it actually hit my fingers, and that would be weird, not to mention bad for my setting.

I spent quite a bit of time depressed while at the beach, watching everyone play ball. It made me feel sorry for myself and very anxious. I tried hard not to show how much fear I was in most of the time. I think I may have managed to do that—but then again, I thought I was hiding my disease, too. Who really cared except for me? As my appointment with the workman's compensation lawyer rapidly approached, I was curious how one gauges the loss of appendages.

Chapter 7

Workman's Comp and Aliens

Before my appointment with the workman's comp lawyer, Mike and I decided to go to John O'Groat's in West Los Angeles for breakfast before we went, which translated into, "I'll make my usual anorexic breakfast before we go and Mike will eat a normal breakfast." John O'Groat's was arguably *the* best breakfast joint in Los Angeles. Mike ordered his favorite breakfast consisting of pancakes, eggs, bacon, and a cappuccino. I envied Mike because I really wanted to eat the same breakfast, but wouldn't dare. I have to say that I make exceptional pancakes. I am known for them. When I was at Passages, the famous rehab in Malibu, I would work the breakfast shift on occasion and every time I did the clients requested my pancakes. The secret to my succulent pancakes is that I fry them in 50/50 butter and oil. Here's the recipe:

White Chocolate Raspberry Buttermilk Pancakes

Serves a hungry family of 4
1 box of your favorite pancake mix, follow directions for
    serving 4 people (I like Bisquick or Kodiak Brands)
3/4 cup white chocolate chips
3/4 cup fresh raspberries, can't use frozen (if you can't
    get fresh, then fresh or frozen blueberries will do)
Butter and vegetable oil
Real maple syrup, warm

Directions: Make your pancake mix according to package directions. Add the raspberries and white chocolate chips, stirring well. In a non-stick or cast iron skillet (I recommend

"See my cheeks? You'd think I had nuts stored in there! I was 15 years old here".

this) add 3 pats of butter and 2 tablespoons of oil. On medium-high heat, melt the butter until golden brown. Pour 2 ounces of pancake mix, adding more according to the size of your pan. Cook until bubbles appear all over the top of the batter and when the sides of the pancake become a crusty golden brown. Flip the pancake and cook for another 30–40 seconds. Repeat until you've used all the batter. Serve with warm maple syrup. Kids love these!

If you desire eggs with this you can serve them either sunny side up or scrambled.

* * *

I was impressed by Mike's metabolism, and even though I knew I had a very high metabolism too, just like my parents, I chose to ignore that fact. When I was a teenager my cheeks looked like a chipmunk's cheeks, or at least I thought so. That's what I called myself at sixteen years old. Too many pancakes as a kid, I guess, not to mention Sara Lee coffee cake, French toast, chocolate chip Baskin Robbins ice cream, and doughnuts: my favorite were crullers. I miss that kind of eating but not really. It was seriously unhealthy. As my disease progressed, I bought pocket guides that listed calories, carbohydrates, and fats. I also started to bring a diary with me when we dined out. I would check out the menu, pick out what I wanted, and log it into my diary. Then when I got home, I would break my meal down and add up the calories I had ingested. If I didn't have time or didn't feel like doing it right away, at least I had what I had eaten written down and could deal with it the following morning. Sometimes I would actually lose sleep over not knowing how many calories, fats, and carbohydrates I had ingested. What a waste of fucking time, not to mention how twisted it was. The *real* trouble began, though, when Mike and I moved into Brentwood. I was already in big trouble in the first place, but when I started "chewing and spitting" food, I was officially screwed. I called it "repulsive disorder" for the obvious reason of how repulsive the act itself was. I later discovered there's an actual name for this— "CHSP", otherwise known as "Oral Expulsion Disorder." It's also a separate disorder from anorexia or bulimia. Fabulous.

It all started with a stupid Mrs. Field's cookie on my walk one afternoon in Brentwood. I could smell her cookies two blocks away and couldn't resist, so I decided to treat myself to a cookie or five. Sweets were generally forbidden; I allowed myself a few per week, but that was becoming more and more rare. And the only alcohol I allowed myself was Fernet Branca, a fermented artichoke digestive with lots of alcohol in it that the Italians use for an upset stomach or help with digestion. If drunk before dinner or lunch, it can stimulate the appetite. And after dinner it literally breaks the food down, and rapidly. I loved the warmth flowing down my esophagus into my stomach, and I would visualize the food I had just eaten breaking up into tiny pieces. It is also a laxative, and that was a plus. I knew I had some Fernet Branca at home, so I was good to go. I never allowed myself sweets for fear my body would cling onto any fat it could, causing me to gain weight. I bought half a dozen of my favorite kind: warm white chocolate macadamia nut cookies. When I got home I had a few bites, but guilt overcame me so I spit it out into the trash.

That's when the sick light bulb went on. It was like I had discovered a gold mine. I could chew anything I wanted, now and forever, and never swallow any of it! I devoured all 5 cookies, spitting out everything—and worse, I found myself completely satisfied. It was strange how fulfilled and exhausted I was after that 'session' as I look back on it, especially by the time I built these sessions up to two-hour chewing frenzies. I drank soda water during these sessions because the act of the spitting without swallowing made me really thirsty. Or maybe my body needed to swallow something. The only good thing about my craziness was I finally started drinking water. Yes, it was soda water but it helped my bowels move. I wondered if the act of chewing those cookies, and the huge amounts of foods I repulsed in the future, actually burned calories. This is where my nine-year full-blown anorexic nightmare began. This is going to sound strange, but I'm grateful I hated puking so much or there is no doubt I would've been bulimic.

* * *

Thrilled with my new discovery, I shared it with Mike when he got home—and with genuine enthusiasm, I might add. I sincerely thought I'd stumbled onto something great. Obviously, he thought I'd lost my mind, and clearly I had. That morning I read a "Dear Abby" letter about a mother who was very concerned about her daughter's bulimia and was troubled about her health and wanted advice on how to deal with the disease and her. Actually, there were a lot of letters being written about this disease, I was noticing. I told Mike I thought I might write to "Dear Abby" and tell her about my discovery. I though maybe it might help others to stop throwing up. I mean, chewing and spitting had to be better for them, right? You're not serious, are you?" Mike replied. "Do you know how crazy that sounds?"

"Yes I'm serious! It's better than throwing up, that's for sure."

"Okay. Do you think what you said just now is sane? Your alternative is not the answer to a debilitating disorder that actually takes lives every day. Eating normally is the only sane answer."

"The strain the body goes through while vomiting is so violent. A person could die puking every day like that. Chewing and spitting is much better for the body."

Of course I had no idea how unsound my idea was and how out of my mind I truly was. Thinking about how sick I was makes me very sad today. I remember Mike's face like it was yesterday. He looked at me like I was certifiably gone. He was almost frozen in disbelief. I'm quite sure he had no idea who I was at that moment. Oh but I did—*not*! I really believed I had discovered a healthier choice for bulimics. Insane though it was, I thought I had the answer.

"None of this is rational, can't you see that? I can barely take it anymore! Your eating issues are totally out of hand. It's been almost seven months since the abortion and almost four months since the accident and you've lost a lot of weight, and I am concerned. You're freaking me out. I'm sorry if that pisses you off, but someone has to tell you. You're in serious trouble."

He was totally right about me being pissed off because I was in trouble.

"You're overreacting. You don't know what you're talking about. You want me to stay fat. That way no one else will look at me. That's it, isn't it?"

"Oh my God, you really are more out there than I realized. I don't know what to do now."

"Don't do anything, okay? I'm just fine. Leave me alone. I'm fine. I've never looked better."

In the coming months, I tried to hide the extent of my repulsive disorder from Mike as best I could. I didn't want him

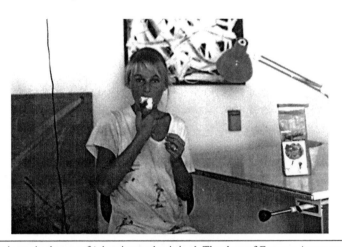

This is me in the act of 'chewing and spitting'. That bag of Famous Amos was chewed and spit into the white bowl hiding behind it and the bag is now being filled with a box of chewed drumsticks. Lovely, not!

to know how often I was doing it. Further along into my disorder, I started to chew and spit while driving just so Mike wouldn't catch me. I'd buy a large bag of potato chips, empty them out onto the street, and then drive around to multiple fast food restaurants, accumulating tons of food and enjoying my bounty on the road. After I finished "repulsing," I would find a trashcan to throw the chip bag into or drive down a quiet street or alley and throw it out the window.

Not only was what I was doing sickening, it was expensive and illegal. Littering is a no-no and to make it worse the bag was full of warm, chewed food in it. Gross! I'd say on average I'd spend a minimum of thirty-five to almost sixty dollars each session. Chewing all that food destroyed my teeth, and I am still paying for that today.

Ultimately my repulsive sessions turned into a ritual making it a fun event. After buying a bunch of crap I would never ingest even in a healthy state of mind, I would place a blanket on the carpet in the living room, turn on the television and have a picnic. In order of my routine I opened all of the food I bought and put it on the blanket. I would then place bowls and/or a large plastic bag next to me to spit the food into. I think it was a thirteen-gallon trash bag. I would then start chewing and when I was done I would spit the food into the plastic bag. After several hours of doing this I would get another plastic bag and put the chewed food into it so that when I carried it to the trash it wouldn't break.

Finally, I couldn't hide the extent of my problem from Mike any longer. We were spending every day off together because we had the same hours. I started chewing and spitting in front of him, as I couldn't help myself. He tried to stop me a few times but he wasn't able to. Sometimes he would join me in driving around town and picking up the food to bring home that I'd chew and spit in front of him while we watched television. In hindsight, he may have enabled my addiction. He just wanted me to be happy, and he hated arguing but loved bantering and still does. Bringing up my disease would certainly start an argument, and the few times he tried to banter with me about it, he had no success. There was nothing humorous about my problem. Even I knew that much. I was way too wrapped up in my own addiction to care what he thought, too. Mike continued to try and stop me, but he finally gave up because he knew it was making me worse. Anyone who questioned my eating habits while dining out or said I was too thin or asked any question regarding my weight just made me fall deeper into denial. Now I know that my retaliation and denial toward Mike and others only hurt me, not them. If I wanted to do it at night, I made sure I ate my 300-calorie dinner first. I mostly did it during the day because I never ate lunch. I didn't want to die of starvation; I just wanted to control my food intake. My jaw was always sore afterward and my teeth throbbed for hours after. That was a major downside, but I was hooked. I can't believe Mike stayed with me while I went through this very long episode. I swear I would have left myself at that point, and I think deep down I was hoping he would. I even tried to blame him later for my disease, and after we broke up I tried to make it his fault. And of course he said he did try but I wouldn't listen. And of course he was right. There was absolutely no getting through to me. He may as well have been talking to a brick wall.

*   *   *

When we arrived at the workman's comp office it smelled like mold. We waited a few minutes in the waiting room before we were called in. An old man with an equally bad odor greeted us. He was wearing a brown suit, a pair of grey shoes, a light brown shirt, and a pink-striped tie. He was also wearing a fedora. He looked like someone out of the movie *Chinatown*, but was nowhere near as handsome as Jack Nicholson. He wasted no time getting right into it though. He opened a large, black, hard-covered book and began reading.

I asked, "What's that?"

"This is the book that will tell me how much we are going to compensate you for the loss of your fingers."

"You're kidding, right? I wasn't expecting this. I thought I was picking up a check. I thought it was a set amount."

"No. It doesn't work that way. I need to look it up in this book and then submit it to workman's compensation and they will cut you a check."

"Wow, that's incredible."

To think a book like this had even been conceived of kind of fascinated me and upset me. But in truth, how else could they determine an amount?

"It would be impossible to have set amounts because people have different points of amputation on the body, making the amount vary greatly. This book will tell me how much that will be for you."

It never occurred to me this how they came up with an amount. I found that interesting and was curious more than ever to find out what my amount would be. I thought maybe three or four thousand would be the most. Why? I have no idea.

He pulled a picture of my hand out of a manila envelope and began looking up whatever it was he was looking for.

"Can I see that picture?"

He handed me the picture and I stared at it for a minute. As I handed it back, I felt so sad. "Can I see that book?"

"When I am finished, of course you can." I was still in awe of the fact that there was a book for this kind of thing. As he was adding up numbers on his calculator, he was making hums and mms sounds.

"What is it? Is everything okay?"

Clearing his throat, he said, "Well, it's too bad as far as money is concerned that you didn't lose your little finger. That would have made a substantial difference in your settlement."

I was beyond offended at his comment. I couldn't believe he said that. I stood up with horns coming out of my forehead and spines coming out of my back.

"Excuse me? What did you say?"

Mike knew I was angry, and he tried to gently pull me back down, but with no success. One thing about me, when someone really makes me angry, I suddenly become full of adrenaline.

Mike said, "Lisa, calm down."

"No! I will not fucking calm down! This man just told me that it was a *shame* that I didn't lose my pinky? Who the hell does he think he is? Do you know how offensive that was? You have no idea what I've been through and you have the gall to sit at your stupid desk smelling like mold and looking like a fucking clown and feeling nothing for me and my situation and you think you can say something like that to me? I'd rather have my fingers back than listen to your shit. And just so you understand me, *any* amount of money the state wants to give me won't help, you asshole."

Mike's head was in his hands at this point, and the guy was clearly embarrassed.

"Lisa, it's not his fault."

"Fuck you! Whose side are you on? He was rude and insensitive."

The poor guy still didn't have a chance to say anything as I continued on with my rant.

"And who decided on the numbers? Huh? People who had multiple missing limbs or were blind? Did these people lose their limbs and extremities one at a time and decided how much a person gets? God, this whole thing sucks."

That poor man. What an angry bitch I was. I knew I was out of control, but under the circumstances and given who I was at that point in my life, I would have been a bitch to him no matter what.

He said, "Well, I didn't write the book and I'm sorry if I have offended you. I am just doing my job."

I knew I had overreacted, but damn it, he was talking about my fingers like car parts you could trade on eBay. After a few minutes, I managed to pull myself together and say, "I'm sorry. This whole thing has been overwhelming for me but that was a bit harsh the way you said that, you have to admit."

"Yes it was, and I'm sorry. Let me explain. The amount you get is determined by how handicapped you are. For example, if you couldn't function on the job like you did before, then you would be entitled to quite a bit more. I was merely saying that you would have received more if you lost your pinky, that's all. I just worded it wrongly."

That made some sense to me, but at that point I was still agitated. Now I couldn't wait to hear the amount I was going to get. After about fifteen more minutes of him calculating, reading, and recalculating, we waited for an answer.

I whispered into Mike's ear, "How much do you think I'm getting? I think maybe three or four thousand?"

Mike said, "I have no clue, maybe five thousand? I think you deserve a hundred thousand, personally."

"That would be something, wouldn't it?" Suddenly, now that money was on the table, I was hoping for a larger amount.

"Okay, I've got a total for you. It looks like you're getting $16,487.47 in compensation."

"What? Oh my God, really? That's incredible, isn't it Mike? I can't believe it!"

"Wow! That's four times the amount you originally thought it might be."

I was blown away. I felt bad that I had lost it on the man and apologized again. I'd never had that kind of money in my whole life. Somehow getting money for what happened did help me some. I felt like there was some kind of redemption, a strange kind of closure. And at the same time, getting money for an accident I knew deep down I didn't cause still wasn't enough.

"So, why such a strange number?"

"It just worked out that way. You also have a fifteen-year window for any kind of DNA work that can be done to help your fingers grow back—and, if you choose, you can be fitted for prosthesis, for free."

"DNA? You mean they may find a way to grow my fingers back like a lizard?"

"Yes, medical science is always working on things like that."

"That's incredible, don't you think Mike? Maybe I'll get my fingers back!"

"Yes, I do! It's amazing, really."

Still, I thought the number was bizarre, and with cents in the total no less. It was like there was tax or something. In my messed-up state of mind, I imagined a board of directors sitting around a table somewhere, maybe making fun of amputees while coming up with these numbers. I was so pissed I'd lost my precious fingers and wasn't thinking clearly. What was more compelling to me, though, was the DNA thing. How cool would it be if they figured out how to re-grow fingers or any other limbs? Somehow I felt encouraged by that information and it brought comfort to me. That idea gave me hope. But I knew for sure I could never wear prosthetic fingers. That wasn't my style, and besides, wearing something like that would bring more attention to my missing fingers and me. That was the last thing I wanted—more attention. That kind at least.

Out of curiosity, I asked, "You mentioned earlier that if I had lost my pinky, I would have received more money. I'm curious as to how much more that would have been."

"$55,000, or close to it."

That was a good amount of money, but I was still happy I hadn't lost my pinky. I still wanted to cook, and I couldn't without my pinky. I honestly wasn't sure I would have been able to use a knife with my left hand.

"Can I see that book now, please?"

"Sure."

He handed me the book, and as I started flipping through it I was fascinated at how they came up with these numbers. If I had lost both eyes on the job, I would have received $220,000. That was the highest number in the book, and nowhere near enough compensation for anyone to never see again, in my opinion. Losing a leg or an arm got a person $100,000. A half a leg or arm was $75,000. I was curious to see what I would have received if I had lost my thumb too. This was considerably more—$115,000.

Pinkies, thumbs, and toes seemed to be very important as far as extremities were concerned. Definitely the dollar amount showed that to be a fact. As I looked at the numbers, I began to calm down because I saw how difficult it must have been to come up with these amounts. It wasn't about making fun of a disabled person, and shame on me for thinking like that. In all fairness, I wouldn't have had a clue how to put a price on losses like these either. Still, the compensation for all of these losses weren't nearly enough to me, but there had to be a number.

I was content with what I received because I wasn't expecting anything at all. I was grateful and pleasantly surprised. Suing was something I did contemplate carefully. But since the produce company that L'Orangerie used had imported the machine from France, I felt okay about it. What I really wanted was a sign at the work station where dangerous machinery was and in all kitchens throughout the United States, warning the user to keep their hands out, even when the machine was off. But my lawyer told me that I would have to sue the company that imported it to get that done. He felt something was very wrong with the machine itself and felt confident we would win. And like I said before, if I got a monetary reward out of it, great—and if not, at least the signs would be a law that restaurants would have to comply with. And the fact that I chose not to go with the team of lawyers that wanted me to sue for millions to never cook again made me feel I'd made the right choice for the right reasons.

*   *   *

Over the next several weeks, while I waited to have my bandages permanently removed, I reflected on my situation, hung out at the beach a lot, and imagined what life might be like when the bandages came off forever. I was imagining it to be not so fun. I was wondering if anyone would notice or if I was going to walk around with a huge sign on my forehead that said, "I'm missing fingers and I'm insecure about it so please don't notice they are gone or dare ask me about it." But before I knew it, it was time. I had also set up the appointment to see the occupational therapist to deal with the machine when my bandages were removed. It was going to be one hell of a week. I was nervous to see the new hand I'd have to live with for the rest of my life, and I prayed that some of the swelling had gone down since I'd first seen it. In truth, I was dreading it. We arrived early, as I wanted it to be over with, the sooner the better. As we waited, I could feel zillions of butterflies fluttering around in my stomach, anticipating the unveiling. Finally, the doctor called Mike and me into his office.

"You look great! You're tan, and it looks like you've been resting."

"Thank you," I said sheepishly.

"Well Lisa, it's the big day! Are you ready?"

"I guess so. I mean not really, but I don't have a choice, do I?"

As he unraveled the bandages, I began to sweat and was lightheaded and thought I might faint because my biggest fear was fear itself. No more bandages to hide the grisliness of what the accident had done to me. Mike noticed me feeling like this and held on to me tight. The fear and anxiety I was experiencing was like no other. Since my imagination is and was limitless, I felt like I was standing at the tip of Meru Peak in the Himalayas, which is the highest peak in the world. Because of my fear of heights, this is the only way I can think of to express how scared I was as that moment. The floor literally felt like it was falling away beneath me. I was so not in control, and I hated that. Many years later, I went rock climbing at Westward Beach in Malibu to try and conquer my fear of heights. It was only eighty-five feet high, but it felt like 200. I used a pulley to scale the rock because I couldn't grip the rock by just using my hand. I cried all the way up and wanted to stop, but the instructor knew how important it was for me that I accomplish what I set out to do and wouldn't let me go back down. Thank goodness he was strong for me. I made it to the top and it was by far one of the greatest accomplishments of my life.

What a heavy moment that was for me to watch my bandage unfold in front of my very eyes. At the same time, the reality was that I was going to be looking at my "new" fingers for the rest of my life. Even today, when I think of that moment, I feel a strange kind of anxiety.

I looked at my hand feeling so many things: sadness, anger, loneliness, fear, and pain. But mostly I felt like a freak. I also felt like a member of my family had died; the idea that my fingers were gone forever was the same as mourning a death. The stitches were black and visible, and my nubs were still very swollen.

I asked, "Why is the top of my middle finger so much wider than the others?"

"That's your second knuckle, which is naturally larger than the others. The overall swelling will go down in time."

"Why black stitches? Why couldn't you have used clear ones?"

"They are the only kind of stitches that dissolve by themselves. In about a month, they'll be gone."

Great, I thought. *People will certainly notice the stitches.* They looked like little black ants crawling along the top of my nubs.

"Will they be sensitive?" Mike asked.

"As I said during our last visit, yes, they will be. And remember to be very careful to not hit the ends of your fingers on anything for quite a while. It will be very painful if you do. It will resemble the feeling of brushing up against broken glass that's on fire if they touch anything."

Again, great news.

"That's great. If I do hit them on something, will a stitch pop open?"

"No."

"When can she go back to work?" Mike asked.

"As soon as Lisa feels comfortable using a knife and the sensitivity doesn't bother her too much. It's really up to her, but I'd say in about six weeks." At this point he turned to me and said, "Lisa, I know you're very upset, but you were very lucky to have survived the surgery at all."

I knew what he meant by that comment. He was referring to my near-death experience in the operating room. There it was, our moment to tell each other what we knew and saw, but neither the doctor nor I chose to share. What was the point? I was sitting there in his office, very much alive.

I couldn't stop looking at my hand. It was so mind-blowing to me that my fingers were gone—and *forever*, which was almost incomprehensible to me. It was surreal. I tried to visualize what my hand might have looked like if he'd been able to reattach my fingers. In my mind, there might have been a maze of stitches, and later scars. I can still see the scars at the end of my nubs and on my pinky to this day. I can still feel pressure at the ends of my nubs and pinky, especially when it's hot or really cold. I feel stress and numbness in my pinky but not sharp pain because of all the nerve damage. When I make a direct hit with my nubs on a wall or some hard surface today, it feels like a surge of electricity going up my arm and they throb for a good half hour afterward. And sometimes I cut them, and that automatically brings me right back to that day. Looking back and having lived with them the way they are for the last thirty-three years, I am happy he couldn't reattach them, but of course I'll never know the difference.

Mike said to me sweetly, "I think they're cute. They fit you and you are still very beautiful."

I cried because his words were bittersweet. I hated what they looked like and it didn't matter what he or anyone could have said to me at that moment because I was pissed. I wasn't happy with my middle finger at all, which was ironic, because I had hated how bent it was when I was eighteen and now that it was half gone, I was still complaining about it. What was that about? Was there anything I was happy with on my body or in my life in general? A loss is a loss and this was no different, but now I would be reminded every day what had had happened to me. As Mike and I were leaving, the doctor handed me the phone number of another therapist: a trauma specialist. He thought I might need it. I guess he knew what I was about to go through, but I sure didn't, and I still thought I could heal myself. Mike took the card for me and we headed out for my parents' house. They wanted to see my hand and to make sure I was okay. When they got home from work, they were anxious to see my hand, which I can't blame them for, but were cautious about asking me. To make it easier on them I asked, "So, do you want to see them?"

Mom said, "Okay. Whenever you're ready to show us, we're ready." I thought she showed me great respect by asking me that question.

"Okay, but be careful with my feelings. I'm super sensitive." I reached my hand out and felt myself blush. God, it was so embarrassing—and they were my parents! How was

I going to react when my friends or strangers wanted to see them or asked what had happened to them?

Mom said, "They are cute! The way you described your fingers before, you made it sound like they were much worse."

Dad said with a crackly voice, "They are beautiful, just like a Jackson Pollock painting. It looks like you'll be able to use them just fine, sweetheart."

I actually felt safe for the first time since this whole fiasco. They really did love me, and I felt lucky to have them as my parents. All in all, they were very cool people. I hoped Dad was right about being able to use my fingers normally again—but at that moment, I didn't know what was going to happen.

Mom said, "How are you feeling, honey?"

"Weird. How would you feel?"

Mom said, "Well, I'd be on my third pack of cigarettes and a bottle of vodka!"

Dad said, "Same here, but a bottle of Scotch instead."

Their comments actually made me laugh for the first time since leaving the hospital.

"So, do you know what the plan is for your rehabilitation?" Mom asked.

"I don't know. I'm supposed to see the occupational therapist next week, on Wednesday I think. I guess I'll know better then."

Dad said, "How soon did the doctor say you could go back to work?"

"I guess when the pain becomes tolerable enough to work. He said I needed to be careful hitting or rubbing the ends of my fingers against anything. He compared the feeling to brushing up against broken glass that's on fire."

"Dear Lord. Please be careful. We will never understand what you're going through, honey, but know we are both very proud of you. You're a real trooper."

"Thanks, but I feel like I've been hit by a Mack Truck."

There was silence, and I could see my family was at a loss for words, as I was. I couldn't blame them a bit.

"Well, are you getting hungry yet? I can have dinner ready in half an hour, and it's your favorite."

"Chicken Marilyn?"

"Really? I can't wait. Whenever it's ready I'm ready, and thanks Mom."

Chicken Marilyn was my favorite meal my mom made when I was growing up. We had it at least once a week until I stopped eating it because of the cream and cheese. But I had lost so much weight since being in the hospital that I felt okay about eating it. Here's the recipe:

Chicken Marilyn

Serves 4
Pre-heat oven to 350 degrees
4 bone-in chicken breasts
Paprika, sprinkled moderately on the chicken
Salt and pepper to taste
Season the chicken and set aside.
Olive oil
3/4 pound white mushrooms, sliced
4 slices Muenster cheese
1/2-cup cream
2 cups plain white rice, cooked according to package directions

Directions: In a cast iron skillet, heat 2 tablespoons olive oil. Place the chicken skin-side down and brown on high heat for 5 minutes. Turn the chicken over and cook another five minutes, adding the mushrooms. Place in the 350-degree oven for 20 minutes. Remove and place on high heat again, and add the cream until it gets a bit thick, about 1 to 2 minutes. Place a slice of cheese on top of the breasts and place back in the oven for 5–10 more minutes. To serve, remove the chicken breasts and place them on a plate. Add the rice to the pan and toss with the creamy mushroom sauce.

Presentation: Place a generous spoonful of rice in the middle of the plate and the chicken breast off to the side. Pour any remaining sauce on the chicken. If there isn't any, that's fine. It will still be amazing! Serve with a plain salad and a nice glass of Sauvignon Blanc. A petite Davidoff cigar and a scotch, neat, afterwards is the way to go.

* * *

While waiting for dinner I wanted a scotch. There's something about the properties of scotch that warms the inside. Mike and my dad talked while I held my kitty, Bootsie. I missed him so. I left Bootsie with Mom and Dad because I couldn't have a pet at our house and honestly, it was enough to move in with Mike; plus, I think they were happy about it. It felt great to hold him though. I missed having a pet.

During dinner, it felt awkward to hold silverware, and the doctor hadn't been joking when he'd said my fingers would be sensitive. Just holding a knife with my right hand hurt, so Mom graciously offered to cut my chicken for me. I resisted, purely out of pride, but I still couldn't do it. It was too painful and I was tired and still traumatized, so I let Mom cut it for me. It's funny how I loved that act of love when I was a kid, but now that I was handicapped it didn't feel all that good. I was ready to go home, but Mike and I stayed for a coffee and another scotch. My mom used a CEMEX glass coffee pot then, and it made a wicked cup of coffee. Mike and I didn't say much on the way home. What was there to say? More of the same old shit? God, how long was I going to feel like this? How boring. I didn't sleep well that night at all, mostly because I was overly concerned about opening my wounds or hurting myself. Until the stitches went away, I wasn't going to take any chances.

* * *

The following week went by quickly, and before I knew it my occupational therapist appointment was upon me. I was to meet the occupational therapist at the restaurant and walk with her into L'Orangerie for the first time in a little over two months. I was nervous because I had no idea how my co-workers would react to me. Before entering the kitchen, the therapist told me what to expect. I was to go to the machine and touch it. Then, when I was ready, I was to start it. No big deal, right? Not! I was doing everything I knew how to show her how cool I was and that I was ready to go back to work, even though I really wasn't. My fear wasn't going to let this thing slow me down. This was the first appointment out of three that would occur over the next two weeks.

When we walked in, Latifa, the woman whose lap I sat in on the way to the hospital, was the first one to approach me, welcoming me with open arms. Some of my other co-workers came over to me to give me a hug, and some ignored me. It felt weird to be there. Even though it had been only two months or so, it felt longer. I also remember how "stale" the kitchen felt. By that I mean the innocence I'd felt before had gone away. It was like the accident had ruined the energy for me and I worried that I might feel that way in other restaurants. It also had a weird odor, similar to that of a sour candy. Someone had created a handmade a sign with a picture of a hand entering the machine with a circle around it and a diagonal line across the hand. Below it, it read, "DO NOT PUT HAND IN MACHINE." I wondered who did that. I didn't ask, and no one offered that information. Too bad that sign hadn't been there before, but even if it were, I might have still stuck my hand in there. When Virgini and Gerard walked into the kitchen, they asked everyone to give me a moment alone with the therapist. I thought that was very cool. Gerard was like a father to me. I had always felt like he was protecting me, even before the accident.

The therapist took my hand, looked me in the eye, and said, "Ready?"

"Yes. Let's get this over with."

I reached out my hand to feel the machine. Get comfortable with it. I began reliving that horrid day as I felt it. I saw it happen again in front of my eyes in a flash of a moment.

"Are you okay, Lisa?"

"Yeah, yes, I'm fine."

"Okay, ready to turn it on?"

Breaking out into a light sweat I said, "Yes." I took a few deep breaths and turned the machine on. All I could hear were the blades cutting my fingers off and that thudding sound again, like running over a small dead animal, and that really sucked.

When I stopped the machine the therapist asked, "How do you feel?"

"Fine! Great! No problem. This is a breeze!" Boy, was I lying.

"You're being sarcastic."

"No! It's easy, really." I was dying inside. I could feel a large lump developing in my throat and was scared I would start to cry. It was like I was going through it all over again. Man, how long was I going to have to feel like this?

"It's okay to cry. You've been through a lot. Let's give it a few more tries and see what happens. Take your time."

"Okay, give me a minute."

"Take your time, you're doing great."

I started the machine again and it was a little easier. Then I started it a few more times after that, and finally I only heard the powerful hum of the machine. The therapist was taking all kinds of notes, and she asked me several times if I was okay. I wasn't okay. I wanted to get back to work and have my life be normal again, or as normal as it was going to be from now on.

"I am ready to go back to work. I am ready to deal with coming back to work. Really, I am totally ready."

She said, "Well, that's noble of you, but I think you'll be ready in a few weeks at the very least. Your fingers still seem to be quite sensitive, and you are too. I'll send these notes to the doctor and he'll let you know when you'll be ready. In the meantime, I'll see you here at exactly the same time next week."

Damn! She saw right through my shit!

"Okay. When will the doctor let me know, do you think?"

"I don't know, maybe less than a week? Be patient. You've been through a lot."

How did she know what I'd been through? I just met her. It felt weird that I had just shared a very private moment with a total stranger.

I wanted to get back to work as soon as possible. Cooking was and is so important to me, and I wanted her to see that I was ready, but I could tell I wasn't convincing enough. Professional cooking is fast; it produces results in minutes. I liked that feeling, and I needed the adrenaline rush cooking gave me. For me, the whole process of cooking is flowing and glorious, and while some patience is required, it's not the total package. In those days and up until a few years ago, I found it hard to sit still. Cooking is a constant physical and creative experience that begins and ends in an eight-hour day.

After we were finished, I met with Gerard. He asked me when I would be coming back.

I said, "Hopefully in two to three weeks. That's if my fingers heal quickly."

"Well, that would be perfect, because we have a guest chef coming in from Bocuse, Paul Bocuse's restaurant in Lyon, France. You know of him?"

I couldn't believe it! I had been reading Bocuse's cookbook at the beach for over a year and thought he was brilliant; I had hoped I'd meet him someday.

"No way! I've been studying his book every day. It's my food bible!"

"He's also looking to take someone back with him to France to apprentice at Bocuse for six months."

That was that. I committed to him right then and there and said I would be back in two weeks ready to work, no matter what. I couldn't wait to get home and share this news with Mike. Maybe my life wasn't over. Maybe there was a future for me after all. When I got home, I flung the door open and said, "Mike! You are never going to believe this! Paul Bocuse's chef from Restaurant Bocuse in France is going to guest chef at L'Orangerie and he's looking for an apprentice to take back to France with him! Can you believe it?"

"Wow! Your dream might come true! Does this mean you are going back to work soon?"

"I'm going back on the schedule. I wouldn't miss this opportunity for the world."

"I'm happy for you, but are you sure you'll be ready? The doctor said there would be considerable pain for a while."

"Yeah, I know. But I want to go back to work. I need get back to some kind of normalcy. I am concerned about my fellow employees, too. They seemed very uncomfortable around me."

"Well, you're going to have to make them feel comfortable from now on. They are probably freaked out this happened to you because it could have happened to them."

"Maybe."

"When do you start?"

"I think February 8th or 12th. I'm not sure, but it's been almost two months since the accident and I'm afraid if I stay away too long I'll lose my momentum. I'll call in a few days to find out exactly when he arrives. In the meantime, I'll continue with my therapy."

I was given a dense little squeeze ball that I had to exercise as often as possible to strengthen my grip. That little thing was so dense it was hard at first to give it a good squeeze. Now my grip is incredible, hard for me to even believe.

"That's great, honey. Well, I have to go to work now and I wish I didn't so we could celebrate. Why don't you come in for dinner tonight?"

"I'll see. I'm still uncomfortable going out in public, especially around people I know."

"Don't be absurd. Everyone will be very nice to you, I promise."

*　*　*

Early that evening I decided to rent Steven Spielberg's *Close Encounters of the Third Kind.* That movie touched me deeply, as it did millions of people, I'm sure. Maybe some people felt more and some less about the content of the movie, but for me it was on a deeply inexplicable personal level. I empathized with the alien. In my mind and for no concrete reason at all, I always thought that if I did encounter one, I knew I wouldn't be afraid. There is no way we can be alone in the universe. After watching the movie, I called several friends of mine and asked if they had ever seen or heard of the movie and how awesome it was. They said it had been out since 1977. I felt like an idiot.

Excited to tell Mike about the movie and eat a good dinner, I put my fears aside and drove to Les Anges, the restaurant Mike worked at, in my powder blue Volkswagen Bug. I loved that car. I grew up with Volkswagens. When I was five, our family drove across the country to Florida in one. My dad put a small mattress in the backseat of the VW so my brother and I could sleep whenever we wanted. I'll never forget the amazing sunsets we saw driving across the United States. Texas seemed like a small country in itself. I felt like it took days to drive through that huge state. When we arrived in Florida, we took a train to Ohio to see my mom's parents. We had a sleeper car. I loved it so much I didn't want to get off. That was the first time I'd been on any kind of train and decided then that was my preferred way of travel.

*　*　*

As I drove down San Vicente Boulevard from Brentwood, I turned right on West Channel Road toward the restaurant. As I drove down the road and approached the stoplight, the light changed from red to yellow to green to red in rapid, sequential order. My car stopped running and the radio shut off with me still in it. As I sat in my car, trying to figure out what happened, I tried to restart it to no avail. Then all of a sudden and out of nowhere, I noticed a huge aircraft of some kind approaching me from the sky. I closed my eyes for a moment and when I opened them, I couldn't believe what I saw. It was a massive spaceship, like nothing I'd ever seen before. The ship was colossal and the lights were beyond the brightest white lights I've ever seen. It was as if the Coliseum was lit up at maximum power. In fact, there is no light on earth that I know of that bright. There was a deep humming sound coming from this humongous beast and it sounded beautiful. The harmonics reminded me of one of my father's music scores. I remember thinking, '*There's no way that's what I think it is.*'

Anxious and full of adrenaline, I got out of the car and stood next to it in the middle of the street. I slowly looked up and marveled at the enormous machine that was suspended over the entire Santa Monica Canyon. That canyon is at least a mile, maybe two miles in diameter, and this ship, or whatever you want to call it, easily stretched over that entire length and beyond. Huge, multicolored lights rotated clockwise around the perimeter of this powerful ship. I had no doubt that I was experiencing a phenomenon I had always hoped I would experience in my lifetime: an alien ship. Was I going to get to see an alien, and would it look like the one in *Close Encounters of the Third Kind*? I felt no fear at all. Feeling full of anticipation and unbelievable excitement, I knelt on the ground and pleaded, "Please, take me. Please, I want to go with you. I want to learn. I'm not afraid. I can handle it. Please, I'm begging you, whoever you are and wherever you came from, I want to go with you or at least meet you." I was relentless in my asking, and I remember saying that I didn't want to be on Earth anymore. I wonder what motivated me to say that.

Did they have something important to tell me? Was there some kind of subliminal information I was to interpret? Was I a messenger of some sort? Something like this doesn't happen to everyone, so naturally I was feeling special. I also noticed that the lights in the houses in the canyon around me were out. There was only the beautiful humming sound that came from the ship, and it was mesmerizing—hypnotic, really. I continued to stand in the middle of the street, waiting patiently for something else to happen and looking for some type of sign to let me know there might be some kind of life form in there. I wondered if anyone else was witnessing what I was seeing. I have no idea how long this event went on, but as I waited for any kind of clue or sign, the stoplight suddenly turned to green.

Then, just like that, my car started without me in it and the radio came back on, playing "Stairway to Heaven" by Led Zeppelin. I remember thinking how bizarre it was that that particular song came on the radio. Then, in almost an instant, the ship lifted up slightly and zoomed off into the sky like a bolt of lightning. As I watched that enormous vessel fly away, I felt elated, invigorated, and energized. I also felt sad it was gone. I stood there for quite a while hoping they would return, perhaps in smaller ships. I wondered if I had been lifted up or transported into the ship and gone to some other planet. Or did I go anywhere at all? I wanted to believe I'd gone somewhere. I looked around to see if the lights in the houses had turned on again, and they hadn't. I got in the car and couldn't wait to tell Mike. Hopefully he wouldn't think I was nuts. I figured no one would believe me, actually. I've always had a vivid imagination, but this was definitely *not* my imagination. This was the real deal. I felt sad that I experienced this alone. But I certainly knew I wanted more of what I saw!

* * *

When I got to the restaurant I wanted to tell Mike so badly what happened but I thought I should wait to tell him in the privacy of our home. The food was always great but that night it was the best I'd had there; the rack of lamb. I ordered it medium rare, and it was perfect. It was served with a fresh port wine sauce and fresh mint. It came with baby turnips, baby zucchini, baby potatoes, and baby carrots. The food at Les Anges was delicious and was headed by Chef Patrick Jamon. He was a very good chef. Claude Koberle was the pastry chef, the same one from L'Orangerie and Ma Maison. He sure did get around back then! I wanted to share my encounter with Mike so badly I could barely stand it.

After dinner, Claude sent out a perfect poached pear tart on homemade puff pastry with homemade caramel sauce. Mike opened a bottle of fabulous French Bordeaux to compliment the lamb. Later, Mike brought a couple of cognacs over and sat down with me for a drink. I decided to share my experience with him right then, and thankfully he believed me. The following morning, while eating breakfast, there was an article about this event in the paper. It didn't say that there was a sighting, but it said there were several power outages reported in the area that occurred in the canyon that night because of some unknown power surge that lasted for almost twenty-four hours.

Mike said, "Wow, that had to be because of what you saw, right?"

"Right! I was there and I know what happened for sure! Maybe I should call the *Times* and tell them my story!"

"No, please don't. They're going to think you've lost your mind."

"Yeah, I guess you're right."

Soon I would be going back to work, and I anticipated a lot of confusion amongst my co-workers. I didn't want special attention. I just wanted to move forward, like nothing had happened. Just like after the abortion. I didn't want to talk about it, but I knew this situation was unavoidable. Over

the next few weeks I worked with my squeeze ball, calcu-
lated my calories, and tried to stay as calm as possible.

Chapter 8
The Road to Spago

After several weeks of reflection, I decided I wasn't going to let my accident hold me back from my dreams. Yes, I was still upset, angry and confused by my loss and would be for a very long time. But as I reflect, I realize I was a hell of a lot stronger than I realized. I was determined to not let the little detail of losing a few fingers get in my way—even though it was a *huge* detail. I refused to let this adversity make me feel like my life was over. At least, I would try my hardest. The days, months and ultimately the years following the accident were the hardest of my life. I had stopped losing weight and I didn't like that at all.

Obviously my weight had reached a plateau. While in the hospital, I liked that I dropped down below ninety pounds, but that didn't last long. Unfortunately, losing weight made me want to work out harder and eat way less food. I went from about 1,000 calories a day to 800 in hopes of accelerating my weight loss. Having time off made me obsess more about food, or the lack of it, which was a dangerous thing. I was discovering new and more exotic foods I could repulsively spit, too. Meanwhile, I felt like I was controlling my intake of calories pretty well, so I used my diary less often when we ate out but used it constantly when I ate at home. That diary was like a child's teddy bear or special blanket; I couldn't let it go for years. Even after I had control of this disease years later and while writing this book, I noticed how easy it was to fall right back into the same old patterns, which freaked me out. I missed the ritual, like the heroin addict that loves the ritual of heating the heroin in a spoon, tightening the rubber band around their arm to get a vein and ultimately shooting up.

I had memorized all of the books I used to calculate how many calories, carbohydrates, and fat I consumed. Still, there was no room for any mistakes. I couldn't afford to add calories to my diet.

* * *

When I returned to work, I felt uneasy. I had no idea what to expect from my co-workers, Gerard and Virgini, or the guest chef. Most everyone welcomed me with open arms, but some seemed to be a bit cautious. I figured that was because they didn't know what to say to me. I didn't know what to say to them either, frankly. Let's face it, we all felt awkward. When we met the chef, he wasted no time giving us assignments for the evening. I was trying to size him up, and what I felt was that he was a seemingly nice guy, but really serious about himself. My job that afternoon was to peel whole Granny Smith apples as an accompaniment to a venison dish. I thought I was lucky because peeling apples is usually easy to execute, but it turned out to be a dreadfully excruciating task for me. The circumference of the apple was cumbersome and painful for me to handle. After peeling a few apples, I couldn't take it anymore and decided to cut them in half and peel them that way. After a few minutes of doing it this way, the chef walked over to me and asked, "What are you doing?"

"Peeling apples, like you asked."

"I asked you to peel them whole."

"I had an accident six weeks ago and lost these three fingers," I said, showing them to him.

"I'm sorry, but I asked you to peel them whole. Now do it." That seemingly nice guy had just turned into a big, huge prick.

I showed him my hand again, stressing, "I don't think you understand, chef." I could feel a rush of blood engulf my face, and it wasn't because I was humiliated. I was pissed and shocked at his insensitivity. I couldn't believe what I was capable of at that moment. All I wanted to do was smash his face in.

"It happens sometimes in this business, but it's no excuse. I don't care. Peel them whole," he said.

"Please, chef. The result is the same, so what's the difference?"

"The difference is I want you to do it the way I told you to do it. I don't need a defiant rebel like you telling me how I want things done."

It took everything I had to not break down and cry, not to mention how badly I wanted to tell him he should go screw himself. I had to hold it together, though, especially if I wanted to go to France and work under master chef Bocuse.

I said, "I'll try." The feeling I felt at the end of my fingers was exactly the way the doctor had described it to me—like shards of broken glass on fire running through my nubs. There was still some swelling, and they seemed to swell more when I had my hand below my heart, which was all the time at work. As I continued to do it his way, he saw the pain in my face and the tears rolling down my face. I hated that I was showing weakness, but it was real. I couldn't help it.

"Lisa, if you can't do it right then go pick thyme leaves. I'll get someone who can peel the apples the right way."

Crushed and totally humiliated, I walked to the thyme picking station, but before I went, I had to go to the walk-in for a minute to pull myself together. Latifa followed me in and told me that Dittier was being an ass and how I was peeling the apples was just fine. Feeling especially melancholy toward Latifa, I couldn't respond to her because I knew if I did I would really start crying hard. After that moment, I definitely knew I didn't want to go to France to work under him, even if it meant meeting and learning under Bocuse himself. If his chef was this much of a pompous ass, what was Bocuse like? A part of me wanted him to ask me just so I could say no to him. There was no excuse for his abrasiveness. I knew then right at that moment that when I became a chef one day, I would let my cooks express themselves even if it wasn't the way I wanted them to do it. If we aren't constantly learning, then we are dead. I realized the importance of understanding technique, but I also knew that each cook would have a new way of doing things that I would have to honor. I wasn't going to be as harsh as Dittier was on me, ever. *Never!* I knew then how important it is to be a team leader.

Latifa told me that working in France under a French chef would probably break my spirit and that I'd be better off not going. Latifa's warning was the additional confirmation I needed to not consider France—that is, if he asked. In any event, I wanted to prove to myself that I still had what it took, so I tried harder than ever to do my best. I spent the next eight hours of my shift picking thyme leaves off their skinny little branches and holding back my tears. To this day, I loathe picking thyme leaves. I was also barred from joining the other cooks at the chef's table because of my behavior. How lame I remember that being. He wasn't Paul Bocuse after all, he was just one of his many chefs.

As the week went on, my nubs adapted to holding a knife and doing other things. Don't get me wrong; they still hurt quite a bit. I put on the "I'm okay" face as much as I could. Even though the guest chef upset me, I didn't want any special treatment, and after the thyme incident I did whatever the chef told me to do. I had to be humble and become more confident, and quickly, so the chef would notice it. In hindsight, it was more for me, not him.

* * *

The fourth night after the apple incident, Dittier invited me back to the chef's table for dinner. By then, I wasn't all that impressed at the idea of dining with him. But I did, of course, and he brought up the opportunity to all of us going to France.

He said, "As you all know, I am looking to take one of you back to France to apprentice with Bocuse for six months."

Everyone at the table had to feel as uncomfortable and curious as I did as to whom he was thinking of asking to go to France. I would've thought he might have addressed this issue in private, and I thought for sure it wasn't going to be me. Looking right at me he continued, "And I have to tell you, Lisa, you have great potential. We got off to a bad start, but I now see you are very open to learning and are actually very fast and good with a knife."

Can I say are you kidding? I guess this was his way of apologizing and I swallowed humble pie and responded respectfully. I still wanted to be the one to say no to him. "Thank you so much, Chef."

"Is going to France something you would be interested in?"

Everyone at the table waited on baited breath for my answer. How bizarre it was that he asked me and not Latifa. She was very good, a stronger chef than I was at that point. In fact, she went on to be enormously successful opening restaurants in Hawaii and Miami. He never really apologized to me, but who cared. I got what I wanted. He asked me to go.

"Maybe, but I would have to think about it."

The energy at the table was mixed. On one hand, I felt like everyone was hoping I would go so they wouldn't have to walk on eggshells around me anymore—or maybe that was my own insecurity talking. On the other hand, maybe they were pissed that he hadn't asked any of them. All I wanted was for my co-workers to treat me like I was normal, like before the accident, but of course that wasn't possible.

"This is a once in a lifetime thing, and I'm sure anyone here at this table would die for the opportunity."

He made it sound as if this would never happen to any of us again, which was a little dramatic. I mean, I was at the beginning of my career, and women were just breaking into a dominant man's world. I was sure this would come up again, especially if I sought it out. My co-workers all nodded their heads yes, like they would go in a shit minute. Going to France to apprentice under a great chef is what most line cooks dream of doing. I did too, but Dittier had put a sour taste in my mouth. The restaurant business is hard and competitive as it is it's an uphill battle all the way to the top. Most every cook wants to become a chef. In fact, they would do just about anything to get there, which was proven to me later on in my career at the most important job of my life, Spago. It was so unexpected, to say the least. "I'm sure they would, but I still need to talk to my boyfriend about it."

"Okay, but I'm leaving in three days and will need your answer by then, if not sooner."

I couldn't believe how much his tone had changed with me, making me think maybe being around Bocuse himself would be worth the attitude. I knew Latifa wasn't interested in going, either. She had left France to cook in America. That said something to me, and there was no way this narcissistic jerk would take a man, no matter what.

"Okay, I'll let you know very soon. I'm honored. Thank you."

I truly was flattered, but I trusted Latifa more than I did Dittier. I didn't want to be jaded and tortured by anyone and for any reason when it came to cooking. I loved cooking and didn't want it ruined by that idiot.

* * *

The next evening I was off. My parents, my brother, Mike, and I went to L'Orangerie for dinner. I ordered the rack of lamb, medium rare, but received it medium well instead. I wasn't about to send it back. What if Dittier had cooked it? The last thing I wanted was to piss him off again. I was still determined to be the one to say no to France.

Dad always ordered oysters whenever we ate out at a nice restaurant. I used to love fresh oysters, until I developed a so-called "allergy" to shellfish during my harsh anorexic days. That was my excuse for not eating any of it. My brother also had the oysters and seared sea scallops with a lobster saffron sauce. Man, I wish I could have tasted that! I had a lot of wine during dinner and was a bit buzzed. I thought it appropriate to go to the kitchen and thank Dittier. I was buzzed. I introduced Mom to the chef.

Mom said, "Hello chef. I just wanted to say how delicious dinner was. It was some of the best food I've ever had."

"Merci, Madam. I'm glad you liked it. Lisa, did you enjoy your dinner? What did you have?" he said in his thick French accent.

I still couldn't believe how nice he was being.

Drunk, I said, "Well, whoever cooked my lamb didn't have a clue as to what they were doing." Right after I said that, I realized I had made a *huge* mistake.

"And why is that, may I ask?"

Shit, I thought. *He cooked it. That was not what I wanted. Damn it, I just blew it.* Now there was no way he was going to ask me to go to France.

"I ordered it medium rare and it came medium well."

"Well, that person who as you said 'didn't have a clue' happens to be me."

I was dying inside. "Are you sure?"

"Yes, I am quite sure. I am the *only* one cooking the meats."

There it went, my opportunity to tell him I didn't want to go. Shit! When mom and I left the kitchen, I knew he was going to be a complete ass to me the next day, and the next day after that. Now I wasn't going be invited to France more than likely and wouldn't have the pleasure of saying no to his pompous ass. I was going to be banned again from dining at the chef's table, and would probably have to pick that obnoxious thyme the next few days. In any case, there was no exchanging his arrogance for an internship.

Actually I did get to find out how much of a jerk Bocuse was. I met him at an awards dinner when I became head chef at Spago. I was there accepting an award for our selection of wine for Spago's maître d' and sommelier, Bernard Erpicum who chose most of the wine along with Wolfgang. There he was, the big and badass Bocuse himself, accepting an award for his wine collection as well. Excited, I stood up to say hello. As he walked off stage I stopped him and said, "Chef Bocuse, I love your cookbook. It is literally my bible of all cookbooks. I am so honored to finally meet you!"

His response ripped and shattered all I had dreamed what he would be like: "I don't know you, and you're too young to know anything."

Stunned and disappointed, I still said with strength and confidence, "My name is Lisa and I'm the head chef at Spago. I work for Wolfgang Puck. I think you are the best chef in the world."

He looked me up and down and said, "You're a young woman and a very pretty one with her whole life ahead of her, so why bother working in the hot kitchen? Find a man to take care of and he will take care of you." He walked off, not even looking back.

Needless to say, I was devastated at his response. It wasn't even close to what I imagined him to be like or what he'd say to me after complimenting him like I did. What a jerk. I couldn't believe how cold and arrogant he was. I didn't want to believe he'd just spoken to me that way. My God, were *all* French chefs in Europe like this? How was I going to feel inspired after my hero basically told me I was an idiot and completely naïve?

* * *

The afternoon after my family and I had the dinner where I stupidly criticized the lamb, I did get my punishment, and exactly how I imagined it to be: I picked thyme, and I was barred from eating at the chef's table again. He didn't even acknowledge what had happened, either. Pride is the ruin of so many people. I was one of those people. Deep down, I hoped he'd still want me to go, but I knew he wasn't going to ask me again. How could he be that mad at me, though? I had told the truth and he knew it. I've learned now that the truth is not popular unless someone else is telling it. After the shift was over he approached me, which surprised the shit out of me. I had no idea what to expect.

"Lisa, even though you insulted me, I still want you to come to France."

"No thanks. I want to stay in Los Angeles and continue at L'Orangerie."

"You don't know what you are saying."

"Oh yes, I do. Believe me."

That felt so good, there are no words! I did get my wish! I got to say no!

"Latifa, I'm sure you want to go, right?"

Latifa said in her thick Algerian French accent sarcastically, "No, not really. Besides, I don't like being second choice." She actually laughed after she said that to him. This is why I love her so. She had no fear and still doesn't.

"Women. You're all the same. You never know what's good for you, even when it's staring at you in the face."

One of the male cooks raised his hand and said, "I'll go, Chef! I'd be honored."

"Chef Bocuse wants a female. Sorry."

Latifa and I broke out laughing.

In French, Chef Dittier said, "What's so funny?"

Again, in French, Latifa responded with a long retort that I couldn't understand. She later told me what she'd said to him, "Do you really think we female chefs want to go to France to be treated like shit by you or any other chef? No matter how talented you are you're still an asshole. This is why I love America. I can say how I feel."

When she told me this I laughed so hard I cried, but I felt sort of bad for Dittier. Maybe he couldn't help who he was. He'd probably been beaten down too, and more than likely by Bocuse and other chefs. When he showed his nice, softer side, I couldn't help but see a nice person in there.

* * *

That evening when I got home, I took a long, hot shower. As I washed my hair, I reached for the shampoo with my right hand and hit the ends of my nubs on the tile. It hurt beyond comprehension. It was far worse than Dr. Handel could have ever explained. I was terrified that the stitches had opened up and blood would come pouring out. I was afraid to look for fear I might pass out. When I finally did look, there was a tiny bit of blood seeping out around my stitches—nothing serious, but at the time it looked like a waterfall of blood to me, and of course it was mostly on my middle finger. Amazing what our minds can do. I flipped out. I crouched down in the shower and bawled my eyes out. Mike came home from work right when it happened and when he found me in the shower crying like a baby, he stepped in with all of his clothes on and put his arms around me.

"What's going on? What happened?"

While crying hysterically I said, "I hit my hand on the tile while grabbing the shampoo. I don't know if I'm going to make it, Mike. I am so pissed this happened and that French chef was such an asshole. Even after I insulted him, he still wanted me to go, and as you know I said no. Still, there's nothing he could have said to me after embarrassing me like he did in front of everyone at work. Nothing he could have said to me would make me feel better about going."

"Screw him. You are a very talented cook and beautiful. Just because you're missing a few fingers doesn't change any of that. With or without fingers, he still would have treated you badly because you are an individual and he's a jerk. You dance to your own tune. You'll get through this, and I'll be there with you every step of the way."

"But what if I can't handle what's ahead of me, both professionally and personally? The mere thought of having to explain what happened and the possible insults I might endure for the rest of my life makes me want to end it all."

"Oh Lisa, you don't mean that. I can't imagine how hard this must be for you, but I know you will figure it all out. It's only been three months, and you have conquered quite a bit in such a little amount of time."

Suddenly I noticed he was soaking wet.

Laughing, I said, "Mike! You're soaking wet! Those pants and shoes are new, and you spent so much money on them. Now they're ruined."

"I can buy new ones, but I can't buy another one of you. And if you didn't notice, you just laughed. You look so beautiful when you *really* laugh."

What a sweet thing to say. I didn't deserve Mike. He was far too nice and why didn't I think I deserved a nice man? I dried off, but I still felt like I'd be better off dead. Mike made me a hot toddy while we watched *David Letterman*. I loved that show. He is such a funny man and I remember that night I managed to laugh to the point of crying.

*   *   *

I had the next two days off and I wanted to try to clean the house and do some laundry. Mike offered to help but I forced him to go play volleyball. He didn't want to go, but I insisted he did. I could see he needed "Mike" time and knew he would never ask for it, especially since I had suggested that I would be better off dead. Doing the usual household chores wasn't easy at all. In fact it was literally a workout, which was the good news. I was burning calories - at least 300 of them to be exact. I had to be especially careful to not brush my fingers against the fabric of the clothes while taking them out of the hamper. Our washer was a community one that was located downstairs and all the way around the side of the building. The biggest challenge was taking the clothes out of the hamper and getting them into the washing machine. Changing the bed sheets and scrubbing things was equally as tricky. I favored my right hand mostly, but consciously tried to use my left as much as I could. I began to realize how much we do with our hands in a single day and how I took that for granted. But how could I think otherwise? Until we lose the ability to use our hands normally or lose them altogether, which *never* crosses anyone's mind, we can't know how precious they are. But after facing those challenges and conquering them, it still felt great to feel self-sufficient.

* * *

I called some friends during my cleaning frenzy and they asked me how I was feeling. I explained how much it hurt to hit my nubs on the tile the night before and how depressed I was. To my disbelief, they didn't believe me, because I was *showing* something different on the outside. They listened to my whining and complaining, probably ad nauseam, and by the time I made the fourth phone call I was over talking about myself. I felt even more pathetic. I was the victim now and I hate victims. It's such a cop out attitude to have in life. Actually, it's super boring to be around. I thought I should just go ahead and kill myself. I just couldn't handle the physical or emotional pain any longer. Just thinking about looking at my monstrosity of a hand for the rest of my life was too much to deal with, at least at the time. It fascinates me how we go to great lengths to trick our minds into eternal despair. I often wondered how I would have handled myself if I had lost my whole hand or even my arm. Probably not too well.

I went to the medicine chest with hesitance because I didn't really want to kill myself. What I really needed was the drama so I could sink my teeth into a McDonald's Big Mac, chicken McNuggets, fries, and a bag of Famous Amos cookies, only to repulsively spit it all out into the trash. I grabbed a bottle of aspirin and a bottle of white wine. I thought about writing a note, but there was no reason really because I figured everyone would know why I did it. But I felt like I should leave a note for Mike. I wanted him to know it wasn't his fault. The closer I came to putting a handful of aspirin in my mouth, the more my heart would begin to race. I tried four or five times to put the aspirin in my mouth, but the truth was I was terrified to kill myself. I really did love myself more than I thought. Still, it seemed to be the only way to end the pain. Killing myself the way I was going to would have probably caused me to throw up, which we all know I loathe. Choking on my own vomit would be the worst way to die besides drowning and crashing in an airplane. All of those scenarios translated into a claustrophobic nightmare for me. I wondered if I had access to a gun, would I use it? I had heard of people living through self-inflicted gun wounds, so there was no guarantee that would do the job, and jumping off of a bridge or a hotel window was nowhere near an option. I hated heights. In truth, I really wanted to get caught by Mike so he'd feel sorry for me as much as I did. I decided I'd wait to for him to come home. Our couch was by the sliding glass door, which was the front door and as soon as I could see him walking up the stairs he would be able to see me put something in my mouth. I wanted him to find me in the act so he could talk me out of it. It seemed like forever waiting for Mike. When he finally showed up and was within eyeshot of me, I shoved the handful of aspirin in my mouth and put the bottle of wine to my lips, but didn't dare swallow. I hoped he had seen me because the aspirin started melting quickly and tasted disgustingly bitter which I wasn't counting on at all. Thankfully, Mike did see what I had done. As soon as he got to me he grabbed the bottle of wine.

"What did you just do? Open your mouth right now!"

I did what he said and began to cry.

"Shit, Lisa! Spit whatever it is into my hand right this minute!

That wasn't a problem to spit it out! He held his hand out and I spit the gooey mess into his hand.

"What were you thinking?"

He grabbed my arm, took me to the kitchen sink, and made me rinse my mouth and spit out any excess aspirin.

Crying and truly relieved, I said, "I can't go on Mike. It sucks, all of it. I was looking at my hand and it's so ugly. And doing household chores is impossibly painful. I can't stand looking at it and there's so much pressure at the end of my fingers and all the time. It really sucks, man."

"Lisa, listen. You really didn't want to kill yourself just now, did you? Even though it would have been difficult using aspirin, you really didn't want to die, right?"

"No, not really. But you have no idea what it's like to be an amputee."

"No, I don't, and it must be very difficult, but don't you ever do this again, do you hear me? Get a grip. You've scared me, and now I'm not sure I can leave you alone. Maybe you should see a therapist."

"No! I can do this myself. It's just very hard."

"You don't seem to be doing a very good job of doing it yourself. Lisa, even though you 'thought' you wanted to kill yourself and waited for me to see you, that's a pretty good indicator that you are depressed. See a therapist at least once, just for me, please? "

"No, I can do this myself. I had a moment, that's all."

"That's more than a moment, Lisa."

"I need a glass of wine."

"No, you don't. It's a depressant."

"Just a little, please? Really I'm fine."

Mike poured me a little glass of wine. We sat on the couch together while he held my hand. I was in awe of Mike's authoritative voice. It was unusual for him to talk to me like that. He always let me do my thing, but I found his tone very attractive and genuine. Maybe that's what I needed: someone to keep me in line. As I look back, I really had very little discipline in my life. Truly, I was and still am a free spirit. Maybe the discipline I was missing then was God's discipline. I seem to always need to be in some kind of trouble in order for someone to set me straight. Maybe that's why I was so screwed up. I had zero foundation for how to live. I was always the "do whatever I wanted" kind of person, and it was not working out well at all. I continued feeling sorry for myself for a few more hours while Mike sat with me. The next morning, when I woke up, I was so happy to be alive and not in a hospital and grateful I wasn't dead. I wondered how I could have considered killing myself in the first place. I realized how much suicide would have been the chicken shit's way out, and how many people I would have left behind. I truly hadn't realized how depressed I was.

* * *

I stayed only three more months at L'Orangerie. It was too hard on me, and definitely too hard on my co-workers. They were always watching me, like they were waiting for the next disaster to happen. Things had definitely changed in my world. It was hard to distinguish what was real or just my imagination. The lawsuit had started to take some shape, too, and almost every day I waited for news about why the machine went off. I took some time off after leaving L'Orangerie, and during that time I had heard that Ken Frank, another well-known chef in Los Angeles and the owner of La Toque restaurant, was looking for a line cook. It was a temporary job—three months, maybe—but any amount of time spent with any great chef was a plus for my resume, if not for my personal growth. He was way ahead of his time too, and his roasted garlic ice cream was one of his signature dishes and very good. I learned a great deal in such a short time working there. The time passed so quickly, and before I knew it the three months were over. It was my last day when Kevin, the chef from The Good Earth restaurant, called me as I was driving out of La Toque's parking lot. I hadn't heard from him in four years and I have no idea how he got my cell number. I carried around one of those huge phones that were popular in the '80s; I think it was a Nextel yellow phone that doubled as a walkie-talkie and a phone. He said that Kazuto Matsusaka, whom I had worked with at Ma Maison, was leaving Spago to open Chinois on Main, another successful Wolfgang Puck restaurant. I hadn't seen or spoken with Wolfgang very much since leaving the hospital, so going to

Spago unannounced was a little weird for me. I wasn't sure how he would react to me, but I was hopeful. Kevin said they were going to need a line cook and that I should drive straight to Spago before word got out. He said to ask for Mark Peel, Wolfgang's head chef at the time. The restaurant was only a mile away from La Toque, so I jammed over in my ridiculously short shorts. It was about ten thirty at night, and the restaurant was still packed. It was such a beautiful place, and it reeked of power you could smell. When I saw Wolfgang, it was like no time had passed between us, thankfully. Seeing him felt like I was home again, and it felt good.

I met Wolfgang just three years earlier after graduating acting school. The day after I graduated acting school a producer asked if I would like to audition for his movie. I was hopeful and surprised at how fast that happened. Unfortunately, the audition was nothing like I thought it would be. He took me to lunch and after lunch he introduced me to the proverbial "casting couch." I resisted, of course, and was told if I wasn't willing to sleep with producers, I would get nowhere with acting. Disgusted and disillusioned, I went shopping. I decided to drive down Melrose Avenue to make myself feel better by shopping. Crying, I saw a quaint, free-standing building. It looked like a cute little dress shop, but there were no cars parked in front. When I walked in I found a restaurant. It had a French bistro vibe to it and a man was standing in the bar area. He greeted me in a raspy French accent while smoking a cigarette. My guess was that his raspy voice was from the cigarettes. He introduced himself as Patrick Terrail, the proprietor of a restaurant called Ma Maison. He asked me my name.

"Lisa, Lisa Stalvey. How come there's no sign outside?"

"We don't need one, and the phone number is unlisted."

I was quite intrigued by that. "How do people know about it then? I thought it was a dress shop."

"Word of mouth. Have you never heard of Ma Maison?"

"No."

He seemed quite enchanted by me, probably because I was so clueless.

"What do you do for a living?"

"Well, I thought I was going to be an actress up until today, but after what I went through I think I'll stick to cooking."

"You're a cook?"

"Yes, I work at The Great American Food and Beverage Company. Have you heard of it?"

"No. Have you been to culinary school?"

"No, should I?"

"Our chef, Wolfgang Puck, is looking for a line cook. Do you know who he is?"

"No. Should I?"

Again, he seemed to be very amused by my naiveté.

"What are you doing tonight?"

Was he hitting on me? He had to be at least fifteen to twenty years older than me. It was a little creepy to me.

"Nothing, why?" I said cautiously.

"You're curious, aren't you? I like that. Why don't you come back and have dinner on me and meet Wolfgang for an interview."

All I could think of was that I was definitely supposed to cook for a living. How is it that I walked in for a dress and walked into an opportunity instead? This wasn't an accident running into him, I could feel it. He obviously knew quite a bit about food and the restaurant business.

"Really? Wow! Thank you!"

"Come at seven tonight."

"Great!"

Feeling like I was on cloud nine, I got in my shit-brown Pinto and drove home. God I hated that car. My dad made me pay for my first car. Everyone else I knew in school had bitchin' cars that their parents bought for them, but Dad made me work for mine. Thrilled by the invitation for dinner and a job interview, I thought about what to wear. What if this Wolfgang Puck guy was cute? I had to look good, just in case. In retrospect, why did I think like that? Maybe I thought if I looked good I might have a better chance at getting what I wanted? When I got home, I told my mom what happened. She couldn't believe that out of all the restaurants in Los Angeles, I drove into the most famous Hollywood eatery to buy a dress, only to get a free meal and a possible job at the hottest restaurant in Los Angeles. I decided to wear my Chemin de Fer jeans, Frye boots, a cowboy shirt and my cowboy hat. Why I felt the need to look like a cowgirl escapes me.

It was almost seven o'clock when I drove into the very full parking lot of Ma Maison with very expensive cars parked in it. I was praying no one noticed me in my car. When I arrived, Patrick sat me in the bar area, offered me a glass of champagne, and told me that Wolfgang would be out in a minute. I waited about ten minutes for Wolfgang and watched movie star after movie star walk through this high-powered restaurant. I couldn't believe I was sitting in such a powerful place, waiting for a job interview with a chef I had no clue about. Then, I saw what I hoped was Wolfgang Puck, walking towards me. He was wearing a perfectly starched white chef's jacket and was devastatingly handsome! I nearly fainted. I wished I had worn a dress. He was drop dead *gorgeous*. He was tanned and had long hair and looked like a tennis player. I found myself instantly attracted to him.

When he got to the table he said in his thick Austrian accent, "You must be Lisa. I'm Wolfgang."

I stood up and gave him a firm handshake and said, "Hi! It's so nice to meet you!"

I remember that handshake well. I had my whole hand then, and I had a firm yet friendly grip, and I could barely say hello without sounding like an idiot.

"So, have you cooked French food before?"

"No."

"Do you like lobster?"

"I guess."

"What do you mean? Have you never had lobster before?"

"No, I haven't. Is that bad?"

Next thing I knew, I was eating a perfectly homemade croissant that was stuffed with lobster and finished with two sauces—buerre blanc and lobster bisque. It was magnificent. I had never had a fresh, homemade croissant before, or lobster, for that matter. Master pastry chef, Claude Koberle made the croissant, the same chef I worked with at L'Orangerie the day the accident happened. I can't begin to describe the succulence and sexiness of that dish except that I can still taste it today. After that evening, I went in every night for nearly three weeks, working on getting a job and tasting the most sublime food I've ever had in my life in the most famous restaurant in Hollywood.

I found myself falling for Wolfgang but I wanted to work for him and thought I might be able to have both like most women think in a situation like this. I grew impatient over those three weeks and finally asked him for a job. He said yes, and I spent the next year, six days a week, learning how to cook the best and the first-of-its-kind cuisine—California French Cuisine. I went home most nights crying. I was making all kinds of mistakes and no one was helping me. Therein began my *real* career. The greats of today worked at Ma Maison too: Nancy Silverton of La Brea Bakery and Mozza, Claude Segal, Kazuto Matsusaka, Hideo Yamashiro (aka Shiro, the man who pulled my fingers out the machine), Susan Feniger, and Claude Koberle. I was among the masters of our day, though at the time even those greats didn't realize where they were headed and nor did I—or maybe they had a plan and I didn't know it. I certainly didn't have one!

* * *

There I was, just three years after working for Wolfgang at Ma Maison, standing at the entrance of Spago and looking right at Wolfgang, who was standing at the bar. Smiling, I said, "Wolf! How are you? It's seems like forever!"

We kissed each other's cheeks, like they do in Europe. It was so great to see him.

Like no time had passed, he said, "Lisa! What brings you here so late and wearing very short shorts?" He always had a great sense of humor, and with that fabulously thick Austrian accent I thought was extra funny. He was my only mentor—or at least the one who made the biggest impression. I was praying he would give me a job. To be working for him again was all I wanted. I don't know where I would have been if I hadn't driven into Ma Maison that day. He always let me express myself creatively and encouraged my passion for the art of cooking.

"I hear you're looking for a line cook and that you're opening a place called Chinois."

"How did you hear that?"

"I also heard that Kazuto is going to be the chef."

"Who told you? Kazuto's last night is tonight, and no one is supposed to know yet," he said in an inquisitive, friendly, and curious tone.

"I heard about this from Kevin McKenzie. Do you know him?"

"No. Mark, have you heard of him? Lisa, this is Mark Peel, my head chef. This is Lisa."

We shook hands and of course he looked at my hand the same way everyone did then. As we shake they look down, flipping mine over to see what's missing. I didn't care because Wolfgang was there. I have no idea why that made a difference, but it did. I guess I felt safe around Wolfgang.

Mark said, "So you want to work here, Lisa?"

"Yes, absolutely I do."

"I have to ask, and I hope you won't be offended."

"Sure, what is it?" I already knew what it was about: my hand. It seemed so many in the restaurant industry knew, but I could be wrong.

"As I'm sure you are aware of, Spago is a very busy restaurant. How's your speed on the line?"

"I'm very fast and am also a very good cook. I'll tell you what. How about I come in and cook one night and I'll let you be the judge of that."

Full of confidence, I couldn't wait to show him.

"Okay, tomorrow at two, and bring your resume. You'll cook on the line next to me, making vegetables for the main dishes. Also, you know how to make sauces, right?"

"Of course I do."

"Great! We'll see you then."

I knew I was going to blow him away with my speed, not to mention my knowledge of and passion for cooking. Wolfgang offered me a glass of wine, but I said no. I wanted to get home and tell Mike. Ecstatic, I took the menu home and prepared myself mentally to blow Mark's mind and hopefully Wolfgang's too. Feeling inspired, the following morning I went my local market in Brentwood, Vicente Foods. I decided to make veal chops for Mike and me for lunch that day—sautéed and finished with a red wine–honey sauce. And to go with the veal, I thought of roasting fingerling potatoes and a making a green salad to go with it. I needed my raw greens. While checking out, I experienced my first challenging and embarrassing moment with my fingers since the accident. For the last three years I had managed to hide my fingers everywhere I went. If I wrote a check at a restaurant, I would put the checkbook in my lap and write it there. My hand was also usually in my pocket. But that day, as I was writing a check for the groceries, the cashier said in front of a large line of people, "I have to ask you something. You've been coming here for the last three years and I've been wondering what happened to your fingers. I hope you don't mind me asking."

What? Of course I minded! I turned a serious shade of red and my heart began to pound. I had no idea if anyone in line had heard her ask me that question. The horror of it all was inexplicable, yet at the same time I was impressed she had the nerve to ask. This was the first time a stranger asked about my fingers.

"Well, uh, um."

"I'm sorry, I shouldn't have asked."

Trying to be cool and well adjusted I said, "No, that's fine. I had an accident at work three years ago."

Loudly, she said, "Oh my God! How did that happen?"

Now everyone in line was listening, and I was forced to be extra cool.

"It was in an industrial type of Cuisinart."

"Oh my, that must have been painful. You've been coming here for a while and, well I . . . Really, I'm sorry."

It was a little late for "sorry," but I could see how embarrassed she was for asking.

"That's okay, and yes, it hurt, a lot." I thought I was going to faint after talking out loud in front of total strangers about what had happened. I felt so naked. I couldn't get out of the store fast enough. I knew that anyone who heard me tell the checker what happened, would tell his or her friends and family about the amputee girl in the store who'd had the freak accident.

After that encounter, it seemed that more and more people noticed my fingers and had the gall to ask me about what had happened. I wasn't all that comfortable with my fingers yet, not by a mile, but clearly something was changing within me. I just couldn't see it. When I got home I told Mike about my encounter at Vicente Foods. In celebration of my opportunity to audition, we feasted on the veal I created for lunch. Well, Mike feasted. I ate only a quarter of the chop and a few of the potatoes and salad. For me, though, that was feasting. Even Mike said something about it, but he had learned a long time ago to not make a big deal about food with me. I actually wondered if I was getting better. Here is the succulent recipe:

Pan Seared Veal Chop with Roasted Fingerling Potatoes and Warm Honey–Red Wine Vinaigrette

Serves 4–6
Pre-heat oven to 425 degrees
4–6 veal chops
1/4-cup honey
1/2-cup olive oil
Marinate for 2 hours.

Honey–Red Wine Vinaigrette

1/2-cup olive oil
1/2-cup honey
1/4 cup red wine vinegar
1/4 cup red wine
1/4-cup honey mustard
1/4 cup Dijon mustard
Salt and pepper to taste

Directions: Whisk well. Just before serving the veal, heat on low heat to just warm.

Roasted Fingerling Potatoes

12–18 fingerling potatoes cut in half
6 king oyster mushrooms, sliced thinly
2 garlic cloves, sliced thinly
1/4 stick sweet butter
1/4-cup olive oil
Salt and pepper to taste

Directions: Sauté the potatoes on the flat side of the potatoes, season with salt and pepper. Place in a baking dish and bake at 400 degrees until tender. Sauté the oyster mushrooms in the same pan as the potatoes with salt and pepper. Set aside. After the potatoes are done add the mushrooms. Toss and set aside. Sear the veal chops on one side for 8 minutes and then turn over and cook another 8 minutes. Roast for 4 minutes.

Green Salad

3 cups baby romaine
1/2 avocado, diced
1/4 cup red onion, diced
1 tomato, diced
1 Tbsp. seasoned rice vinegar

2 Tbsp. olive oil
Salt and pepper to taste

Presentation: Place the veal chop on one side of the plate.
Place a fourth or sixth of the potato mixture next to the veal
chop. Place the salad on a side plate. Drizzle a little of the
vinaigrette on top of the veal.

Enjoy this with St. Francis Claret or a nice velvety Pinot
Noir or *Whispering Angel* Rose. A petite cigar with a nice
cognac would be good after dinner.

* * *

Later that afternoon, I showed up early for my audition,
which was unusual for me. I'm always fifteen minutes late
for everything. I was pumped to show Mark my skills and
also wanted to show Wolfgang how much I'd grown. I was
nervous, yet confident. I was certain Wolfgang knew I had
what it took, and it helped me a great deal just to know that.
I couldn't believe what my eyes saw that night. Fresh pizzas
were made with homemade dough and looked perfect every
time, not to mention how delicious they looked and were
handcrafted by head pizza chef, Ed La Dou, God rest his
soul. He was also the creator of California Pizza Kitchen's
pizzas. The other pizza chef Serge Falistch turned out equally
amazing pizzas. The Chinese air-dried duck we served was
finished in those ovens too, creating a deep, cherry- caramel
color with thin, crispy skin that had a shiny lacquer finish.
That duck was by far the best duck in the world—at least, I
thought so. When I got home I told Mike about my encounter at Vicente Foods. It consisted of a perfectly baked pizza
crust spread with crème fraîche and topped with house-
smoked salmon. Then it was finished with chives and Servuga caviar. *Amazing* is all I have to say. The sauté station
was fun and easy for me, thank goodness. I was responsible
for the white butter sauce called buerre blanc in French. The
base of the sauce is made with a reduction of white wine,

cream and shallots that is reduced in steps. When that's done, you would then whisk in unsweetened butter on medium to low heat, making a flavorful, creamy sauce. Add salt and pepper to taste. The French use white pepper to season, but I like black pepper. We used it as a base for some of the other sauces, and that meant it called for twenty pounds of butter—yikes! I was also responsible for all the vegetables that went with each dish.

* * *

I started my audition by blanching all the vegetables. This technique stops the cooking immediately and preserves the color of the vegetable. I then trimmed the sweetbreads, the pituitary gland of a cow, which was something new for me, and a major pain in the ass to clean. But when they are done right—nice and crispy—they are amazing. I prepared the garnishes for all of the dishes and finished the huge vat of buerre blanc and was ready to go—and early, to boot. I was pumped up. I'd never felt that kind of adrenaline before. The anticipation of cooking in an open kitchen also excited me. We could see the customers' reactions to the food, which made it more fun to cook, especially since everyone seemed to be enjoying their meals. Cooking in an open kitchen was quite an energizing experience, as the energy of the dining room directly affected the energy in the kitchen and vice versa. That was a rush I have to admit. It felt like we were all putting on a show and we were. The evening started and ended faster than any other shift I'd ever worked. Not only did I do my job, I found myself helping Mark put food on the grill, pulling tickets down for him to put in line for firing, and stoking the mesquite grill when necessary. I felt like I'd been working there for years. After it was over, I walked to the back kitchen to put my stuff away. Mark stopped me and said, "Lisa, I have to tell you that you did a great job. I am totally impressed with your speed and organization. You were great."

"Really? I'm so glad! I tried so hard."

Actually, I found it very easy, but I was on a mission to get the job and didn't want to sound to confident. Why not, I wonder?

"I noticed."

"So, what do you think? Do I get the job?"

"Of course you have the job."

I wanted to hug him so badly, but instead I thanked him and told him I couldn't be any happier than I was at that moment. That day was by far the best day of my life. It marked the beginning of my true professional career.

Chapter 9

Spago

My first day at Spago was the following Wednesday after my audition, so I had about four days to learn the menu. I wanted to be prepared with a few specials just in case Mark or Wolfgang asked me if I had any ideas. The culinary influence was new and a refreshing change from what was "in" then. Wolfgang broke the mold with California Cuisine, working with flavors from France, Japan, and Italy. I thought a summer type of soup would be refreshing and fun:

Cold Cucumber-Fennel-Cilantro Soup with Crème Fraîche and Fennel Sprigs

Serves 4–6
1 1/2 hothouse cucumber, sliced and partially peeled
1 fennel bulb, reserve the top herbs chopped
2 bunches cilantro leaves
1/2 red onion, chopped
1 clove garlic
1-3 cups chicken stock
1 cup crème fraîche
Salt and pepper to taste

Directions: In a Vitamix, immersion blender or other high-powered blender, place 1/2 of the ingredients listed above, except for the salt and pepper. Puree well. Add the rest of the ingredients to the already pureed mix. I like to leave it a little chunky, but you can strain this through a colander if you prefer a smoother soup. Season with salt and pepper to taste.

Garnish with fennel sprigs. Enjoy with a cold, high-quality Sauvignon Blanc or Sancerre.

* * *

I barely slept the night before in anticipation of my first day at Spago. I had the menu pretty much down, and was confident I was ready to go. I wanted Wolfgang to be proud of me and the confidence I had built since we'd last worked together was in a good place. Deep down I wanted to eventually be the head chef, so I did my job as well as I could in hopes it might happen someday. Wolfgang's new ideas as far as the culinary world was concerned were exciting to me. The fusion between French and California Cuisine cooking was oddly familiar to me. It felt natural to cook the way he wanted us to. One of the best and most popular dishes on the menu was the boneless half-chicken. It was a super simple and remarkably tasty dish. I'd never seen a chicken filleted like that before. It was a half chicken without the bones. I couldn't wait to learn how to do that. It was stuffed with garlic slivers and Italian parsley leaves under the skin. It was so juicy and clean tasting. Besides the pizzas, the chicken was right up there in sales. The grilled salmon was equally amazing. It was cooked on the mesquite grill on grids that were the thickest and widest I'd ever seen, making it a challenge to cook the fish just right before turning it over. This is when I learned how to grill fish properly. It's important to flip it over only one time, instead of turning it over and over again. Cooking to its finish on the first side makes for a fabulously marked piece of fish and a juicy one too. This also applies to grilling steak, chicken, liver, etc. The same rule pertains to sautéing as well. I'd never worked with a mesquite wood grill before, and standing right next to it was as hot as I've ever felt before. The pizza ovens were right next to the grill, raging at 900 degrees, which didn't help.

The first night I worked it flew by, just like it did the night of my audition. A lot of stars dined at Ma Maison, but I couldn't see them unless I went to the restroom. Barbara

"This was taken at the first Meals on Wheels event called The Great American Food and Wine Festival in a tent on the parking lot of Spago Sunset. I was just a line cook then."

Lazaroff, Wolfgang's wife at the time, designed the first exhibition kitchen in the United States for a fine dining establishment. I also couldn't believe I was working at the hottest restaurant in town. Seriously, it felt almost unreal to me. Only four short years before, I had been a line cook at The Good Earth. I would never have guessed I'd be working at Spago, for goodness' sake. Night after night, I watched Mark expedite and grill food, taking mental notes for when I would be the chef someday. I was more than willing to work my butt off to get there. I wondered if Mark would ever leave though. Why would he? I wouldn't. He was in a great position. Watching Ed and Serge whip out fabulous pizzas was poetry in motion. They made it look effortless.

* * *

About six months into cooking at Spago, I was promoted to pasta chef. I had so much fun working the pasta station. It was my own station, meaning I expedited from there and worked in coordination with Mark. If I had to guess, I probably made around two hundred orders of fresh pasta dishes a night for over a year and a half. I got very good at cooking pasta, and was surprised to find out how difficult it was to cook fresh rather than dried pasta. It cooks faster, and if you overcook it, it turns to glue by the time it gets to the customer's table. Coming up with a special pasta dish every night was challenging but something I loved doing. I finally got to make my cucumber soup that I had created before starting at Spago. I also tried to never repeat my specials. Meanwhile, my eating disorder was hitting a new plateau at that point—actually, an all-time low. I had dropped another four pounds, and I was one pound away from my goal, which was 90 pounds. Each pound was like five on me because I was so thin—or at least that's what my disease told me. I was working out longer and harder than ever before, and consuming less food. People began to notice it, too. They were asking me if I'd lost weight, and of course I said no. It's like asking a person who is overweight if they are pregnant. The anorexic mind takes any type of comment about our bodies very personally and defensively, maybe more so than overweight people, but of course I can't really know how an overweight person feels when someone insults them. I'm sure it's horrible.

* * *

I got Mike a job interview at Spago in 1985 and he got the job as a waiter just before I became the head chef. By this point we were actively searching for a place to have the ceremony and reception for our wedding. The hardest part was who was going to marry us, since we both didn't belong to a church. My mother recommended the priest from the church we had gone to years before the whole Sunday school fiasco. I couldn't believe he was still alive.

I still had reservations about marrying Mike, but I figured we were too far along and we must be good together, and why not? We'd been together for five years, and I thought it was the right thing to do. Besides, I was still going through the pain of the loss of my fingers and was convinced no one else would want me like Mike did. I was so focused on my career and my disgusting disease that to think about leaving him and going through all the painful stuff that goes along with a breakup was too arduous to think about. Like getting married and divorced wasn't going to be arduous! Then there was meeting the new guy at this stage of my disease. It was unfathomable to imagine.

My eyes were still roaming around—not for a serious relationship, but for a fling. I had to know if any man still found me attractive. The fact that I was still looking around wasn't a good sign either. Mark and Nancy from Spago were engaged too, and were making plans for their wedding as well. When Mark gave his notice, I naturally prayed I would take his position as head chef. Quite often, after the shift, Wolfgang would invite us to sit together for a glass of wine after cooking. The night Mark gave his notice Wolfgang asked all of us in the kitchen to join him for a champagne toast to celebrate Nancy and Mark's future together.

While we all toasted to their success, I still hoped I was going to be the one to take his post.

"And as you probably know, I am going to need a new head chef, and I've made a decision," Wolfgang said.

My heart was pounding a million miles a minute. I wasn't sure I was qualified to run a restaurant like Spago, but I wanted it to be me and I knew I could do it. Serge could definitely do the job, and a great one too. Did I have a shot?

Then Wolfgang said, looking right at me, "And I've decided to give Lisa a shot!"

I nearly fainted, but instead I cried tears of joy. I put my head in my hands and held back a full- blown cry. I could not believe it. I was going to be Wolfgang's head chef at the hottest restaurant in Los Angeles! I stood up and ran over to Wolfgang, hugging him and kissing him on both cheeks. The feeling I felt at that moment is truly inexplicable.

"Oh my God! I can't believe it! Thank you, Wolf. I really can't believe it! I swear I'll do a great job."

"You better!" he said in his wonderful Austrian accent. I relished in the moment.

It was like I was bathing in the warmest sun and sitting in the brightest moonlight. That was undoubtedly *the* single most important and phenomenal day of my life as it brought me to a new level in my craft. I was now a part of an elite circle of amazing chefs, accepted and respected by a tremendous community, and most importantly by Wolfgang Puck. How could it get any better? Things were looking up. It was 1985, five years after the accident, and I felt on top of the world—maybe a little too much so. The ego is a delicate thing. It can make us soar or it can destroy us. Not only was my life about to go to a whole other level, so was my ego. My anorexia was obviously out of control and unbeknownst to me, I was headed straight for disaster. Well, maybe disaster is a bit strong—but several events I experienced later proved my ego was definitely in a misguided and lost place.

* * *

During the two months before Mark left, he trained me how to do what head chefs do like how to do inventory, and how to order food and in what amounts. Then there was the importance of food rotation, the cleanliness of the walk-in, and scheduling. I was supposed to make sure the kitchen manager was doing his or her job as well, and he stressed that I should trust no one. Everyone will want my job, and I should never forget that. If I was going to be the head chef of a restaurant of Spago's caliber in the future, that meant I was responsible

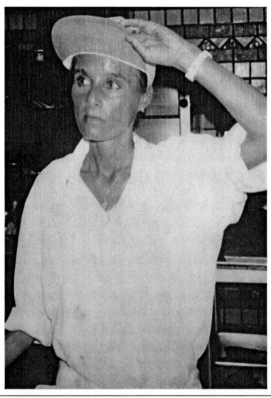

Me in the kitchen at Spago Sunset while I held position as head chef and was more than likely at the worst of my anorexia. See how drawn my face is?

for everything. So now I was under pressure to be the best I could be. I worked the grill the last few weeks Mark was there and learned how to stoke the grill, which was the hardest part of the job. It meant pulling out the heavy grill, which may have weighed easily over a hundred pounds. Adding logs of mesquite wood to the fire was also a challenge. I was thin but strong, and because the grill was in a weird position, it made it easy to pull out and push in.

During this period, Arnold Schwarzenegger had a private book signing for his new book "Pumping Iron" on the patio for a 100 people. I met him at Gold's Gym in my teens while I was dreaming of becoming a body builder. I think that's hysterical now that I think about it. At the time, I was regularly eating a 16-ounce steak and 6 eggs for breakfast, lifting weights and putting on muscle. My back was ripped and I had to get all of my jeans taken in at the waist. Now I was terrified of food? I think that's hysterical! I wanted to go say hello so badly, but I was nervous that he might have forgotten me, as it had been eight years since he'd seen me, but I took a chance. As it turned out he actually remembered me and even gave me a signed copy of his book. I still have it today!

* * *

Mike and I had a trip planned in August, way before I knew I was to be head chef. We had tickets to Kauai for a vacation. Amazing timing, I thought, since Mark was leaving in September to marry Nancy. I had a feeling I wasn't going to get a whole lot of time off for my honeymoon, especially since I was going to take over as head chef, so we decided to use our trip for our honeymoon. I was still a friend's with my second boyfriend, Terry Taylor and in retrospect it is amazing to me. Here I was, twenty-seven years old, and still in contact with him after ten years. His mother had a cottage on Kauai in Hanalei Bay. Terry invited Mike and me to come join him, his fiancé, and another couple there for a week. The cottage was right across the street from the bay, and both of us being a strong swimmers, I wanted to go for a swim the minute we got there. Hanalei Bay is a relatively large bay, and it looked nice and calm. As soon as we unpacked we all went to the beach. We jumped into the ocean with enthusiasm and joy, looking forward to the warmth and beauty of the ocean of Hawaii. We started our swim and immediately found ourselves totally outside the bay within minutes. Mike was way ahead of me too, which was scary because we both had equal strength in swimming. Frightened, I decided to turn around and swim back to shore.

I noticed I was making absolutely no headway and quickly became exhausted. I looked at the shoreline and it seemed to be miles away from me. Our friends looked like little tiny dots in the sand. I could faintly see them waving their hands frantically, yelling something at me, but I couldn't hear what they were saying. I looked back and saw Mike swimming towards me. It helped me but he too was trying to tell me something I couldn't hear. I saw somebody on the shore jump in the ocean and could see they were feverishly swimming towards me. Of course I began to think there might be a shark nearby, so I looked around hysterically for a shark fin, but there wasn't one and thank God. Exhaustion finally overcame me, and with little strength or desire left in me, I gave in and slowly began to sink to the bottom of the ocean. It didn't seem that far down, as I remember, because I could see to the top of the ocean easily.

As I looked around, I began to feel that same peaceful feeling I'd had in the operating room. Was I going to see the light again? Was I dying again? Dang it! Was it possible that I *still* wasn't getting whatever I supposed to learn in the operating room? Was I *that* much of an idiot? Suddenly, I saw an image of a deck of cards playing a sort of movie, flashing my entire life right in front of me. I could even hear it shuffling. I saw my childhood, my teens, my accident, and my entire future being revealed to me. I liked what I saw, especially the future. I don't remember the future the deck of cards showed me, but I knew I had to live so I forced myself to push off the ocean floor and come up for air. I looked forward to my future hoping there were many great things coming my way. I felt I had a very interesting life ahead of me and when I popped up out of the water, I released a huge amount of air from my lungs only to find Terry's best friend, Richard, treading water next to me looking very relieved I was there and alive. I was relieved to say the least

Richard said, "Lisa! Oh my God! We were so worried you were dead."

"You were worried? How long was I down there?"

"Not sure, but it seemed like five minutes. We're all in a very big riptide right now, so let's all swim to the left, towards shore, right now!"

We all did, and before I knew it, we were all on the shore. It seemed effortless swimming sideways than straight towards the shore. Still freaking out I found myself still swimming in the sand and thanking God for yet another chance at life, even though I still didn't believe in God. It is amazing to me that He kept saving me. I was beside myself that I had been given yet more information about my life—and underwater, for goodness' sake, and through a flashing deck of cards. I couldn't remember any of it, but the feeling I felt was positive. When I calmed down and got my thoughts together, I asked Richard, "How long was I down there?

"I don't know, about five minutes. You shouldn't be here, you know—unless of course, you can hold your breath that long."

"Wow."

"The currents were going in several erratic directions and clashing against each other, causing a rip tide. This one was really bad."

"It looked calm, though. Why didn't you say anything?"

"I thought you knew. You said you guys were good swimmers."

All I cared about was that I was alive, and by a miracle. The week zoomed by, and when we returned from Kauai I started my job as Wolfgang's head chef. It was still hard to believe that I was the head chef. After being gone a week it seemed even more surreal to me. I pondered this thought and realized it shouldn't have seemed that outrageous that I had that position. I earned it, after all. But I was too insecure to think I deserved something so amazing. After a few weeks, Wolfgang changed the menus, putting my name at the top. It was dreamlike. I was able to bring my ideas to Wolfgang openly, and he actually considered them. I thought that was cool. There was this one dish he really liked—and so did the customers. It was a scallop dish that became a permanent item. I'm proud to share the recipe with all of you.

Seared Jumbo Sea Scallops on Sautéed Spinach with a Toasted Hazelnut-Frangelico Sauce

Serves 4
The Scallops:
12 jumbo (U10) sea scallops
Olive oil
Salt and pepper to taste
The Spinach:
8 cups fresh baby spinach, about 2 ½ pounds
Olive oil
Water
Salt and pepper to taste
The Hazelnut Sauce:
1-cup hazelnuts
(Roast in a 350-degree oven for 20 minutes. Cool and
    rub off the skin. In a mini
Cuisinart, puree into a fine meal. Set aside.)
1 cup white wine
1/3 cup Frangelico
½cup heavy cream
½pound sweet butter, soft
Salt and pepper to taste

Directions: In a saucepan, reduce the wine and Frangelico by 1/3. Add the cream and reduce it by half. Whisking vigorously, add the butter on low heat. Add the hazelnut meal to the sauce gradually, off the heat, with a whisk to create a nice consistency and strong hazelnut flavor.

Presentation: On a large, beautiful plate, separate the spinach into fourths in the center of all four of the plates. Place three scallops on top of the spinach and finish it with the hazelnut sauce.

Enjoy with a crisp glass of Sancerre or a Lillet on the rocks with this dish. I love a light cigarillo after dinner with a lovely cognac.

* * *

My anorexia had suddenly started creating interesting digestive issues. I'm quite sure the years of physical abuse didn't help. I'd never had this problem before. I was finding myself constipated more than normal too. Most likely that was the result of not drinking enough water or not eating enough food to "go" everyday, not to mention I was so tightly wound up from controlling everything I couldn't take a poop anyway! I had also become addicted to Fernet Branca, the Italian aperitif; it tasted very bitter because it is made from fermented artichokes, but I loved how empty it made my stomach feel. I also discovered that it acted like a laxative, which was a good and bad thing. Then out of nowhere Fernet Branca was recalled because it had too much absinthe in it, which is highly addictive and was illegal in the United States at the time. That's probably why I craved it all the time. After that, I had nothing to break the food down in my stomach anymore. I could actually feel the food in my stomach digesting, causing the food to travel a lot faster through my system than normal, which was exactly what I wanted. The less time food was spent in my body, the better. For a period of six months, I was without my precious drink, and surprisingly I experienced mild withdrawals from not having it, causing me to be more irritable and on edge than I already was. Carrying around 3 percent body fat can do that to you, more so than the lack of Fernet Branca. I wasn't drinking that much, only a few ounces a day, but it was enough for me to crave it. It became increasingly difficult to hide my disorder, too, which makes me sick to think about today. I was so sick. Looking back, I was sicker than I care to admit today. My shoulder blades were beginning to sink in deep and my chest bones were protruding out complimenting my boney rib cage, like a super-skinny model, and there was no hiding that.

* * *

Things with Mike were gliding along at a steady pace thank goodness, but my main focus was on food and the ever-growing restrictions I continued to put on myself each day. I went to bed hungry every night, and by my *choice*. Now, I think of all the people who don't have a choice and go to bed hungry and wake up hungry every single day of their lives. Those poor people, dying young and there isn't a damn thing they can do about it. And yet there I was, *choosing* to not eat and actually enjoying the feeling of hunger. At the same time, the feeling of hunger was so painful—emotionally and spiritually. If Mike or any of our friends made dinner plans past 5:30 p.m., I would flip out. I would literally ruin the evening by rushing to order and eating quickly while showing how miserable I was by not socializing and being a bitch. Our friends eventually stopped making plans with us, and for good reason. That's how starvation can affect our brains. I can't believe I never passed out from how low my blood sugar was and the 3 percent body fat I had. I lost my period during my last year at Spago because of it too. I wasn't myself on any level, which bled into not enjoying anything anymore. I only loved cooking, and even that was becoming hard to enjoy because of the mere fact that I loved and hated food. Even volleyball wasn't doing it for me anymore. My eating disorder always came first.

Meanwhile, I knew I shouldn't be marrying Mike and not because I wasn't in love with him—because I was far too sick and irresponsible to get married to anyone. It was all about me, me and me.

I was in a real-life dilemma about everything. I should have cancelled the wedding but was too afraid to take action. I was afraid to tell Mom and Dad, too, because we didn't have a lot of money and they had already spent thousands of dollars so far; I thought they would be angry with me if I cancelled. I wanted to think I could handle what was about to happen, so I went into further denial, just like everything else. I could always get a divorce, I argued to myself. If there was ever a time to find God, it was then. Being a pretty, twenty-seven-year-old girl with three missing fingers who is the head chef of the most famous restaurant in Los Angeles, is about to get married, has a raging eating disorder and was also totally devoid of any kind of faith was a pretty scary place to be. A fling was never more on my mind. I was equating marriage with death, when I should have seen a joyous union. I would have no more freedom, I told myself, which of course is ridiculous. I mean cheating wasn't what one is supposed to be thinking about before getting married. I think I was afraid I was going to have to stop being me and become a "Stepford Wife," which would never happen. The urgency to have a fling was overwhelming, almost as over-whelming as wanting to really eat again. I had several opportunities at Spago to hook up with someone, but I didn't. I was trying very hard to be good and I was until after we were married. I was more selfish than ever then, and a big fat liar to boot, and I would pay for that later in a very harsh way. With my wedding day two days away, I did my best to see how lucky I was to be marrying such a nice man, but instead I was wondering how I could succeed at having my cake and eating it too.

Chapter 10
The Wedding and Finally the Settlement

With the "big day" finally here, I wanted to remember how happy I felt when Mike asked me to marry him the first time in 1981. The way Mike proposed to me was unusual and done with such wit. I loved his dry sense of humor. He took me to a place in Orange County called, Chez Cary, when he proposed to me. It was decorated in the typical late '70s early/80s décor,' complete with swiveled chairs, a footrest and a menu that had no prices on it for the ladies. I'd never seen that before, and I thought it was rather presumptuous that a man should be expected to pay. My parents never told me a man should always pay. What if the woman wanted to pay? L'Orangerie had the same type of menus. Maybe that was the last frontier of chivalry. There was even a strolling violinist. It was cheesy but still romantic. In its day, it was considered an expensive place to eat. A salad and a fish entrée were $20 per person. It's incredible how prices have risen since then. Mike had some money then, and he always had enough to take me out several times a week and give me gifts. It was all on credit, but he loved carrying around cash for tipping waiters, valets, hosts, and busboys. When he kneeled down to propose, which I was not expecting at all, he put a plastic Mickey Mouse ring on my finger and asked me to marry him. The ring threw me off a little bit. Maybe it wasn't unusual, as he knew I'd get it. I'm sure he wasn't sure I would say yes. Why else would he give me a Plastic Mickey Mouse ring to ask my hand in marriage? I remember feeling so happy. A few months later, he took me to L'Ermitage, my favorite restaurant in Los Angeles at the time, and by surprise he proposed again, but this time with a platinum wedding band. I knew for sure then that he gave me a plastic ring in the first place because I must have given him a strong idea that I might say no. It's interesting to me to think about that now.

* * *

When we were planning our wedding, we got lucky when it came to choosing where the ceremony and reception would be. An old client and dear friend, Dr. Zackalini, God rest his soul, offered us his huge backyard in Bel Air, California, which was convenient because it was a block away from the Hotel Bel-Air. That was where we were going to stay for our so-called "second honeymoon." We were lucky with the food too: Spago catered our pizzas, and Wolfgang gave us a seriously discounted price. We also had sushi given to us as a wedding present from an old beach friend, Bob Styles. As for the cake, Patrick Jamon from Les Anges, where Mike worked before Spago, gave us a serious break and included an array of pies, tarts, and petite fours that were all made by Claude Koberle, the fabulous pastry chef I knew who had made that wonderful lobster croissant at Ma Maison. Finally, we had beautiful Hawaiian birds-of-paradise hanging from a huge oak tree in the backyard. It was quite beautiful, unassuming, and elegant.

* * *

Now that the wedding day had come I was very nervous. Tropical thundershowers were predicted throughout the afternoon, right at the time of our ceremony. I took my bridesmaids and my maid of honor to my gym for a workout before the ceremony when it was only six hours away. I was taking niacin at the time, and I asked all the girls to join me while we rode the stationary bikes for an hour. I told them it was a great feeling to rush on niacin. Those poor girls, they must have hated me. After my wedding party dealt with my manic requests before the wedding, we left for the house in

Bel Air. When we got there, everything looked great. The Hawaiian birds-of-paradise looked gorgeous hanging from the trees and were right above where we were to be married. The clouds had broken up just in time and looked exactly like the clouds I had seen as a teenager in Hawaii after a tropical rain. Thankfully, it had cooled down a bit too.

While the guests began to trickle in, I found myself developing considerable anxiety. This wasn't about Mike—it was about me and how I was about to drag him into my messiness. But to my credit, he knew what he was marrying; he must have. I had also reached my goal weight, and one pound lower, too: 89 pounds, and on my wedding day. What could have been better than that? I was more proud of that accomplishment than the idea of getting married. And because of that, I wasn't worried about taking a bite of the wedding cake or eating a slice of pizza. I could afford to eat that cake now. I had actually obsessed over how I was going to spit it out after Mike fed a piece to me, but now I didn't have to worry because I had reached my goal weight, and one pound less to boot. Yahoo! I was in a major deficit.

* * *

With the ceremony about to begin, I was amazed at how beautiful everything looked, and on such a small budget too. As I watched my maid of honor and my bridesmaid's walk down the aisle, I thought how lucky I was to have such great friends and how beautiful they looked. Thank goodness the niacin had worn off by then but it actually gave them a nice afterglow. The guests were finally seated. The wind was gently blowing, and the breeze felt great. Thankfully, there was no rain. The air smelled clean and fresh mixed with the smell of the baking pizzas in the backyard. There's nothing like the smell of baking pizza. The crust has an especially awesome smell, igniting the appetite. Of course there is the smell of bacon, onions, and garlic, which trigger childhood memories for many. Needless to say, I was starving. My feeling of

Mike and me on our wedding day in 1986.

hunger was more constant and noticeable now, but I loved it. When I wasn't all screwed up about eating, all it took was the smell of bacon, garlic, pizza dough, or onions to make me salivate. As I waited to walk down the aisle, I wished I were that person again. I wanted to genuinely look forward to eating great food again without feeling guilt or remorse, but that idea seemed like a distant memory. I remember noticing how emotional Dad was as I was walking down the aisle. He had tears in his eyes. I never remembered him being like that when I was a kid. It was sweet to see. Maybe he liked Mike more than I thought, and somehow that helped me, but only a little. Mike was wearing a light sage-green suit from Ted Lapidus in Beverly Hills. We shopped together for his suit. He wanted me to pick out three suits I liked that would go with my dress and then make his final choice by himself. He wanted me to be surprised, as he was going to be when he saw my dress. I was glad he'd picked the sage-green one because he looked handsome in it and the color matched one of the colors in my dress perfectly. I could see that his eyes were flooded with tears as I walked towards him, making me feel worse than I already did.

I noticed the sushi display on the way down the aisle and I thought how striking it looked and how I couldn't wait to dig my teeth into the Hamachi. It felt weird, everyone watching me walk down the aisle with my father. The pressure was intense. I felt like a phony. When I got to Mike, I had a frightening revelation: I wasn't sure I was going to be able to hold my true feelings back any longer. I prayed for strength to hold my actual feelings in but it was too late. I knew I wasn't going to be able to control myself. Then it happened. Halfway through our vows, I involuntarily said, "I do, already." I had absolutely no control over what came out of my mouth. I turned around and walked back down the aisle, *by myself*. When I reached the first row where Mom was sitting, she grabbed my arm sternly and whispered, "Lisa, it's not over yet. Just get through this and we'll talk about whatever this scene you are creating is about later." I remember not being aware of what I had done at that moment. How Mike must have felt. Totally embarrassed, I turned back towards Mike, and when I got to him he said, with tears rolling down his face, "Lisa, if you want an annulment, that's fine, but let's get through this right now, okay?"

"I'm so sorry, Mike. I don't know what came over me just now."

At that moment the priest said, "If there is anyone here who objects to these two getting married, speak up now or forever hold your peace."

His timing was surreal. Out of all the words he said, those were the only ones I heard. I thought about saying "I object," but I didn't and thank God. We finished our vows and started our reception. What the hell was wrong me? Seriously. Mike was and is a really great guy. Mike was classier than ever.

Me getting ready to smash a piece of cake in Mike's face.

I'm not sure what *I* might have done if he had done what I did to him. I think it would have been horrible, given the place my pride was in at the time. After we got our pictures taken, my bridesmaids and maid of honor asked me what the hell that was all about. Lying, I told them I freaked out and that I was fine. I highly doubt they believed me. As if that wasn't enough, things got worse, if that's possible. When I think about my wedding day it's hard to imagine it happened at all. My father—my sweet, dear father—experienced his worst nightmare right after the ceremony. After I downed a few glasses of champagne, along with some pizza and sushi, I noticed my dad was standing alone at the bar looking upset and teary-eyed. I thought he was feeling melancholy about the marriage, so I went over to him and asked him what was up.

"Dad, are you okay? You look sad."

"I'm fine, honey. You look so beautiful. My little girl is all grown up."

That was definitely something I had never heard him say ever.

"You don't look right. Are you okay?"

He lowered his head and said something I could have never imagined him or anyone saying on anyone's wedding day, "Your mother just asked me for a divorce."

What? Really? This wasn't the mom I knew. What could have possessed her to tell him she wanted a divorce that day, or even at all? They'd been together almost thirty years!

"You're joking, right Dad?"

"No, honey, I'm not."

"But why today? It's my wedding day?"

"Things aren't great, but I didn't think it was this bad. Honey, please, go enjoy your party, okay? I shouldn't have told you."

"No Dad! You should have told me. You know I would have pestered you until you did! I'm so pissed."

"Honey, please don't say anything to her now. Go have fun."

"I can't have fun Dad unless I say something to her now. Be right back."

Disgruntled and angry with her, I walked over to her and said, "I can't believe you just asked Dad for a divorce on my wedding day! Why today? What happened?"

This wasn't like my mom. She must have been going through a midlife crisis.

"Why did you walk away from Mike in the middle of the ceremony?"

She always had the wherewithal to call me on my stuff no matter what was going on and always changed the subject in her favor, confusing me, my whole life. I still loved her with all my soul, anyway. I wasn't happy with Mike, or actually,

I wasn't happy with myself in the relationship to be honest, only she didn't know that. I was afraid to be on my own, and missing three fingers and all, I was sure no one else would want me. What a shitty reason to get married.

"Don't change the subject."

"We'll discuss this later. Go enjoy your wedding day."

How was I supposed to do that? I walked away shaking my head in disbelief, saying nothing, and when I told Mike what happened, he said that it was the icing on the cake of his day. I let it go the best I could, but what happened wasn't the greatest example of what marriage could be, and it definitely wasn't what I needed to hear that day.

* * *

After the party was over, Mike and I went to the Hotel Bel-Air. Our room was by a private pool shared by four cabanas. It was a beautiful room, and the view was unsurpassed in its loveliness. Mike wanted to take a swim but I didn't want to go, so I changed and turned on the television, which was rare. About twenty minutes went by and I couldn't hear him swimming anymore, so I went outside to see if he was okay. What I found freaked me out. I found him at the bottom of the pool with his legs crossed.

I screamed, "Oh my God, Mike!"

I jumped in and dived down to the bottom of the pool to get him. He seemed aware of what was happening, but for some reason he couldn't move. I grabbed his hand and started to swim toward the surface in hopes that it would get him to move and it worked. Within seconds, thank the good Lord, he was able to free his legs and swim up by himself.

"What happened? What were you doing at the bottom of the pool? You weren't trying to, you know . . ."

"No! I cramped. I guess it was too soon to go swimming after eating all that pizza."

"Your legs cramped, not your stomach. If it was the pizza, your stomach would have cramped."

I wasn't surprised one bit. One of my biggest issues in our relationship was his cramping, which usually happened during the semi-finals of the countless beach volleyball tournaments we entered over the years. I would get so angry when he cramped. We would get all the way to the semi-finals only to lose because of cramping. It took many games just to get to the semi-finals if you didn't win them all, and over an entire weekend. I hated losing volleyball tournaments. When we got back to the room, Mike handed me a gift wrapped in yellow paper with a red ribbon. I opened it to find a very sexy pink negligee. It was hardly my style, but very pretty nonetheless.

"It's a La Perla."

"What's a La Perla?"

I was still very much a tomboy then and wasn't as into fashion like Mike was. For me, a bra under any brand was fashion. He loved high-quality and stylishly tasteful clothes. He definitely had a style of his own. I loved jeans, T-shirts, and funky tennis shoes.

"La Perla is a French lingerie company. They make high-end bras, underwear, and lingerie."

I wasn't feeling sexy at all, and I said, "Oh. It's beautiful. Thanks. I'm really not in the mood though. Are you?"

One of the worst things about anorexia is that low body fat ruins the sex drive—actually, it makes it almost nonexistent. I simply wasn't interested.

He looked rather disappointed, but I'm sure he wasn't surprised at all. He said in his usual unconditional way, "No, not really. It's been a long day."

I was wondering how much he really loved me. Of course this was my insecurity talking. Was he just as much of a cheater as I was? It made me angrier than I thought it would if I knew he was. This could have been what motivated me to look for a reaction from him. Anything to let me know he cared. I could see that he was lying that he was tired, yet I had a feeling he was hoping that night would have been different. So why didn't he say something? I think he hated arguing, in hindsight. He'd rather get along than fight. I will never understand the total acceptance he had for me, even when he was disappointed. But I was even more disappointed, really. This was a constant about him, and as I look back, it was what I needed, as I was so self-absorbed which more than likely caused my appalling behavior.

"Are you okay? It's been a rough day for you, hasn't' it?"

"Yes, it has. Mom must be going through some kind of horrific midlife crisis. I hope when it's over, he'll forgive her and take her back. They've been through so much it would be a shame to divorce after so many years."

Feeling bad, I suggested we at least have champagne by the pool. He agreed and we talked like we were old friends for a short while, which we actually were.

* * *

The following morning I woke up full of anxiety and distress because of what had happened with my mom and dad, and I couldn't keep my feelings in any longer so I jumped out of bed, locked myself in the bathroom, and called my mom. There was a phone next to the toilet and I loved that. When she answered she said, "Is everything okay?"

"No, everything is not okay. I can't believe you asked Dad for a divorce on my wedding day. That is just flat-out disrespectful!"

"I'm sorry. I just couldn't wait another minute. Please forgive me. Somehow, watching you walk back down the aisle in the middle of the ceremony alone gave me the courage to ask your father for a divorce."

It took me a minute to ingest what she had said. She thought that was logical and fair?

"Why, may I ask? Lord knows you've had a rough road, but hasn't everyone?"

It was so disturbing to have this kind of conversation with my mom because it was painful for me to think they were separating, possibly divorcing. Even so, that's how mom and I were: Deal with whatever it is as soon as possible and move on.

"Do you know how devastated Dad is right now? You broke his heart—and on my wedding day, no less! How is this supposed to translate for me?"

"Well Lisa, all I can say is when you get to be my age, you'll see."

Really? What's that supposed to mean? That's her excuse for behaving like an idiot?

"That's your excuse? That's pathetic. You and Dad have been together for almost twenty-seven years. What could possibly have happened that you can't get through now?"

"Someday you'll understand. Now, is this really why you called me?"

"Yes!"

"It's none of your business."

I couldn't believe it. This was the first time she hadn't opened up to me. I was actually sickened by the thought of Mom and Dad not together.

"You made it my business! Come on, Mom. There's got to be a way to work it out."

"Look, it is what it is. It's my life, and shit happens."

I had spent years trying to keep the family together when I was teen, and in a very codependent way. This is probably another reason why I became anorexic: control, control, control. Even if I didn't go so far as to be anorexic, control was the theme of my life. A lot of good my controlling did for me. It was the very thing that pushed him and others away. I know now that nothing is in my control—not one thing. I wish I'd known that sooner, I might have saved myself a lot of aggravation. She was acting so casual about it all, which totally sucked. It really wasn't my business, but it became mine because of the way it went down. She was still my mom, though, and I had to respect that.

"So, Lisa. Do you want to tell me why you really called me the day after your wedding?"

"What do you mean?"

"Come on, it's about Mike, isn't it?"

She had me on that one, but she was changing the subject again.

Continuing, she said, "You left him standing at the altar saying 'I do, already.' It doesn't take a genius to see you didn't want to finish it."

"I can't understand why he stays with me, Mom."

"Love is usually blind, and I think he really loves you. But I'm not sure you do or ever really did. I actually like him. But if you don't love him the same way, you have my blessing. When did you start having reservations?"

"Well, since the accident, really. I thought no one else would want me."

"That's why you married Mike?"

"Yes partly and other reasons, and because I thought you and Dad would have been angry with me if I cancelled and would have made me marry him anyway."

"We can't and have never been able to *make* you do anything, and that's a shitty reason to get married."

Realizing I couldn't argue with that, I hung up and reflected. I felt like I was in an episode of *The Twilight Zone* and *One Life to Live* after we hung up. I was totally confused, more than ever before. She not only validated my fears of being married by her asking for a divorce, she was living proof that I was right about love and a lifetime commitment. Now that I saw that nothing lasts forever, I was really in trouble. I know I keep repeating myself, but poor Mike, man. I was the coward, really. I didn't have the courage to be real. When I came out of the bathroom, Mike said he had heard everything.

I said, "Look, don't panic. It just might be the cold feet thing. It happens all the time. I will go talk to the therapist and I'm sure I'm just having a moment."

"This is more than the 'cold feet' thing. You walked away in the middle of your ceremony and said, 'I do, already,' Lisa. If you think anyone or I didn't notice, you're wrong. If you want to annul the marriage, just tell me the truth and we'll go get it done today. I can handle it."

I could see that was the last thing Mike wanted, and above all, I didn't either, even though I knew in my gut we wouldn't make it—not because of Mike but because of me.

"Mike, I don't know what I want. The last five years have been so hard on me, and I am very confused. I just became the head chef a week ago at the most famous restaurant in Los Angeles. I just got married and I'm still dealing with my accident, as unbelievable as that may seem to you right now. Everything happened so fast."

"While we are being open with each other, your accident was six years ago, and I have to tell you that you have a serious major eating disorder and I'm not sure how much longer I can live with that. But I love you and you are my wife now and I'm willing to help you any way I can as I've tried to before yesterday. Honestly, that's what you should see the therapist about, not this. The reality is this; your problem is with eating, not with me."

When he said that, it was like a punch in the gut. I excused myself and went back to the bathroom. I noticed in the hotel booklet, there was an on-call therapist. I called the concierge and asked if there was one available they could call for me. Lucky for me, there was one that could come to the hotel in an hour, so I made the appointment for that afternoon.

What he was saying was devastatingly true. But it still didn't change anything, and moreover, I knew he meant what he said and that scared the shit out of me. He was that fed up with my anorexia and me. I had no idea it was that bad with him. He had been so accommodating all these years.

With pride *screaming* through my heart, I said, "I can't believe it! You've never said this before."

"I have said this many times to you before. You just didn't want to hear it or believe it. Because I love you and love conquers all. Why did you bother marrying me?"

"Why did you bother marrying me?"

Silence took over. What could I say to that? Shit. I was terrified to tell him it was mostly because of my accident. He never talked to me about how he felt about my disease like this before, and I should have been as honest with him, but couldn't answer his question.

* * *

As I walked to meet the therapist, I felt so bad. Mike had been so patient with me all these years and I was so not with him. During the session, I told the therapist that I thought I loved him but was afraid of intimacy. That was big for me to say. She didn't seem very interested in that. She was more interested in finding out why I was so thin. I became defensive and told her I was there to see if my marriage could be saved, not to talk about why I was so thin. She insisted my problems had to do with my very unhealthful weight and not with my marriage per se. Angry at her truth, I stormed out of there. When I returned to Mike, he asked if I talked to her about my eating disorder. I lied and said the therapist thought we would be just fine and thought we should give us a solid try.

"She did? She couldn't see how thin you are?"

He had brought up my disease over the years, but always knew it was useless. His words sounded different this time, like he was letting me know how serious he was about my disease and our relationship and how unhappy he was watching me hurt myself.

Lying, I said, "No! If I was obviously sick, I'm sure she would have brought it up."

I could see he didn't believe me and I didn't care. He trusted me, but I wasn't trustworthy. I trusted him but not myself. Looking back, I realize that I always looked to my significant other for happiness, which of course doesn't work. Happiness comes from our own happiness. No one can make us unhappy unless we allow him or her to. Yes, it's hard to do when someone around us isn't happy, but the best way to help that person is to not be dragged into his or her crap. Thinking *I* was God and *I* knew it all and *I* had the answers to everything was a very empty and lonely place for me. After my disastrous appointment with the therapist, we checked out and headed straight for the beach to play some volleyball. It felt good, but I was feeling sad because so many emotionally challenging things had happened in such a short period of time. Now that Mike had told me the truth, the game had changed for me quite a bit. There was an actual possibility he might leave me. He was as serious as I'd ever seen him.

*   *   *

On Tuesday, I was back at work. I wanted to get back into my normal routine desperately. One thing about anorexia: regimen and discipline is everything, without it we are lost and feel completely out of control. Being in an unknown environment without a schedule is like being in the middle of the ocean treading water, even if it is the Hotel Bel-Air. I was lousy at relaxing. That same day, I finally got the phone call from my lawyer. It was incredible, really. I'd been waiting forever for that call—actually almost five years, to be exact—to hear the answer as to why my accident happened.

He said, "Hi Lisa. How are you?"

"Great! What's up?

"Well, are you ready? The answers you've been waiting for are finally here."

I sat down feeling tons of butterflies in my stomach. I had no idea what to expect.

"I'm so excited and ready, I think!"

"Okay, here it is."

My heart was racing with a strange kind of anxiety. I almost didn't want to know.

"The machine started because the machine itself was faulty."

My relief was beyond comprehension.

"The watch you were wearing that day had a magnet in it, as did the starter on the machine, and because of that a current was created, starting the machine on its own."

I couldn't believe what he said. I had totally forgotten I had worn a watch that day.

"How did you know I had the watch on?"

"Well, the hospital keeps records of everything, and it's my job to investigate."

"Wow, so what does this mean?"

"It means that the machine itself was defective. The company that imported it into the United States never had it safety inspected before selling it to L'Orangerie, which puts them at fault."

"So anyone's watch could have started the machine, is that what you're saying?"

"Yes, if it had a magnet in it."

"If I hadn't worn the watch, would the machine have gone off?"

"Probably not, I'm sorry to say."

I never wore any jewelry to work prior to the accident. Why did I that day? I must have been really out of it, like Virgini saw. I felt sad because if I had been a healthier person, I wouldn't have worn the watch and I'd have my fingers today. It was unbelievable to me that the mystery was suddenly over and just like that, and all because I had worn my watch that day.

"Are you ready to hear what your settlement is?"

"I hope I got what I wanted."

"Yes, you did. There will mandatory signs placed next to dangerous machines in kitchens from now on. But there's also a financial reward."

"That's great—and there is?"

"Yes. You'll receive $240,000."

My jaw dropped. That was the largest amount of money I'd ever received in my life and had altogether in my entire life. I couldn't speak.

"Lisa? Are you there?"

"Yes! I don't know what to say right now. I'm in shock."

"Well, minus my legal fee and other expenses over the last five years, you'll end up with a total of $186,000, and because it was awarded from the court, it's tax-free."

During the past five years, he used his own money to find out what happened. I thought that was cool.

"Thank you for believing in this and working for nothing this whole time. I am very grateful. Thank you."

"It was my pleasure. I wish there could have been more money for you."

"Are you kidding? I'm overwhelmed right now!"

"You need to come sign some documents."

"I can come tomorrow morning."

"Congratulations, Lisa."

I was beside myself. Just like that I was rich! Well sort of just like that and $186,000 was a lot of money then, or so I thought. I reflected on how this could change my life, but it never occurred to me how fast that money could leave me. The journey of waiting was over, and getting that amount of money definitely made me feel much better. There was some closure, but I would've rather have had my fingers back, quite honestly. I got what I really wanted though; mandatory signs explaining the danger of those machines. It was a good day. As I sat alone relishing in the finality of it all, I was still sad I'd worn my watch that day. I was already spending the money in my head, too. I promised myself I'd get some CDs and bonds. I wanted to be disciplined, and wanted none of it to go to my head. When I cashed the check, which was immediate, I was taking out cash here and there and found myself recklessly spending it. Right off the bat I bought two cars with *cash*. I bought a Suzuki Samurai and a Chrysler Le Baron convertible. Mike drove whichever car he wanted, even though he had a car of his own. It was I have to confess, a very cool feeling to buy cars for cash. I paid off Mike's credit cards, which was an unexpected surprise for him and for me, but I didn't mind. I was his wife, and I knew he would have done the same for me, and then some. I more than likely paid off my Christmas presents over the past six years! Mike never assumed any of that money was his. He felt I had earned it and never said a thing about how I spent my money. But I was generous with it. Let's not forget about my ego, which was already working overtime, and now that I had money, I was acting like an idiot. I was showing off by buying dinner for my friends and buying stuff I thought was important. I also thought I was indispensable at Spago, just like I thought I was at Ma Maison and L'Orangerie, and of course we all know we are not. Being the head chef at Spago was by far the best time of my life. It felt great standing at the helm of a great restaurant. I was creating food I had never dreamed I was capable of cooking or creating, thanks to Wolfgang's encouragement. I received that money a few months after we were married and took over as head chef. My ego took a full-blown turn for the worse and my judgment hit an all-time low. About a year into being the head chef, I was offered a job to be the executive chef of my own restaurant. A regular customer who frequented Spago offered this opportunity to me. During this time, I simultaneously had to hire a kitchen manager, someone Wolfgang recommended. After several weeks of pondering what to do about this offer, I thought I'd confide in my kitchen manager. Big, huge, ignoramus mistake. Of course she thought I was ready to go on my own and that it was a sign that it was my time to make my mark. A few days later, I decided to give my three months' notice to Wolfgang after the shift and the night before I was to leave for my first vacation since my wedding—without Mike, I might add. I was going to Club Med in Ixtapa, Mexico with my friend Davida, who was a bridesmaid at my wedding. It was a week's vacation and I was looking forward to it. She also worked at Spago as a waitress. I thought a three-month notice was more than fair.

* * *

After the shift was over, I asked Wolfgang if I could speak with him. As I recall, his energy and attitude wasn't the usual awesome one; it was different. He looked pissed off. What happened was nowhere near what I was expecting. He had never been angry with me before, at least not like this. He was always so tolerant and forgiving. He was so angry after I gave notice that he fired me instead. He said he wasn't going to let me quit. In a word, I was totally *devastated*. I'm not sure that devastated is a strong enough word, actually. I gave him three months, not three minutes to leave. My heart sank deep into the pit of my stomach. I thought I was going to vomit. I couldn't understand why he was so angry. I was giving him plenty of notice. I had to force myself to hold back the tears I knew would explode as soon as I left the building. I asked him why he was so angry. Well, what he said shocked me but then again it didn't. He told me that my so-called "trustworthy" kitchen manager had told him I was never going to return after my vacation. That my intention was to screw him over—which is of course was a lie and nothing I would ever do to Wolfgang or anyone. She stabbed me in the back for her benefit that bitch. But as far as *he* was concerned, I had stabbed *him* in the back. He said I should have talked to him about it first, and he was totally right. I was such an idiot then. I never thought things through, and it never occurred to me that she would tell him and add a lie to it in order to get what she wanted. Was I so wrong? I tried to make excuses, but he wouldn't hear of it. In hindsight, I probably wouldn't have either. He probably felt like he had been good to me, which he had been, and I just basically showed him no respect. My betrayal was something he couldn't look past and accept, and honestly I can't blame him. I blamed the kitchen manager for my demise for a long time. But now I know it really was my fault he fired me. What was I thinking? What made me think I could trust her, and why didn't I have the courage to tell Wolfgang first? I had no courage. I didn't trust myself. And there's another reason why. I knew that if I went to Wolfgang first, he would've talked me out of it, and for one reason and one reason only: to stay another two or three years to build my credibility and gain respect in the community, which of course was the right thing to do. He constantly reminded me of this during the three years I was there. After quitting and getting fired at the same time, what was I going to do now? I had just blown the biggest job of my life because I trusted my kitchen manager, had a huge ego that was totally out of control and had no balls. Now I was on my way to Club Med with no way to communicate with Wolfgang. Where would I work that could compare to Spago?

Chapter 11

Goodbye Spago, Hello Club Med
Ixtapa and the Divorce

I flew to Mexico the following morning beyond depressed. I could've cared less if the plane crashed. What was there to live for? I just ruined my career, so I thought. I was the chef at the hottest restaurant in town! What the fuck did I do to my life? Plus, I was a fingerless loser. My eating disorder was going to get expensive again too. All that free food at Spago was gone. I was sharing a hotel room with Davida, which meant a whole week with no chewing and spitting. Deep down, I was hoping it would break that awful habit, but it didn't. That's how bad things became, and *seemingly* almost instantly, overnight. I know this is repetitive, but I want to drive home the point the despair I was feeling. I couldn't believe I was gone from the most important and most significant job of my career forever—and just like that. Here today, gone tomorrow was now my reality. The feelings I had were markedly similar to how I'd felt when I lost my fingers, except this time I had *caused* the situation. I didn't see either event coming, yet they were both permanent. The irony was I respected Wolfgang immensely, and for more than being a great chef—as a person, too. He had been my friend and mentor, and I had blown it. The whole way to Mexico, I cried. My vacation now had a dark cloud over it when it should have been an amazing time.

* * *

We landed in Guadalajara and were greeted by eight members of the Mexican army outside the plane and all of them were sporting machine guns, pointing them towards the plane and us. That scene didn't create a sense of security for me at all as I'm sure anyone else. These men who were taking us to Club Med Ixtapa then escorted us to the bus. My imagination went absolutely wild. I imagined we were being taken somewhere to be killed. I envisioned my friend and I being raped by horrible men and then shot, left for dead in some remote place in Mexico. Ever since I can remember, I've had an incredibly huge imagination, playing out violent scenarios in my head. As an example: I could be taking a walk in a park or on a trail alone and would begin to feel frightened and vulnerable. I would imagine what I would do if someone was hiding in the bush to attack me. I would then begin mentally preparing, envisioning how I would defend myself. I could see the whole struggle in my head—seeing myself using my elbow to hit him in the nose or face, using my nubs to push in his eyeballs, or kicking him in the balls to get away. I have a rather high amount of adrenaline. To this day, I never assume I'm safe anywhere alone or with someone. I try to carry around an energy that says, "Don't screw with me or you'll be sorry." I didn't share my thoughts with my friend for fear that my thoughts might come alive if I said them out loud. The bus reminded me of the one in the movie *Romancing the Stone* when Kathleen Turner gets on the wrong bus and ends up in the mountains in the middle of nowhere after it crashes into Michael Douglas's chicken coop.

* * *

On the way to Club Med we drove through a small, quaint town called Oaxaca. The streets were made of cobblestone and every other business seemed to be a cheese store, because Oaxaca is famous for their cheese. I asked the driver if he might let us walk around for a bit, but he said no. We were on a schedule, he said. Then, when we approached the highway again, he relentlessly and literally "pushed the pedal to the metal" the entire way, scaring the hell out of everyone. I was praying he wouldn't lose control of the bus causing it to crash into the deep, narrow ditches that were along the road the whole way there. After the most stressful two-hour bus ride I've ever been on, we arrived. I wasted no time getting down to destroying myself physically and emotionally that week. I went straight for the bar after the orientation and started drinking Fernet Branca, no less. It was a miracle they had it. I signed up for almost all of the sports they offered that week, one of which was sailing. It was a small sailboat, but I learned how to navigate it, along with the sailing instructor. Apparently, so did every other girl that week. I caught him several times during the week having sex with other girls—once in a tree on the beach and twice when I was supposed to be coming to his room for sex and the door was locked. He wouldn't answer, even though I could hear him with someone. What's even sadder about this story is that I knew this and *still* had sex with him! How the instructor found the time I have no idea. I had no clue what went on at a Club Med, but what I learned was that that particular Club Med was known for hedonistic acts. It's now closed. All I knew beforehand was that it was an all-inclusive and affordable vacation. Also, being anorexic it was important to me that it was an active vacation. That week was by far *the single* most *empty* and *meaningless* week of my life. I was active though.

* * *

Cheating no longer felt good the way it used to. I used to like the element of danger, and the sex felt good to me. What a dilemma. How was I going to feel good now? Was I actually beginning to grow a conscience? Being married and cheating was actually making me feel great shame and regret for the first time and it felt disgusting. Before Mike and I were married, I would tell him when I cheated and he'd forgive me each and every time. He said that when I turned thirty years old, he wouldn't be so forgiving. I believe now that I did those things just to get a rise out of him, to get angry and not forgive me—*anything* to get him to react. I must have been unknowingly angry with Mike about this because it translated into him not caring about me. Truthfully, the lack of arguing might have caused me to do hurtful things to myself, just to get him to fight. Still, here I was placing blame. I'm not saying this was healthy, not even close, but it does explain why I might have been so sick. Right. Keep on blaming him for my disease. The pain was so deep I can't even put it into words. Still, how I felt that week didn't stop me from continuing to act like an ass. It was like the voice of reason didn't exist in me. I should have known better than to have sex, unprotected or not! Idiot. I was married, for Heaven's sake. What was wrong with me? I'm not a stupid person but I sure knew how to destroy myself. The abundant exercise, the controlled drinking, the endless pouting, the meaningless sex and starving myself were nowhere near fixing the issues I had. But what were my issues? What was so horrible in my life that it made me become addicted to drinking too much, pouting over nothing, having stupid sex and starving myself to death? Talk about instant karma. Like having sex with a total stranger on vacation was going to make me feel better about losing my job? The week flew by and I couldn't wait to get back to see if there was any shred of hope for getting my job back.

*   *   *

We landed early in the afternoon, and I didn't want to wait to get my last check so I called Wolfgang on the way from the airport to see if I could come and get it. He was surprisingly nice to me, like I might have a chance of getting my job back—actually, my career back. He'd had a whole week to think about it. When I arrived, there were no hard feelings, but I didn't get my job back. It was over. He said it would be setting a bad precedent to let me come back. I understand that now, but I didn't then. I just wanted to go backwards a week and pretend that what happened, didn't. I can't begin to express the sadness I felt and how badly I wanted my position back as Wolfgang's head chef. I'm not sure he knew how much I regretted my actions and how horrible I felt. I came close to begging, but I had to show some kind of dignity. As I was leaving, I prayed that the kitchen manager, who would undoubtedly take my position, would make Wolfgang feel like he had wished he had taken me back, regretting his decision for the rest of his life. I wasn't feeling bitter about the whole thing, though, but I was definitely bitter and angry towards my kitchen manager, and I let her know it. When I walked passed her she was surrounded by her co-workers crying. I'll only say this: I was so evil towards her that I can't repeat what I said it was so vile. It took many years to forgive myself for being that wicked and years to forgive her for being so devious. When I got home from Spago, Mike was happy to see me, but I wasn't as happy to see him because I had a huge secret and I was growing a conscience, which meant he probably could feel I had done something bad. More than likely it would come out but when? Who was I, and what had happened to me? I'd had a conscience as a teenager—although that was *before* I'd had sex the first time.

* * *

I decided I would take some time to off to reassess my life. Having some money afforded me the luxury of time to think and reflect on what I wanted to do next. There were no other restaurants that I really wanted to work in. I was spoiled after Spago, and only the best would do. My "reflection period" turned into a year to be exact. I wasn't in a hurry to work, and after seven straight years of it, it was a welcome time off. I found myself restless at night, though. I was used to cooking and sweating and socializing. All of that excitement was gone. If I didn't have the money from the accident, I would've had to have found a job immediately. I thought

$186,000 was going to last a lifetime back then. And further, if I had been a healthy person mentally, I would not have acted the way I did at Spago. I missed Wolfgang terribly, as well as the energy of Spago.

* * *

Mike didn't stay at Spago much longer after I was gone. It wasn't very comfortable for him after what went down between Wolfgang and me. I think Wolfgang was fine with him being there after I was gone, as Mike was an excellent waiter, but I don't think Mike was. He found a job at The West Beach Café in Venice, California. That place was great. The food was incredible, and the restaurant was always packed. It was so hot it was almost impossible to get a table after 5:45 every night of the week, the best time for me to eat. I loved eating at the bar. Lots of artsy types hung out there, making conversation quite interesting. But my marriage was starting to fall apart slowly. Maybe Mike didn't feel it, but I certainly felt it. I didn't know how much of a secret I was holding in until three weeks after my return from Mexico. My boobs started swelling, and I was putting on the "weird" weight I'd gained when I was pregnant before. I knew I was pregnant. It was almost impossible to comprehend that idea. Worse, whose was baby was it? Before I left for Mexico Mike and I had had sex. It might be his. When I found out I was pregnant again, I had to tell Mike. Naturally I thought he thought it was ours. I wouldn't be able to hide this one from him because he would've had to take me to the hospital for the abortion. I could've had a friend take me but that would be highly suspect, I thought. I had a feeling he didn't believe me. I refused to use birth control after the first abortion, which was another stupid decision I'd made in the long list of many. When he reminded me we hadn't had sex in something like three or four months, I was surprised he was keeping track, but I reminded him we had sex the night before I left for Mexico. I would've had a hard time believing me too, since we only had sex one time in four months. He offered to pay for the abortion, but there was no way I was going to let him. My conscience wouldn't allow it. I had the money and I had no problem paying for my stupid mistake. Mike knew he couldn't talk me out of that abortion too. He couldn't the first time, so he didn't even try or fight for this one the second time—more than likely because he knew it wasn't his.

* * *

This situation didn't help my disease either. Then I remembered my encounter with God. How was He thinking about me now? That's if He was thinking about me at all. I imagined not too well. A second abortion couldn't possibly please God, let alone one. I thought for sure I was going to live in eternal hell. The guilt made me want to eat even less. That abortion was so much more painful for me, emotionally and physically, than the first. Mike took care of me, passing no judgment and not questioning me, which made me feel even worse about myself. I knew then that, sooner than later, this was going to be the death of our marriage. Secrets like this never turn out okay. Lying always finds its way to the surface. There's a certain feeling couples get when someone's lied or cheated. There's no way he couldn't have known. About two weeks after the abortion, I needed time alone, so I decided to visit a friend on Oahu, Hawaii. I needed to figure out what I wanted to do with Mike and our marriage. I was already halfway out the door, but I hoped some time alone would give me time to find a way to come clean and hopefully save the marriage. I had no intention of fooling around, and couldn't anyway. The doctor said I couldn't have sex for a month or even go in the ocean. Not listening, I went in the ocean anyway, causing an gnarly infection. I can't remember what it was but it required an antibiotic. And the thought of having sex hurt. I felt dirty enough, and adding another SDT to the list of shit I'd done, wasn't what I had in mind. I booked a room at the Hilton, which is a large and busy place. It's like a small city. I had a huge suite with an ocean view. I went straight for the beach and was looking forward to my big date of chewing and spitting that evening. I was going to try everything on the menu and almost couldn't wait until the sun went down to start. I usually didn't care what time of day it was when I wanted to chew and spit, but I was in Hawaii. Beach time was important since I loved it so much. I went down to the snack shop and bought three bags of large potato chips. That night I emptied the chips into the trash so I could spit my dinner into it. I remember ordering over $150 worth of food. That may have been the worst episode I ever had with my repulsive disorder. My teeth and jaw were exceptionally tender afterward. When I was done filling the potato chip bags with my macerated food, I called housekeeping and asked them to bring me a large trash bag. I filled the trash bag. I snuck out that night and dumped the trash bag into a large trashcan by the pool at around two o'clock in the morning. No way would I have let the housekeeper empty that bag! She would have looked to see if there was a body in there, it was so heavy. It's so gross to think about it today. I spent the week pretty much repeating that night for the next five nights. I saw my friend only once. But I did manage to enjoy *swallowing* the ahi tuna "poke." It's one of Hawaii's well-known dishes, and it's low fat, and therefore a guilt-free pleasure. Here's the recipe:

Ahi Tuna Poke My Way

Serves 4 appetizers
1 pound sushi-grade ahi tuna, diced into 1/4-inch squares
1/4 cup chopped cilantro
1 avocado, diced into 1/4-inch squares
1/4 cup minced red onion
1/4 cup thinly sliced scallions
3 Tbsp. lemon ponzu sauce
1 tsp. toasted sesame oil

1 tsp. chili oil
1 tsp. wasabi mayonnaise
1 Tbsp. black and white sesame seeds

In a medium-sized bowl, toss everything together gently. Serve with Maui onion potato chips on the side. Place a small teaspoon of the poke on a chip and enjoy with cold sake.

* * *

When I returned home I still didn't know what to do about everything. What I did know was that it was becoming increasingly difficult to pretend everything was great. I was out almost every night with my friends or by myself, as Mike worked five nights a week. I was no good at alone time or relaxing. It was like there was always a fire under my ass. I wasn't cheating, though, which was huge. I spent some of my time painting again. I loved painting, but during this time I found myself losing interest in creativity. I also continued to chew and spit on a regular basis, which sucked. I was spending more time at the dentist office getting cavities filled than I preferred. I was also playing less volleyball. I went out to dinner a lot too, finding myself getting hit on a lot more than I expected.

* * *

After a year of denial and procrastination, Mike and I went to The Charthouse in Westwood for his birthday. My secret had become unbearable to live with and I could see that Mike wasn't his usual self. He seemed very preoccupied, nervous and distant. Maybe the truth would come out after a few drinks. I felt like he wanted to ask me about my trip to Mexico, so I thought I'd let him. Better than me offering up the information. I wasn't a big drinker then, but I decided to try the infamous Navy Grog, which had three types of rum, including a floater of 151 rum and Meyer's Dark

Rum on top of that. My parents used to love that drink when we went to Kelbo's Restaurant in West Los Angeles. They used to light the drink on fire at the table there. I thought that was so cool. I started sipping from the top with a straw, where the 151 Rum was floating around, because it tasted so good, but it went straight to my head. We sat down at a quiet booth in the bar, and finally Mike asked me the dreaded yet very welcome question. I wanted so badly to tell him the truth and hoped I would have the courage but I also sucked at lying. I wasn't sure he was going to accept this one, but I had no choice.

"So, I've had something on my mind for quite some time now."

My heart was racing.

"What?"

"Did you have an affair in Mexico? Tell me the truth."

With astonishing ease, accompanied by slurred words, I said, "Yes! I had an affair in Mexico. There, I said it. GOD! What a relief that is! Boy do I feel better. Man!"

The disappointment was all over his face. I could tell I had hurt him for the last time and beyond repair, and that didn't feel good at all. I thought I'd be happy, but I wasn't. I sounded like an idiot. I was happy that *I* felt better? I never considered *his* feelings. Wow. I could see he was over my immature behavior, cheating ways and more than likely, me.

"I'm glad you feel better, but I don't. At least it's out in the open. I had a feeling deep down. I told you I'd forgive you until you turned thirty years old and before we were married, not after we were married. I cut you some slack and gave you an extra year for your shenanigans. I can't do this anymore. I got you in your early twenties, which shouldn't be an excuse for your cheating or me accepting it. I will forgive you but I can't go on in this marriage any longer. It's over, Lisa."

Wow, did I feel like a trailer-trash piece of shit. Why did he let me off so easily all this time? I think I wanted him to argue with me- defend himself. I thought I wanted him to agree with everything I did, but I really didn't. He should have left me after the first one. I would have. There were so many mixed feelings I had about myself. I thought I was the catch of the day, but I also thought I was absolutely disgusting. The weird thing was that when he told me he was done, I found him more attractive than ever.

"I understand, I really do. I don't know how you've put up with me at all. Why did you?"

"Whose baby was it?"

Ugh. Thank goodness I was drunk.

"I really can't be sure. It may have been yours."

Wow, I felt like a guest on Dr. Phil just then. I hoped he'd fight for us, but it was too much to take and he really was done. I kept drinking, and so did he. He had this weird look on his face like he was so angry with me he was smiling. My dad did that when he was really angry. That's when you knew you were in real trouble.

"I don't know what to say."

"I'm an asshole. I don't deserve you."

"I'll agree with that."

"Why have you stayed?"

"Well, believe it or not, I love you. But I love me more."

Feeling bad went to feeling horrendously bad.

"But I forgive you."

Feeling like I may have a shot I said, "Really?"

"Yes, but it's over. You know that, right? There's no going back. I can't do this anymore. Between the cheating and the eating issues, I'm done."

"I haven't cheated since then."

Like that was going to make it all okay.

"Good for you."

Feeling nauseous and spinning I said, "Mike, I don't feel so good."

"I'm sure you don't."

"I mean that literally. I think the rum got to me. I'm spinning."

"How bad is it?"

"Bad. When will it stop?"

"Okay, we better go."

Mike carried me out of the restaurant. So embarrassing. I was spinning so bad I thought I was going to hurl, and when we got home, Mike made me lie down on the bed with one foot on the ground. He promised that the room would stop whirling if I kept my foot on the floor. I was praying it would work. Thank the Lord I didn't get sick and the room finally stopped spinning. Mike was, however, beyond angry. I had never seen him like that before, and I knew he was gone. I felt so gross and disgusted with myself I couldn't say anything, so I took a shower thinking maybe it might wash the shit off of me.

*   *   *

The next day, I pleaded with him to not leave. I told him after that nightmare I had already decided to never be unfaithful again. I promised I was going to change and be a faithful wife, but it was too late for all of that. He probably saw me as a cheap person, never to change. Lying, I took it a step further and announced I was going to start eating again. That I was sick of people looking at me walking down the beach every day wondering if they thought I was fat or skinny. After saying those words, I knew I might have been an a habitual liar. I truly believed my lies were truths. But I knew deep down I had to start eating or I could lose a kidney or something. I already had so many problems with my teeth, and if I didn't start eating like a normal person, I really started to think that dying could be a reality. Mike could see that I was full of shit too, and for the first time he couldn't care less. He made arrangements to stay with a co-worker that day, and said he would come back for the rest of his things in a few days. Even though I was the one who screwed everything up, I was devastated. I suggested therapy as he walked out the door, but no way. The shame of it all was relentless, eating me even more alive than ever. It was hideous what I did to him and myself. I deserved exactly what I was getting. How could I possibly have seen things in a healthy way when I was so sick? So many parts of me were starving—not only my stomach. It was very difficult to watch him walk away even though I wanted him too since before we were married. I found the next six months after he was gone one of the loneliest times of my life. This is how deadly the cycle of any addiction is. What it does to people's lives is damaging and unforgiving.

* * *

I stayed in our place for about a year or so after Mike left. Then one morning, a miracle happened. I saw what I really looked like in the mirror for the first time in 7 years. I was bone-thin. That image scared me to death. I couldn't believe my eyes! I've always avoided looking in the mirror while changing clothes for fear I'd see all the fat that I thought was there. I happened to glance that day while getting dressed and saw bones. How could I have seen a chubby, fat girl all these years? How could I have seen a chubby, fat girl all these years? I immediately went to the market and finally made that burger I promised God I'd make when was about to go into surgery. It tasted divine, just like it tasted in my mind. Making that burger was the first promise I actually kept even though it took seven years to accomplish. Better late than never! I wondered if I'd made God happy that day. I relished every single bite. I felt like I had a chance to conquer this disease. I thought I was cured that day—but I wasn't, not even close. I managed to digest the burger mentally and physically. It was tempting to take an enema, but I didn't. I toughed out the fear and allowed myself the joy of the feeling of eating. I fell in and out of eating better, and quite often. Over the next four years, I forced myself to eat. Mike moved to Hawaii six months after we separated to surf. That's something I made a living hell for him when we were together. Why was the idea so threatening to me that he went surfing? What, was he going to meet some surfer chick in the water? Not. When he eventually returned, I tried to win him over again. I wrote Mike a love letter telling him I would use birth control. I thought he would understand that I was willing to reignite our sex life and restart our marriage, but it was no use. He just couldn't trust me anymore. It was another year before we finally got a divorce, and when we did, it was quick and amicable. Volleyball also came to an end for me, and that was sad. Mike was still going there and it felt awkward to be around him. It was the end of a season. That period of my life was amazing, even with all the pain and disappointments during that time. We both know now we were great friends and still are. I was burned out and was working on feeling better about myself. II had a long way to go, but at least I was aware of how incredibly skinny and screwed up I was enough to know I needed help. I was slowly beginning to heal, and I wondered what single life was going to be like and what was in store for me professionally.

Chapter 12
The End of a Season

After the divorce, I was attempting to seriously get a grip on my disease and decided I should try to embrace it spirituality. How was I was going to go about that, I wondered? I was on a slightly healthier path food-wise, and it felt awkward and uncomfortable to be in a slightly healthier state of mind. It felt strange to put on 5 pounds. I hadn't caught up with my want to stay skinny and my desire to be normal. The fight to not go out and exercise obsessively or take an enema or panic about gaining weight every minute of the day was unreal. I made a conscious effort to eat later than usual about two to three times a week, which was huge. No more chewing and spitting except for maybe once a month, which was also a big and welcome change for my teeth and jaw, and I virtually stopped going to the gym. I replaced the gym and volleyball with bike riding and power walking. To this day, I still can't walk into a gym. I joined Jane Fonda's Workout on Robertson Blvd. about that time. What a workout that was. I was drinking more water too and stopped sleeping with men altogether. I still wanted to burn calories and had a couple of major relapses later on though. It was the "one step forward and ten steps backward" thing, but something important had shifted: I wanted to get better.

* * *

During the year following my divorce, I went through quite a bit of growth. I began looking at myself and what I saw was a good person inside, but I was still so hardened on the outside and couldn't tell which was the real me, making it hard to know which person I was and so desperately wanted to be—honest, self-loving, trusting, spiritually sound and healthy. How was I going to do this without tools? I was still flirting, but that was all it was—flirting. I was also sick of trying to get into the next relationship. I like relationships and prefer to be in longs ones, but some of these I didn't think through. I was addicted to sex, romance and the idea of love, as if an eating disorder wasn't enough. If I'm going to be really honest here, I didn't know what I wanted so I fell for whomever came after me and who I thought was the shit. If the sex was great then it must be love. That's a good reason to start a relationship, not! During this "season," as I like to call it now, I had some horrible and major unexpected disappointments when it came to men. I wasn't prepared for what was coming as far as dating men now that I was an amputee. Yes, I'm missing only three half fingers. By comparison, missing a leg or an arm is way worse, but missing a body part is still a missing a body part. Mike kept me sheltered from the harmful comments, reactions and just plain old mean statements that came my way. I knew I'd eventually have to confront the reality of my situation without Mike and how men would think about me while on a date. I was in no way prepared for the reality of it. There were two dates in particular that were painful and yet strengthening for me.

Even though I thought I was unattractive, I thought maybe I was being a bit tough on myself, even though I had parts of my fingers. I mean, I wasn't that insecure really, but I made a drama out of the fact that I was. I know Mike thought I was attractive, or at least I thought so. Two unfortunate, yet eye opening experiences, happened on dates with men. The first episode happened on one hot summer night about six months after the divorce. I was sitting at the bar of The West Beach Café, starving and wanting my usual ice-cold Caesar salad, my veggie platter with sides of sauces to dip them in, and my one drink, which was normally Fernet Branca or Fernet Menta. I loved Caesar salads. When I wanted something healthy but fattening, I ordered a Caesar. This is my version of the Caesar salad:

Lisa's Caesar Salad with Rye Croutons, White Anchovies, and a Soft-Boiled Egg

Serves 2
1 head romaine lettuce, chopped
2 slices rye bread, cut into 1/4-inch pieces, and browned in olive oil
Salt and pepper, for seasoning the croutons
4 white anchovies, sold at Whole Foods or specialty Italian stores, chopped
2 soft-boiled eggs (cook six minutes in already-salted boiling water)
Parmesan cheese, grated however you like
Caesar dressing (recipe follows)

Run the hot eggs under cold water. Peel carefully and cut in half with a sharp knife. Place the romaine in a large bowl. Add the seasoned croutons, chopped anchovies, and salad dressing. Add the dressing slowly, as you don't want to overdress the salad. Top with the halved eggs, allowing the liquid yolk to spill out onto the lettuce. Sprinkle with shaved, shredded, or grated Parmesan cheese.

Caesar Dressing

   1/4 cup lemon juice
   1/4 cup Dijon mustard
   1/2-cup olive oil
   1 tsp. balsamic syrup (most stores carry this now)
   1/4 cup Romano cheese
   1 Tbsp. sherry wine vinegar
   Salt and pepper to taste

Whisk together and let it sit for at least 2 hours to 1 day before using. I would recommend a light red wine and no cigar with this.

*   *   *

It was already busy at 5:45 p.m., but there was one seat open at the bar. I sat down and ordered an Appletini instead of my usual Fernet Branca The guy sitting next to me was already drunk and was talking loud and sounded like an idiot. He started hitting on me almost immediately, and I didn't appreciate the way he was going about it. I wasn't feeling it and was also feeling ornery, so I decided to "test" him. At the time smoking was still allowed in restaurants, including cigars, so I decided to light my cigar. It was a good one and my favorite—a Monte Cristo 2 torpedo, a big and strong-smelling cigar. After I took a few puffs he said he thought it was very "sexual" the way I was smoking that cigar.

He said, "So, it looks like you know how to suck on that cigar pretty good. What else can you suck that good?"

I was disgusted, and so was the bartender. The guy got up and left—I thought for good, but he returned. While he was gone, the bartender said he didn't like the way he was talking to me and he'd be right there for me if it became a problem. He'd been trying to eighty-six the guy for a while and had no reservations about kicking him out. When the guy sat back down, he said, "So what do you say? Let's go back to my place, honey." I hate it when guys call me honey. I'm no one's honey except the man I'm with. Right then I switched hands, taking a huge drag of the cigar with my "nub" hand, blowing the smoke right into his face. I said, "Is that right?" And when the smoke cleared, he saw my nubs. The look on his face was priceless and hurtful. It looked like he'd seen, I don't know what, but it wasn't good.

He said, "Oh my God! You're disgusting!"

"I'm disgusting? Really? I thought you wanted to take me to your place. What's changed?"

"You're missing fingers! It's so ugly!"

"Is that a fact?" I was so disarmed by this guy's manners that I couldn't help but aggravate the situation. I had not been confronted like this since Mike and I divorced, and it forced me to overreact. I wish, in retrospect, I had known what it meant to take the high road. Instead, I became just as ugly as he was.

Pissed, I put the cigar in my other hand while I slapped him across his face as hard as I could. That was the first time I'd slapped a man, and it didn't feel as great as I thought it would feel. In the movies it always looks so empowering. But really, it shows how much of a bitch a girl can be. The bartender came out from behind the bar immediately and kicked him out. I clearly wasn't anywhere near adjusted to my fingers, and it was ten years after the accident. Not a positive experience at all.

* * *

The second incident happened when a friend hooked me up for a date. We met at the Paradise Cove Restaurant in Malibu on Pacific Coast Highway. I'll never forget what he wore. He had on cut-off blue jeans, a plaid shirt and beige work boots with white knee socks. When I sat down, we shook hands. I could see he knew something was up with my hand but didn't say anything. But like most people, he followed it around as I talked. We ordered drinks, and as we talked I could see he was preoccupied with my hand. I didn't have the courage to confront him and break the ice. I ordered a lemon drop martini and he ordered a beer. When we lifted our glasses to toast, he saw my nubs wrapped around the stem of my glass and said, "Your friend never told me you are an amputee!" Really? No one up until that point had ever referred to me as an amputee. You'd think a grown man would have more manners than that. The hurt I felt was indescribable.

"Amputee? Really? Well, I don't know how to respond to that."

"Well, it would have been nice to have been warned."

"Why? What does missing three half fingers have to do with me?"

"It has everything to do with you."

"So if you had known, you wouldn't have wanted to meet me?"

"Yes, definitely!"

"How?"

"I wouldn't have taken time out of my life to bother meeting you."

Angry beyond words, I stood up and threw my martini in his face and said, "Well if I had known I was meeting someone as classless as you, I wouldn't have bothered either. And for the record, you're an ass."

He sat there in shock, dripping wet, as I walked out of the restaurant. I bawled my eyes out all the way home. I knew at that moment that I wasn't anywhere near okay about my hand. Why should it matter if they were there or not? What did that have to do with me as a person? Looking back, maybe I was more okay with my fingers than I realized, but those men made me feel as though there *was* something wrong with me. But how those men saw me physically kept me from seeing how beautiful I truly was inside. What a rotten excuse. No one can make us feel bad about ourselves, only we can. For the first time I realized that beauty comes from the inside, not the outside. Unfortunately, therein lay the real issue: was I unattractive inside because of my lack of self-esteem, or was I just full of shit and drama? Yes. How was I going to become beautiful inside while I was still feeling so much pain? How many more times would I endure this kind of shallowness before meeting someone who didn't care whether or not I had missing fingers, even though Mike loved me anyway? I was still a mess but I decided I wasn't going to look for love. I was going to wait for it to find me.

* * *

I started to focus more on my recovery after those two hellish experiences. I found a job at Rebecca's restaurant, across the street from The West Beach Café. When Mike returned from Hawaii, he worked in both places and we managed to be friends, but our divorce was still raw for me, more than I had realized. I noticed that Mike was starting to date.

How dare he! My pride was definitely alive and well. There was one girl I remember seeing Mike out with, and it particularly devastated me. She was really pretty. Piercing blue eyes and blonde hair I could see fifty feet away. I was on a date that night with George, who was to be my boyfriend for the next eleven years and I became instantly jealous. I began to cry and got very angry, and I made sure he saw it. I'm sure George was very uncomfortable. I excused myself and ran outside, embarrassed and humiliated. Mike came out after me and asked me what my problem was. What could I say?

I said, "It hurts to see you with someone and someone so beautiful, that's all. I didn't expect to feel like this."

"You should have thought about that before you cheated on me the last time."

Gouge. Stab. Ouch. Beyond humiliated, I knew it was really over. Truth was, I really didn't want him back, I was just jealous that the girl he was with was so incredibly beautiful—and worse, wasn't missing any limbs. I'm sure Mike felt pretty darn good seeing me like that, but I sure didn't.

* * *

Feeling empty spiritually, emotionally, relationally, and financially, I desperately tried harder to find myself. Who was this person I'd become? Wandering around aimlessly hoping someone would save me was not working. I wanted some answers, and I wanted them immediately. So I decided I'd go see a past-life psychic a good friend had told me about; if anything, I'd be entertained. And I would get to hear all about me—my favorite subject. I hoped she might be able to shed some light as to why my accident happened in the first place. Again, I just couldn't let it be. I needed answers. I wanted to know if there was a deeper reason for everything I'd been through. I wanted to understand why I had been so promiscuous, anorexic, and self-destructive for so many years. I wasn't capable of taking personal responsibility for what I'd done. It was all about ascribing it to something outside of me, something I could blame to make myself feel better, free from the guilt flaring up inside of me. Plus, I was still angry about the whole thing, even twelve years later. I was pissed about it and wondered if I would truly ever be at peace with it.

* * *

When I arrived, the psychic got right down to business. She asked me for a piece of jewelry I wore all the time. I gave her a gold ring, a frog that wrapped around my finger with emeralds for eyes. It was my mom's, and for years I had begged her to give it to me. She finally did when I started high school. Soon after holding it, the psychic went into some kind of trance and spoke as if she couldn't control what she was saying. This went on for almost four hours— the whole time I was with her. I barely got a word in edgewise, and that wasn't easy for me. She told me many things, but several of them stood out: I would write several books by the time I turned forty, and would create something later on that would feed the world. I did end up writing two cookbooks for Paul Newman and developing two products for Newman's Own when I turned forty years old, amazingly enough. What else was coming? Then she got finally down to the bare bones of what I really wanted to hear. According to her, during the 1500s I was a servant for a king who sold me to another king who wanted to marry me. I'd never met him, and that alone made me angry, according to the psychic. A servant came to escort me to the king who I was to marry. When the servant and I met, we fell instantly in love. About halfway there, we couldn't hold ourselves back any longer and made passionate love. We thought we could hide our love from the king by the time we arrived, which was another two weeks away. When we finally met the king, we could see he knew.

* * *

Though I loved the story she was telling me, the more my bullshit meter was going off. This self- indulgent moment was costing me $300, so while the story was nice and all, I started to wonder why I came at all. How lame of me to think this person I didn't know could save me. I said, "You know, this is ridiculous." Just as I got up to leave, she said, "Wait, and there's something else. You had an abortion before your accident, didn't you?"

I didn't see that one coming. I couldn't believe she knew that I'd had an abortion. Anyone can make up a story like she did but not this.

"Yes. How did you know?"

"This is what I do."

At that point she went back to the past-life story. According to her, I'd lost my three fingers in that life as well. The king, whom I'd betrayed, had done this to me as punishment for humiliating him by falling in love with another man and getting pregnant with my lover's child. With only bandages and no doctor's care, the king threw me back into the dungeon. As if that weren't enough, he hit me in the stomach, causing a miscarriage. I spent the rest of my life, which didn't last very many more days, stuck in the dungeon to die.

I was speechless. What a horrible story.

"That's just awful. But what does that have to do with my accident?"

"Nothing. But your abortion has everything to do with your eating disorder."

Angry, I said, "My eating disorder? What does that have to do with why my accident happened? That's what I want to know about. And I don't have an eating disorder."

"Anyone can see that you are anorexic. It's the abortion that caused you much harm, physically and emotionally, not the loss of your fingers. I'm not saying that didn't help perpetuate your issues further, but it's the abortion that is at the root of *all* your issues. You recovered well from the accident even though you don't see that. You are much stronger than you realize. Your accident was just that—an accident."

I was *not* happy with my reading at all, or her accusations. My abortion had caused my eating disorder? For me it seemed that the accident was the more painful of the two. Everyone could *see* that loss, but no one could see the loss of my child. The whole thing was a waste of money. As I stood up to walk out, she stopped me and said she had something else to say.

"You want help with *why* your accident happened or not?"

"Yes, I do!"

"Was there some kind of jewelry you wore the that day? Something you would normally never wear?"

Wow. Okay, she had my attention again.

"Yes, I did. It was a watch I wore. How did you know?"

"I've told you before. It's what I do, and God gave me the gift of healing through Him. There are no mistakes in this world, only blessings. Your accident happened for a reason."

Dumbfounded, I said, "What reason could possibly explain it any way but bad?"

"And you died for a bit, didn't you? You saw the light, too."

Man she's good! "Yes, I did."

"But you didn't grasp that you were self-centered, am I right?" I couldn't say anything I so shocked. "That's your real lesson here. Faith means believing in something you can't touch or see, and since control is what anorexia is all about, faith was and still isn't an option for you, at least not right now. You must have faith in the fact that there is a very good reason why this accident happened, but that realization will come in God's time, not yours. One day, it will become clear."

Okay, I finally got an answer as to why it happened, but I already *knew* the machine had gone off because of that watch. What I wasn't expecting was the "lesson and the blessing" part of my accident even though I had died and saw the light. Why was I blocking that out? Did I enjoy being in the dark? That certainly wasn't what I wanted or expected to hear. In retrospect, I have no idea what I wanted hear—it just wasn't that.

* * *

I left bewildered, sad and confused by what the psychic said, and by her insights as to why I was the way I was. She mentioned God, faith, blessings and lessons. I had almost died twice—once in the operating room and once in Hawaii. On both occasions, God revealed Himself to me and I refused to see that as a sign to change my life. I had no faith, obviously, except my own. *I* was still "God." *I* still had all the answers. *I* still knew better when it came to making decisions. I, in fact, hadn't grown one bit. I was still ignoring what I needed. What *I* didn't know was how important it was for me to believe in something more powerful than me. Clearly *I* wasn't making good decisions, not even close. I never saw any blessings, only pain and drama—and was that really the way to live? I never learned any lessons, not even in school. We said the *Pledge of Allegiance* every day, and I never once understood those words. When it came to studying, I didn't care. I wanted to make up my own history, math, and vocabulary. History, for me, was someone's idea of it. I never got why it was so important to understand where we came from in this world. I learned nothing in history except that it bored me to death. I fell asleep all the time, which produced my one and only F in school. And the bible was only a book after all that was written by a bunch of fictitious characters.

* * *

After spending twelve years ignoring God's messages, I continued to do so for another twenty some odd years. Even though I was intrigued by the idea of why God was showing Himself to me, I wasn't interested enough to find out. I'd heard the phrase "Let go and let God" over the years from time to time, and I never totally got that idea, especially since I didn't believe in God. The letting go part scared me and for an anorexic this is terrifying. What if I fell apart when I let go of everything? The irony was that controlling every aspect of my life, struggling every bit of the way unnecessarily, was what caused me to fall apart, but I couldn't see it. How was I supposed to feel joy while wanting to be in total control? I was in a constant state of conflict. What was I gaining from this attitude? Nothing, nothing at all except misery and isolation. I wanted to learn to let go, but I resisted and didn't really know how. It seemed too hard to change so drastically. In the deepest depths of my soul, I did understand her, but it sounded way too hard to live like that. Who wants that kind of responsibility or way of life? To be accountable to God for everything seemed really hard to conceive of and a ridiculous notion. To think that God knew everything I did every minute of the day seemed scary and rather unrealistic to grasp onto. Was it really because I was *afraid* to let go? Afraid of what, exactly, is the question. Why was the thought of talking to God about my problems or my dreams and turning all of it over to Him such a scary idea? Because I liked using my free will. It made me feel powerful and in control and okay about being a bad girl, an exciting girl. The kind of girl all men wanted, or at least the kind of men I can't imagine being around now, not even close. After that reading I find myself thinking about my abortion every now and then and how that incident did play a very serious role in why I was so self-destructive. It actually made tremendous sense to me over time, and having a second abortion really was the nail in the coffin for me. How was I going to ever forgive, I mean truly forgive myself?

Epilogue

Although it took me many more years to find Faith and understand genuine forgiveness, I plugged along anyway down many spiritual paths, especially after the reading from the psychic. Even though she didn't mention anything about my promiscuity, she helped me see how empty my spiritual "house" really was. I was lacking any real understanding of how much I needed to believe in something other than myself. New Age beliefs are largely based on this belief. While this can help many people as it did for me, it wasn't permanent. I wanted a permanent solution. What I didn't understand then, nothing is permanent. Relying on myself for decision-making and knowing it all clearly brought me problems and dissatisfaction. Sex, food or the lack of it, wine that turned into booze later on and smoking cigars way too often wasn't doing the job for me anymore. I wondered what it would be like to enjoy life without excessive behavior. I vowed to myself that I would be faithful in my next serious relationship, or at least I would try. Clearly, thinking *I* had total power in my life was absurd. If this were the way to live then I wouldn't have been in this shithole of a mess. I knew I needed to move forward in my spiritual house, but had no idea where to start or how to do it. So the journey began and it started with Louise Hay. Her affirmations and positive thinking had healed many from deadly diseases, so I decided to *try* and recite Louise Hays's affirmations in hopes I would grow spiritually and change the way I thought about myself.

I worked hard at believing in the words I was "reciting." Even though I kind of didn't understand how changing my negative thought process would "cure" me, I continued to recite them anyway. But to my surprise her methods did work, and I experienced their power when using them for anorexia. What I did like about how Ms. Hays is how she saw things was how she spelled disease as "disease." If I really think about that spelling, I was in a state of disease within my body, soul, and mind. But at the time it was the best I could do, continue writing these reaffirmations on Post-it notes and placing them all around the house, mostly on my bathroom mirror. It was the first thing I would see every morning, yet I managed to ignore them often. It was hard to read them. It meant change and acceptance, and I wasn't ready for that, not for a very long time. It was like I thought I could rub a lamp and some genie would pop out and heal me in an instant. I wanted immediate results in every part of my life. I knew I didn't want to have to go through the pain of soul-searching, but it was inevitable. I've always known that hard work is necessary for growth. Anything that's worth a crap is. After a while I gave up reciting affirmations and kept wandering in and out of the light and the darkness.

I put on ten pounds, which felt like fifty pounds for me. That took a while to get used to. As much as she helped me, I wasn't feeling it in my heart or soul at the deepest level for permanent change—the places that were truly at the root of my disease and lack of self-confidence. Logically, they made sense to me, but there was no *real* commitment from me. I needed something much bigger than what I recited to heal-even though that did help. I needed something supernatural and powerful. I thought having that alien encounter was my new source of information, but that really didn't cut the mustard either. I wanted a real core connection with something that felt right and natural.

* * *

In 2000, I decided I'd give the Dalai Lama a try. As faiths go, he seemed easy for me to understand. For the first time, I listened to a well-respected spiritual man about life that paralleled the way *I* wanted to live my life, hoping I was able to apply his wisdom in my life. There was also relief in believing in reincarnation because I thought I could come back and do it all over again as someone else and that I would get to choose whom that would be. That was a weird way to think, especially after almost dying twice and seeing the great peace that God and Heaven had to offer in Eternity. It was like I chose to forget that even happened just so I could convince myself that I could come back right after death. I was excited by the notion that I would be able to come back and do whatever I wanted to, over and over again, in many different lifetimes, which translated into not caring how I treated myself or others in my present life. Even though the Dalai Lama has many empowering things to say, I knew that I wasn't going to get another go-around like I thought I was. There was still emptiness inside of me—a big hole in my heart. I was still rough around the edges. I had an altar I hoped would magically change my life and save me from having to go through the agony of change. No such luck. So many words have come out of my mouth that I wish hadn't. All the swearing I did and the nasty things I said to people were ridiculous. It got so bad that an old friend gave me a coffee table book called *The "F" Word.* For some reason when I got that book it suddenly made me feel embarrassed. I felt like a joke. It wasn't so funny anymore that I swore incessantly, so I threw it away. To this day I wonder what people thought what was so funny about my truck driver's mouth. People never forget the words we say to each other. That old saying "sticks and stones may break my bones but words will never hurt me" is a bunch of bullcrap too. I have pretended that words never hurt me, but they have, and deeply. Not to mention the words I've used to hurt people. But how could they have known if I didn't say something after all? I mean really. I was the end all teacher of these people by calling them on their shit? I think not. Ultimately, I knew that if I came to God that would mean admitting all of the wrongs I had done in my life, and I didn't want to ad-mit them to anyone, especially God! It would be too difficult to look at myself that intensely and honestly.

* * *

Then I became fascinated with the metaphysical aspects of why we become sick with disease. I've always been afraid of sickness, and honestly, I still am. Anorexia is all about denying the self and with extreme fear, self-hatred, and rejection—all of which is the sad and painful truth, and I will never know the damage I did to my body. Now I take great care of it in hopes I can live a long and healthy life. As I learned more about disease, I began to see the connection of how important it is to feel good about us in relation to health. But still, it wasn't enough. Soon my fascination with metaphysics and the Dalai Lama dwindled. So I learned how to throw tarot cards in the aftermath of a horrible and heartbreaking breakup in 2002 to a *married* man no less. That's a whole other story I won't share here. Man oh man, what was I even *thinking* it was okay to see a married man? I still hadn't learned a thing. Pathetic.

There I was again, trying to find answers and thinking *I* could get them by throwing a deck of cards. I've spent countless of thousands of dollars on psychics. I was so lost. I mean I wouldn't doubt they had a Post-it note by the telephone at The Psychic Eye Bookstore in Sherman Oaks that read "Lisa Stalvey is calling again, the huge sucker that will believe anything we tell her." As I reflect back on all of the incredibly thoughtless things I've done to myself and others and how many I've hurt, I am also grateful to have persevered in my journey to become a better person. Further, I now know I needed to go through all of it to come to where I am today, which has given me major comfort. I now see how blessed I have been in my life. To name a few blessings: Not everyone gets to be Wolfgang Puck's head chef at the hottest place in town, and as a woman, to boot. Not everyone gets to meet Paul Newman and co-write two cookbooks and develop two products for his company. Not everyone get to develop spices for a meat company that is still on the shelf today.

Not everyone gets to live a life doing what she truly loves to do in life. My talent as a chef is truly a gift from God. I always wanted to be a better person, I just didn't know how. I cared about stuff, but caring would have meant I couldn't do what I wanted to do and with a clear conscious. Now I care so much, I feel everything. My compassion for animals is almost too much to tolerate. I pray that I get to work with orphaned lion, tiger and panther cubs some day contributing my time to saving these species from extinction.

*   *   *

I was desperately trying to climb out of the abyss of pain and fear I was in for years. I noticed that I was still fighting with my boyfriends, and in my current relationship it was still happening. I was also a flake- I'd make plans and then cancel with some lame excuse. I was not a reliable friend. I hadn't let go of my need for drama and was literally exhausted from all the arguing. It wasn't fun anymore—in fact, it was starting to wear on me physically. My eyes were dull and showed no joy, only pain. I wanted to know what I looked like happy all the time. It's hard to believe that I needed to fight to *feel* and actually thought it was fun. My soul was damaged and I needed help. Finding work also became hard. I never had a hard time with that, but when the recession hit in 2007, it was. I allowed this thinking to creep in, causing hardship to my life. But with my attitude of fear, negativity, gloom, and doom I was feeling during that time was scary. I was terrified of being homeless even though my current man, Frank, would have taken care of me and he did. I still got work occasionally but not enough to make ends meet, which made me terrified. I had no Faith at all. Whether we like it or not, these feelings can keep work away not to mention love, happiness and joy. How could anything positive happen to me while I was in that state of mind? Who would want to be around that, especially if I'm cooking their food? I wanted to live in peace.

* * *

Then one day, thirty years after the accident, I woke up. It was like I had no choice any longer. I had to face myself and look to something more powerful to help me. I had no idea what to do or what that meant, but for the first time I knew I needed God. I opened up with my friends about this new revelation with a sense of resolve. My dear friends Nancy and Cathy, who are Christians, suggested I try going to the Pasadena International House of Prayer. It's a place where people pray for you. I wasn't thrilled about going, but I thought, *Why not? How could it hurt?* Saying the word prayer or God and especially Jesus wasn't easy for me to say, but I was being called to it. How ironic as I experienced Him in the operating room. I felt like if I didn't go do something and soon I would live the rest of my life without joy, happiness, or love. Nothing up until that day had been such an emergency. More importantly, I knew I needed a miracle. I was at my bottom. There was nowhere to go but up!

* * *

I was nervous going because this was a serious thing for me, to go to a church and hope to find an answer. When I walked into the building, it wasn't a church setting like I thought. It was a nice space. Two women greeted me with open arms, directing me into a seating area. I was ready for a transformation, and honestly I hoped it would start with these women. I felt a kind of cleansing come over me as they spoke, and all that "dirtiness" I felt earlier in my life seemed to disappear. I felt as though everything I had done before that was bad was forgiven. It was weird. It was like the highest high I'd ever had and it felt incredible. I like to describe my experience with these women at that moment as a "humbling place of hope." What I experienced was nothing short of a miracle. My heart was filled up with love within seconds. It was a healing on the soul level, something not found of this world. No one was pressuring me to convert either. They were just there to help me. Their *actions* alone were proof for me because of the genuine love they showed toward me. They asked why I was there and I told them: for help. I was exhausted and tired of trying so hard to please people just so they'd like me. I was tired of my pride and ego, which resulted in bad results. It took me a while to understand that attempting to please people was futile and actually damaging to them and me. There is emptiness in that kind of existence, but it kept me busy and away from my own problems.

*   *   *

As they talked and prayed over me I felt the same warm breeze I felt in the operating room. God was there with me. I wanted more information and an understanding of what it would be like to be outside of myself and not in control completely. The way they were talking was in a way I'd ever heard anything explained to me before. There was no judgment, no making me feel bad about myself, or like I'd *ever* done anything wrong before. They said that God was pleased with me and had been my whole life. How could He be pleased? I was a reckless person and a non-believer for 30 years. Then I began to see that I was in fact at that moment being released from my pain, and I found myself completely free. I started to cry. It was truly a miracle. I was intrigued by the idea that I could trust something I couldn't see. This is what they meant by faith. As scary and weird as it sounds to live life in faith, it's the only idea that has softened my heart and calmed me down. Nothing I tried before influenced me like that, and I wasn't trying.

After listening to these two women talk for a time, I asked, "So how does one let go and let God?"

One of the women answered, "It's simple. Live minute to minute, not thinking about the past or the future and knowing God is there with you. Just *know* that there's a plan for you and all the planning and worrying you do won't change what will happen. We all have a destiny, some come sooner than later. Do you understand?"

"Sort of."

"What do you do?"

"I'm a chef."

"Is this what you wanted to be in life?"

"No. I studied to be an artist. Actually, I wanted to be a fashion photographer."

"Why weren't you?"

"I don't know. I would imagine it is a really hard profession to break into?"

"Did you once think that cooking was a hard profession to break into?"

"Actually, no, now that you mention it."

"You know why?"

"No?"

"Because it was effortless, am I right?"

"Actually, yes, now that I think about it. I still went through a lot of pain and hard work though."

"Of course, that's normal. The ease in which the opportunities showed themselves to you and how you couldn't explain to anyone why you were so gifted in many areas of your profession seemed odd to you, didn't they?"

"Well, yeah, I guess."

"That's what faith is, and what 'letting go and letting God' means. You naturally followed the path that was given to you without questioning or ever understanding why, right?"

"Wow, right. I tried to leave it several times, but it brought me back."

Those beautiful women helped me see that my life was exactly the way it was supposed to be, and that I had been given a gift and never once asked myself why. I realized at that moment that I chose to torture myself because I couldn't understand why everything was so easy for me. I actually felt guilty about that. I was on my path, my gift from God. I knew and saw so many around me my whole life struggling with what they wanted to do with their lives or what their purpose was. I could see what their God-given talents were, even though they couldn't. Wondering what our purpose in life is can be very frustrating and scary.

"But your plan is still ongoing. There's more to come."

"Really? Do you know what that plan is?"

"No, and it's not for me or you to know. We all have the same ongoing plan from Him. You just have to let it all go and let God. Have faith and trust Him entirely. That's all. And don't be afraid to talk to Him just like you would your best friend. Everyone these days makes a big deal out of *how* we are supposed to pray. There are no rules. He's next to you all the time."

"I've never prayed before, but I'm liking the idea of just talking to Him like a normal person."

I liked that idea a lot, but I knew it would take me a while to understand the power of prayer and how it would feel to *trust* and let it all go to something I couldn't see. Faith and trust have been two difficult things for me to comprehend throughout my life. I had been burned so many times, and mostly because of my own doing. Over time I decided to test the idea of living just one whole day in faith, and when I noticed how powerful it was to live like that I began to do it more often. Now I do it all the time. I thank Him constantly. Over time I began to notice the blessings I was receiving but all along He had been giving me blessings even while I didn't believe. He is so forgiving. Talking to God was working in my life, and better than I could have ever imagined it to be. There it was—the true messengers I'd been seeking my whole adult life, and I found them in a small, obscure building in Pasadena and not at The Psychic Eye Bookstore in Sherman Oaks. That day I met God.

* * *

After that incredibly fulfilling experience, I found myself craving an In-N-Out burger! So that's what I did—I pulled into the healthiest fast-food joint I know of and had a Double-Double, "animal-style," and fries. Not one ounce of guilt came over me. I even ordered a Coke! Still, it took about a year after that day for me to fully understand the extent of what they were speaking about. My life has changed greatly in the last few years, and for the better. I noticed as I started speaking freely about my newfound beliefs, they weren't as welcomed as I thought they might be. That was a bit surprising. I guess I shouldn't have been surprised because I didn't welcome this belief when I was younger either. I guess I've changed more than I thought. I mean it's not like I'm walking around asking people if they've found Jesus. I don't bring up my beliefs with my friends unless the conversation lends its hand to talking about God. Many have noticed a certain "glow" or "energy" or "transformation" in me. When they ask me what I've done, I tell them. I'm not afraid to share my Faith, not one bit. I tell them I don't believe in "dis-ease" anymore. They then ask me why, and I tell them I've found God and all of my worries and fears are in His hands now; I trust Him implicitly to take care of me on every level. Some argue, some blow over it and some want to know more. I ask Him to show me the way every morning and if needed and all day long. It's a relationship, not a religion. That's it. That's a lot for anyone to take in, especially for me because of who I used to be. I am walking and will continue to walk on what seems to be an ever-narrowing path in life, and that's okay. At least I am at peace. I am working on being a better person. I'm not going to become a nun or anything—or maybe I will! I don't know. All I know is this: I love God and how I've been feeling since finding Him. No one can keep me from feeling this way and from sharing how God has changed me. I want others to feel like I do and feel that it's my responsibility to share what God has done for my life.

* * *

I used to get angry when people talked to me about God and Jesus too, so I don't judge anymore. This is God's job, not mine. I was threatened because I had no idea what they were talking about and placing my entire life into the hands of someone or something I couldn't see was insane to me then. Now I can't live in this world anymore without Faith. I'm *of* it, not *in* it. I struggled somewhat with needing people in my life to feed me drama during this transformation, but God literally removed them from my life—and effortlessly, as if they vanished into thin air—I see why now. Some of these people were friends of mine for over 20 years. I never guessed these people would ever leave my life. But I guess it's a part of the big picture and His plan for me. I have much more to accomplish, I know that now, and I can't wait to see what unfolds. I miss them dearly, and how long they will be absent, only God knows. I accept and trust Him totally. Whomever He chooses to take from me or bless me with, I know it's for my good. Whatever door He closes, a better one is about to open. Actually, it's a very exciting and peaceful way to live!

*   *   *

I now understand that what I received that day in the operating room was a blessing and an amazing gift but my head was too far up my ass to see it. We are fragile souls, and we live within such a stream of unconsciousness that to realize the Mightiness of God within us in an instant would be virtually impossible to withstand. Change like I experienced that day at the Pasadena International House of Prayer couldn't have happened overnight or at any other time. It was perfect. Looking back, I now realize that all the different roads I had took over the last thirty years were necessary for me to grow. Every nuance, heartbreak, pain, sadness, disappointment, the loss of my babies and my fingers and all painful circumstances I experienced were totally necessary for me to get where I am today. The key is to be patiently impatient, which is almost impossible. Waiting for our illumination becomes lost in our daily need for survival. I never saw this or could have ever understood this, and I feel sad that I missed many days of my life by being impatient. Well, better late than never. Always looking at the future and the past and never living in the present I know now was in fact what caused my emptiness. I also know now that no matter how dark my past has been it has now been erased, and just like that. I no longer feel shame or guilt. I feel like a child, full of innocence and clarity. The fire was lit under me that very afternoon, and it will never go out again. As I come closer to living with God, the darkness tries to creep in often, and I fight it with a vengeance, but this time I'm not alone. The energy in that room was awesome. Letting it all go has freed me from the chains of unhappiness, jealousy, anger, and the need to impress others. I still have the choice of free will, as we all do, and I hope I am making better decisions, but it feels better to leave everything to God now. If it weren't for my accident, I might have found myself in much darker places than I ended up in. It could have been much worse, so much so I can't think about it. It's gone now, all that pain, and now I look forward to each day and thank God for it. I look back at who I was and I can't believe it. I live each day now as if I were flowing down a river in a boat. I have two choices: hit the millions of rocks I have on my wide path, or take the narrow path and walk simply, avoiding the things that aren't good for me. Too often we make life more difficult on ourselves than we need to, but then again we are human.

* * *

In closing, I have no idea what the future holds for me now and I love that. Only He knows my last day here on Earth. The future for me now is in the present moment—literally. I look forward to whatever God has planned for me each day and only this day. I am fearless now, which is a miracle and feels so freeing to feel like that. It is impossible for Fear and Faith to live together. Knowing that I am not in control of anything in my life is such a relief I can't begin to articulate it. That was the *real* reason why I was anorexic. All the years of denying myself joy and being frightened to the point of arrogance and rejecting the idea that there was something way more powerful than me was the highest form of pride and self-importance I could have ever known. Something God isn't and doesn't want us to be. He wants us to be humble and grateful. Sure, there will still be obstacles throughout the rest of my life. Feeling connected to God is amazing. I laugh at the obstacles and the hard and painful times now because I know it won't last forever. Nothing ever does. I go to sleep thankful for having another day on earth and look up into the clouds and the stars thanking God for it, for this life and everything I've been through and am about to experience. I live the way I do now because living any other way is virtually impossible. I had a glimpse of the *old* Lisa recently, as recently as few short months ago. I decided I was going to get a personal trainer for strength training. My friend Linda is excellent at it. During the first week I began to notice the obsessions coming back. I wasn't happy with the way my arms looked. Age is a bitch. But by my third session, I told her I couldn't go on – that I was obsessing over what I ate, thinking I should run longer and take up swimming. Most importantly, I was depressed and miserable over the *idea* of restricting myself from enjoy things. I told her I wasn't going to give up my joy for the sake of looking good and feeling like this. It wasn't worth it at all. I cried over this. Thankfully, what I realized was that I was saying goodbye to my disease yet *again* and knew I would *always* have to keep it in check for the rest of my life. This was a shocking discovery to say the least that 2 sessions of training could bring me back to where I was over 30 years ago. Now I look at tragedies that arise in life as blessings, such as the experience I just explained to you. Pain is an opportunity to grow and is preparation for what He wants us to do next. There is definitely a reason for everything and the end result of each trial is always for our benefit, even if we can't *see* it. It can wake us up to a better way of life. Mine thankfully did. It's only been since 2012 that I finally embraced my fingers as a whole part of my body, which is a miracle to me. They are beautiful and artistic, and all by the Grace of God. I've accepted the loss or losses now, so much so that I rejoice in their imperfectness. I'm so happy I found Him and I am grateful that He never gave up on me. I hope you find your way to supreme bliss. It's a wonderful feeling.

Review Requested:
If you loved this book, would you please provide a review at Amazon.com?

RESTAURANTS

L'ERMITAGE

L'ORANGINÉ

MA MAISON